DOOLITTLE RAID DOCTOR

A Firsthand Account of
Bombing Tokyo and Escaping
Occupied China from
Flight Surgeon "Doc" White

MAJOR THOMAS R. "DOC" WHITE, MD

WITH GABRIELLE ADELMAN AND
JOHN FREDRICKSON

4880 Lower Valley Road
Atglen, PA 19310

Copyright © 2025 by Gabrielle Adelman

Library of Congress Control Number: 2025930101

All rights reserved. No part of this work may be reproduced or used in any form or by
any means—graphic, electronic, or mechanical, including photocopying or information
storage and retrieval systems—without written permission from the publisher.
    The scanning, uploading, and distribution of this book or any part thereof via the
Internet or any other means without the permission of the publisher is illegal and
punishable by law. Please purchase only authorized editions and do not participate in
or encourage the electronic piracy of copyrighted materials.
    "Schiffer," "Schiffer Publishing, Ltd.," and the pen and inkwell logo are registered
trademarks of Schiffer Publishing, Ltd.

Designed by Jack Chappell
Cover design by Brenda MacCallum
Type set in Helvetica/New Frank/Arial/Times New Roman

ISBN: 978-0-7643-6989-6
ePub: 978-1-5073-0581-2
Printed in India
10 9 8 7 6 5 4 3 2 1

Published by Schiffer Publishing, Ltd.
4880 Lower Valley Road
Atglen, PA 19310
Phone: (610) 593-1777; Fax: (610) 593-2002
Email: Info@schifferbooks.com
Web: www.schifferbooks.com

For our complete selection of fine books on this and related subjects, please visit our
website at www.schifferbooks.com. You may also write for a free catalog.
    Schiffer Publishing's titles are available at special discounts for bulk purchases
for sales promotions or premiums. Special editions, including personalized covers,
corporate imprints, and excerpts, can be created in large quantities for special needs.
For more information, contact the publisher.
    We are always looking for people to write books on new and related subjects. If you
have an idea for a book, please contact us at proposals@schifferbooks.com.

CONTENTS

ACKNOWLEDGMENTS

ANYONE WHO EXPENDS the effort to write down a 40,000-word wartime memoir does so in hope the manuscript will be preserved, treasured by posterity, and shared with others. The descendants of Dr. White honored that wish by safekeeping the original document, protecting the corresponding artifacts, and hereby sharing the epic tale with others.

The morning of April 18, 1942, eighty airmen staked claim to a unique niche in the annals of warfare by fearlessly launching their sixteen B-25 bombers from the deck of aircraft carrier USS *Hornet* and then attacking the urbanized heartland of Japan. Some died during bailout over China, four expired as prisoners of the Nipponese, while others survived the raid but perished in subsequent (but unrelated) wartime events. Sixty-one Raiders survived World War II and subsequently celebrated their audacious accomplishment at periodic reunions. Most gatherings were annual parties mostly open to the public. As planned, these events ceased after the demise of the last Raider. None remained after the passing of Doolittle's copilot, Richard "Dick" Cole, at age 103, on April 10, 2019.

Retired NBC television news anchor Tom Brokaw coined the term "Greatest Generation" in 1998 to describe the people who lived through World War II. Postwar exuberance created the massive "baby boom" generation. Later in life, many boomers lamented, "My parents never shared their wartime experiences." Some elders may have assumed that their military (or civilian) contribution was too insignificant (or too boring) to merit telling. For others, powerful emotions swirling deep within made the memories difficult to articulate. Many military veterans found empathy, solace, and comradeship within service organizations such as the VFW (Veterans of Foreign Wars) or the American Legion.

As a recipient of military awards including the Silver Star and Distinguished Flying Cross (DFC), Dr. Thomas Robert White diligently captured his wartime recollections in writing while they were still fresh. The family correctly assumed that this was a normal and healthful means to clear his mind of troubling memories, while noting errors discovered in the accounts of others.

The psychological injury of war inflicted on some veterans has variously been called "melancholy" in the Civil War, "shell shock" during World War I, "combat fatigue" during World War II, or, more recently, "posttraumatic stress disorder" (PTSD). Estimates of the percentage of military people impacted by PTSD vary widely; however, Dr. White was without symptoms and simply wished to move forward with professional and family obligations while pursuing other eclectic interests—and did so with grace and dignity.

Family members suspect that the memoir began on a apron pocket sized notebook filled with dates, times, and locations intended as source data for preparing military pay and travel expense vouchers. The simple diary was expanded in the wake of Ted Lawson's 1943 book, *Thirty Seconds over Tokyo*. Updates, additions, and editing continued until the last referenced date of June 1944. Ted Lawson, with a leg amputation and other crash-related injuries, was Dr. White's most seriously injured patient. The pair were linked for the balance of the trip after their two aircraft (numbers 7 and 15) separately ditched on the China coastline. As an attending physician, Dr. White normally downplayed his personal fears, political opinions, or religious convictions despite seeking out advice, sustenance, and shelter from other English-speaking Westerners— who were often missionaries.

Like a diamond in the rough, the manuscript required polishing. Edits were needed because Americanized English has evolved since 1942, to add context and untangle certain events. After eighty years, some words became obscure or obsolete or assumed unintended or unflattering connotations. Also, fact-checking uncovered some misstatements. These are either footnoted or scrubbed out. We regret any errors that escaped detection.

The terms "Japs" or "Jap" are pejorative—but universally used (and historically accurate) during World War II, as was abundantly evident in newspapers, radio broadcasts, movie newsreels, signage, and everyday dialogue during that era. The Japanese then called their country Nippon. They now call it Nihon. In other Pacific nations, the term "Nipponese" (as in All Nippon Airways) is common and abbreviated Nip or Nips. The terms "enemy," "foe," "invaders," and "Shipu-men" (Chinese slang), also found herein, are euphemisms for the Japanese military.

Dr. White's natural granddaughter, Gabrielle Adelman, took leadership by having the historic manuscript crafted into a book. John Fredrickson, the author of five other published aviation history books, willingly stepped forward and embraced this new project. Primary proofreaders included Adelman and Carl Fredrickson. A Seattle-area physician, Dr. Hilton Chen, reviewed the medical aspects of the transcript.

Fredrickson found himself on hand with the Boeing B-52 bombers at U-Tapao Airfield, Thailand, during the Christmas bombings[1] of December 1972. The POWs came home in April 1973 because of President Nixon's decisive aerial assault on Hanoi and Haiphong. The door was then open for American forces to exit the self-inflicted quagmire that was Vietnam. Working as an aircrew life support specialist within the Air Force (and later at the Boeing Company) provided insights into the survival situations faced by many in Doolittle's cadre.

Photographs were obtained from stock photos, online public-domain images (NARA[2] and others), Boeing Historical Archives, private collections, and the White family. Most of the photos identified as "Boeing" are from the North American Aviation (NAA) collection within the Boeing Historical Archives and are used with permission. Unattributed photographs are from Fredrickson's personal collection. Artifacts purchased by Dr. White remain with the family and are depicted in photographs and captions. All dollar amounts (and prices) quoted in the text are exactly as written by Dr. White. No inflation adjustments have been made.

White's manuscript was augmented by other accounts of early war in the Pacific. Sources consulted include other unpublished firsthand accounts, oral histories, interviews, online references, and books. Two volumes of Japanese origin were informative. The first is in English, dated 1955 and titled *Midway: The Battle That Doomed Japan, the Japanese Navy's Story*, by Japanese naval historians Fuchida and Okumiya. The second is a detailed account of the Raider's bomb damage, written by Shibata and Hara. The small paperback is dated 2016 and currently is available only in Japanese.

INTRODUCTION

ON DECEMBER 7, 1941, the United States suffered a military defeat of such magnitude that the meaning of such words as "dastardly" and "infamy" was forever altered. The Japanese juggernaut ran rampant in the months that followed. Nothing seemed to blunt the rapid and ruthless advance. Successful Nipponese attacks were being executed on a broad swath ranging from the Aleutians on the north, to New Guinea on the south, to Hawaii on the east, and almost to India on the west.

The ire of the American public was aroused by the embarrassing sneak attack on Pearl Harbor. Delivered with stealth, cunning, and surprise, the well-choreographed aerial assault was a rout that truncated the lives of 2,403 young Americans. Antiwar sentiment had been strong. The gauntlet was laid down. Would a nation of the unwilling and those of dubious resolve rise to the occasion? Emotions rose to a fevered pitch. A stunned nation was down but not out. US citizens of every stratum expected and demanded swift retribution.

The debacle at Pearl Harbor triggered the equally audacious (but much less devastating) Doolittle Raid. By 1941, Depression-era underfunding yielded a decimated US military properly categorized as undersized, poorly equipped, and unprepared. The 17th Bomb Group of the Pacific Northwest was a notable exception. Unlike the National Guard and other reserve forces, the aircrews were full-time aviators, experienced, well trained, and already proficient with their freshly acquired B-25 Mitchell fast-attack bombers.[1] The formidable North American B-25B was one of the most lethal new warplanes then entering service.

Jimmy Doolittle personally picked the most-capable aircrew members. Officers seldom perform in an enlisted position; however, crew size limitations dictated that Dr. White (a physician) be trained as a top-turret gunner before being assigned to airplane number 15. By mutual crew agreement, the three initials "TNT"[2] were painted on the nose of the airplane bearing tail number

40-2267.[3] Each volunteer aircrew pampered and prepared their assigned plane because, to a man, they each aspired to make the final cut. The only B-25 aft of "TNT" belonged to William Farrow and crew. The late addition was squeezed into position number 16.

The single-file march of the Raiders up the gangway and aboard the Pacific Fleet's newest aircraft carrier—USS *Hornet* (CV-8) at Alameda—came on April 1, 1942. Lacking means of concealment, sixteen of America's most advanced fast-attack bombers graced her deck for all to see at a moment when the war was still fresh and the outcome uncertain. Many of the Navy deckhands were newly recruited and eager for their first cruise. Most everybody assumed that the planes were being ferried to Hawaii. Accompanied by cruisers, destroyers, and an oil tanker, the flotilla appeared invincible at dockside and could be headed anywhere.

The task force brazenly departed by steaming under the Golden Gate Bridge in broad daylight[4] and then set course for a midocean rendezvous with the legendary USS *Enterprise* (CV-6) and escorts. Only when at sea were the Navy men informed the mission destination was Tokyo. The cheering was spontaneous and heartfelt. The assignment of Task Force 16 was to penetrate to within 250 miles for a close-in attack on the heart of the Japanese Empire; however, the plan was derailed by an encounter with an enemy trawler, one of a string forming a defensive perimeter surrounding the Japanese main island of Honshu. An immediate but premature takeoff was ordered.

By the standards of today, the size and weight of a North American B-25 Mitchell are diminutive and roughly the same as a modern-day Cessna Citation X. It takes all sixteen of Doolittle's fully loaded B-25s to equal the full weight of a single battle-ready Boeing B-52 Stratofortress. The Japanese Empire was then at the apex of its military ascendancy. Nobody declined a mission akin to plunging a bare arm into a hornets' nest. Eighty brave souls entrusted their lives to these little airplanes to deliver a gut punch deep into the cultural, military, religious, and political heartland of Nihon.

On April 18, 1942, sixteen B-25s appeared at low altitude, spread over a broad swath of urban Japan. The hydraulic systems came alive with a whine. The bomb bay doors on each of the sixteen aircraft swung open upon approach to target. Four bombs weighing 500 pounds each were delivered individually. Like the Americans at Pearl Harbor, Tokyo's defenders were also caught napping. Under the capable planning and leadership of James R. "Jimmy" Doolittle, not a single attacker was brought down or even seriously threatened.

Nightfall comes quickly in the tropics. Things went seriously awry in the hours following the successful bombing mission. Darkness overcame daylight just as all of Doolittle's planes ran short of fuel. The extra and unplanned air miles between USS *Hornet* and Tokyo consumed the precious fuel intended for final approach into waiting Chinese airfields. Most aboard donned parachutes and bailed out over China. "TNT" ditched off the coast. Five aviators scrambled out of their sinking hulk and onto an emergency life raft. Dr. White instantly realized he was the only able mariner aboard the floundering rubberized boat. Shivering in the chilly darkness, the aircrew luckily made it to shore and onto an island inhabited by impoverished Chinese subsistence farmers.

The Doolittle Raid is an epic World War II drama that, while familiar, remains compelling. This account is specific to the crew members aboard a pair of airplanes named "Ruptured Duck" (number 7) and "TNT" (number 15). At the core is the wartime memoir of Dr. Thomas Robert White, MD, a Harvard-educated physician, a flight surgeon, and the only medical officer to participate in the Tokyo raid. Dr. White's saga combines selfless service to others mixed with the vicissitudes of life on the lam in war-torn China, where menacing Japanese soldiers were frequently in hot pursuit.

The US military of World War II was awash in young males. As is typical, their daily vernacular was thick with profanity.[5] Furthermore, there was probably disagreement between these feisty young men of equal rank regarding appropriate next steps as they slowly trod the breadth of China. Dr. White spares the reader from these squabbles. Despite the unemotional writing style typical of a practicing physician, the result is a gripping account of wartime escape and evasion in an exotic land.

Doctor White's stellar education included Harvard Medical School (1937), with an internship as a surgeon at Johns Hopkins. White joined the Army Air Corps and eagerly sought out an assignment aboard the top-secret mission as flight surgeon, gunner, and crew member. He was often called "Doc" by others within the unit, and his unique story was captured on paper while still fresh in the 1940s. Hidden away for eight decades, the memoir begins with stateside preparations and training. Dr. White and pilot Edward York joined at the third stop (Eglin Field, Florida), where the late arrivals became valued additions to the team.

Born into wealth, educated in science, bestowed with an appreciation for the arts, and endowed with a natural curiosity, Dr. White savored the sights, sounds, and cuisine of the exotic Chinese route traveled by his cadre of downed aviators. Some were hobbled by serious injuries. No longer overlords above or masters of the Asian skies, those lucky enough to survive and avoid capture next found themselves afoot and at the mercy of rag-clad local peasants. Betraying a single Raider entitled any Indigenous Chinese to a generous reward from the ruthless invaders. Luckily, peer pressure combined with a mutual seething hatred of the "Shipu-men" were sufficient disincentives.

The turn of the twentieth century was a time of Chinese turmoil. The last Qing emperor abdicated. The situation remained a mess during 1942. A new republic was declared, but regional powers soon arose and struggled for supremacy. Colonial violence continued at the behest of the Europeans, rival gangs, and US Navy gunboats on river patrol. The Sino hinterland remained home to a smattering of tenacious Christian missionaries and a few other persistent Western aid workers.

As the political elites debated about future trajectories for their society, average citizens were confronting threats to their survival that included a ruthless invader (Japan), concurrent with civil war between the Nationalist regime of Chiang Kai-shek and the Communist factions of Mao Zedong (formerly spelled Mao Tse-Tung). Deepening economic connections to the capitalist industrialized world that brought along modern Western technology including automobiles, railroads, telegraph, radios, and airplanes imposed further fissures upon this most ancient of Asian cultures.

As is common for the human condition, large numbers of perpetually poor Chinese endured in their communities amid a smattering of wealthier neighbors. Both rich and poor shared contempt for the Nipponese invaders. Both factions collaborated at the risk of torture and death to assist the Americans who fell randomly from the sky and into their midst. The helpful peasants barely subsisted off the land—yet proved themselves as fearless saviors during an alarming number of close encounters with pursuing Japanese troops. The long trek to safety was a life-or-death ordeal that began on foot as it proceeded westward across China. Like a recurring nightmare, walking, hiding, and fording water obstacles made the escape excruciatingly slow but never seriously eroded Dr. White's indomitable demeanor. Whenever the opportunity arose, his favorite diversions included scholarly observations, tinkering with guns, or frequent visits to retail bazaars.

Doctor T. R. White became one of a celebrated band of aviators[6] collectively remembered as the "Doolittle Raiders." To this day, a physician assigned to an Air Force flying organization is called a flight surgeon. The term "surgeon" is a misnomer. Very few routinely practice surgery; however, all perform flight physicals and are experts with the physiological aspects of flight. It is unprecedented for a medical officer to participate as a crew member aboard a high-stakes combat mission. As later acknowledged by Doolittle himself, having a physician aboard was fortuitous for the subsequent survival of four seriously injured comrades.

Doc was quick to adapt to being on foot in a weird alien landscape. Despite strange surprises lurking everywhere, he assumed leadership of his small party under trying circumstances. Dr. White's unwavering commitment was always to his patients. Chinese generosity repeatedly arrived in the form of aid and assistance. Everybody, from poor farmers to wealthy noblemen, pitched in. In-kind help included transportation, food, shelter, clothing, and, most importantly, secrecy and safe passage.

While the actual damage inflicted upon greater Tokyo by the raid was a mere pinprick, the impact on American morale was significant. The American airmen, in flying over Tokyo, even though avoiding the Imperial Palace, had violated Japanese dogma because nobody is entitled to "look down" upon the emperor. The Nipponese militarists, despite their ire, had failed the emperor and were forced to shift some offensive assets into a defensive role. The fallacy that their island nation was immune to attack (called "divine wind" or "kamikaze") was debunked. Furthermore, there are hints[7] that Japanese naval master tactician Admiral Isoroku Yamamoto (1884–1943) was flustered enough to bungle the planning for the pivotal Battle of Midway (June 4–7, 1942), where the Imperial Japanese Navy stumbled and never fully recovered.

Doolittle's audacious raid remains high on the list of celebrated World War II events. Even with an unlimited budget, the epic around-the-globe journey detailed herein can never be replicated because the world as it existed in 1942 is forever gone. White's manuscript augments the familiar Doolittle tale with a fresh account of survival, escape, evasion, and a grueling transcontinental trek across mainland China.

CHAPTER 1

MEET DR. THOMAS R. WHITE, MD (1909–92)

"**MY PARTICIPATION IN** the Doolittle Raid on Japan was largely a result of an old habit of sticking my neck out," wrote Dr. Thomas R. White, MD. He continued, "There were many times during the months that followed when I had qualms about volunteering; however, now that it is over, I wouldn't take anything in exchange for this adventure of a lifetime. Having been born in Hawaii, I considered the dastardly Japanese sneak attack on Pearl Harbor as a personal affront."

Doc was born in the territory of Hawaii at Haiku, on the island of Maui, in 1909 into an accomplished American clan. Family roots have been traced back to barons Richard de Clare, Gilbert de Clare, and John de Lacie from the Magna Carta days, and even William the Conqueror. The family name traces back to Thomas White of Sudbury, Massachusetts, in 1638. Rooted in philanthropy, his grandfather Thomas H. White (1836–1914), of Cleveland, was the founder of the White Sewing Machine Company and the White Motor Car Company (1900–80). In the tradition of Henry Ford, White (of sewing-machine fame) was short on formal education but a savant as demonstrated by mechanical and entrepreneurial skills.

Thomas Howard White (of Cleveland) was wed to Almira Greenleaf, and the couple conceived eight children. The fifth born was Clarence Greenleaf White (1869–1957). The passion of Clarence was agriculture—including the commercial growing of Irish potatoes in northern Florida, followed by a pineapple plantation in Hawaii. Also financially well set, the Clarence White family made its permanent home east of Los Angeles in a suburb called Redlands. The tradition of philanthropy continued by underwriting the Redlands Bowl, one of the most enduring musical venues in America.

White attended a special elementary school called Kingsbury School in Redlands. The school still exists. It is where reciting the Pledge of Allegiance first became a daily ritual that later spread nationwide. With prominent ancestors also named Thomas, Dr. White shunned his first name and embraced his given middle name of Robert. Better yet—friends and family called him "Bob"; however, Army decorum demanded proper first names, and only then did he revert to "Tom" or Thomas. Easily finishing prep school at Redlands High School in 1927, T. Robert White's undergraduate matriculation was at the nearby California Institute of Technology at Pasadena. The school (sometimes called Caltech) describes itself as a "world-renowned science and engineering institute."

California enjoyed a prosperous economy starting with the Gold Rush of 1849 and continuing into the Hollywood era. Oil wells, thriving agriculture, and an aviation boom in Southern California made the Golden State an especially idyllic place for rearing young people. T. Robert White was a big youngster with broad shoulders. His freshman interest in football later shifted toward a passion for chemistry, science, and flight (then called aero club). Graduation from Caltech came in 1931.

Young Thomas White was blessed with a sharp mind, good grades, ambition, and financial means. The passion for science drove him to Harvard Medical School, followed by an internship at Johns Hopkins. A commission as a lieutenant in the Army Air Corps sealed the deal by melding medicine with aviation. The circuitous route via medical school and the internship found Dr. White a decade older than the other lieutenants who were his Air Corps patients, peers, and constant companions. As a group, they were each handpicked as some of the most capable aerial warriors America could muster.

Under the Law of Armed Conflict and various treaties, some categories of military service qualify as noncombatant. People afforded protection on the battlefield include military medical people and chaplains. Dr. White eschewed this status. Even though all physicians are pledged to healing, Doc deported himself as a combatant by willfully manning the guns aboard "TNT." In any case, he knew that the Japanese ignored protocols regarding noncombatants. If ever captured alive by the Japanese, a well-educated practicing surgeon would be a godsend to any combat unit; however, Dr. White, when clad in a flight suit, could expect the exact same fate as any other downed aviator.

Dr. White wrote, "My quest towards war began in February of 1942 when my outfit, the old 89th Reconnaissance Squadron, and our parent unit, the 17th Bombardment Group (Medium), were being transferred from Pendleton, Oregon, to Columbia, South Carolina. While in transit, the combat crew members were approached and asked to volunteer for a 'secret and dangerous' mission. We were the number one priority outfit for overseas duty and had just finished a stint of maritime surveillance missions out of Tacoma's McChord Field in search of Japanese submarines lurking in the nearby Pacific Ocean. Maritime patrol had served to whet our appetites. Naturally everyone volunteered when the opportunity presented itself."

CHAPTER 2

JIMMY DOOLITTLE

Our purpose was to give the folks at home
the first good news that we'd had in World War II.

—James H. Doolittle

THE SHREWD BUT AMIABLE Dwight D. Eisenhower and a reformed ruffian, James H. "Jimmy" Doolittle, were two of the most universally recognized general officers to emerge from World War II. What were their shared attributes? Both were brilliant planners with the ability to inspire others. As an accomplished pair with stellar reputations, it was said that Eisenhower[1] ("Ike" to most) chain-smoked too many cigarettes and had a terrible temper; however, the tantrums were normally well hidden from public view. Jimmy Doolittle was already an aviation icon and achieved celebrity status after scripting and executing the Tokyo Raid of April 18, 1942. Separately, Eisenhower rose from prewar obscurity by planning and orchestrating amphibious invasions, first in North Africa, then Italy, and culminating with the onslaught at Normandy (France), commencing with the massive invasion of Europe starting on June 6, 1944 (now remembered as D-Day).

Like the White family, the lineage of the Doolittle clan also traces back many generations into American history. Jimmy was the only child of Frank Henry Doolittle (1869–1918) and Rosa Cerenah (1869–1930). As father and the traditional family breadwinner, Frank Doolittle was a carpenter and a restless soul frequently on the move in search of a better life. Chasing the Alaskan Gold Rush brought the family to the Wild West "hell on wheels" mining town of Nome just prior to 1900. It is where Eskimos, agog at the massive influx of new Caucasian arrivals, struggled to maintain their identity. Bars and bawdy houses prevailed as the inevitable camp followers sought to mine the miners.

A small boy with girlish looks, Jimmy was a natural magnet for bigger boys, who delighted in pushing him around. With lightning reflexes, the young Doolittle learned to swing fast and punch hard whenever menaced. Young Jimmy traveled with his father on a trip to Seattle, where he witnessed amazing things: streetcars and houses with paint. Rosa returned to Los Angeles in 1908, partly so Jimmy could get a better education. At age fifteen, Jimmy got involved in a street riot and was hauled off to jail. "Keep him there until Monday morning," his mother told the police. "I'll come get him in time for school." She felt that a weekend in jail might set him straight. It did. Henceforth, Doolittle vowed to defer to reason ahead of emotion—and sometimes he succeeded.

Yet, a propensity toward either brawling or organized boxing lingered during his formative years as new interests arose: motorcycles, flying, and a romantic interest in Josephine "Joe" Daniels. A long courtship ensued. As the other passions faded, it was love for Josephine and passion for flight that remained through seventy-one years of marriage.

Despite a ne'er-do-well reputation (especially with Josephine's parents), the bright little guy (stated height, 5 feet, 6 inches; actual height was closer to 5 foot 4) also had a knack for education, flying, and surviving close calls. He completed high school in California and then studied mining engineering at the University of California at Berkeley. Marriage to Josephine came in December 1917. Like many young men of his era, Jimmy also succumbed to the siren song of wartime service against the despised Germans and enrolled for pilot training in the US Signal Corps aviation section.

Ground school was completed in January 1918, at San Diego's Rockwell Field. Jimmy, accompanied by an instructor pilot, taxied out for his first flight in a Curtiss JN-4 Jenny. Nearby, they heard the shocking sound of crumpled wood and metal hitting the ground. It was a midair collision. Doolittle and the instructor exited their craft and rushed to the nearby first heap of wreckage. A student solo pilot lay dead in the wreckage. A short distance beyond, the second heap was occupied by an instructor and student—both still breathing. Jimmy helped extricate the victims from the wreckage just as an ambulance arrived to evacuate them to a hospital. After a very brief pause, the instructor then motioned for Jimmy to remount their plane.

"I was shaken by what I had seen," Doolittle later recalled. "If there is such a thing as love at first sight, my love of flying began on that day at that hour." Thousands of young men aspired to wartime adventure. Many of those who experienced the horrors of trench warfare intermixed with poison-gas attacks came to loathe it. The bloodbath called the "Great War" ended on November 11, 1918, before the eager young lieutenant arrived. The US Army brass bestowed upon Doolittle more freedom than normal for air racing and other stunts, first because he was a gifted aviator. Second, in their quest for congressional funding, the Air Service was always eager for good publicity.

As a confirmed overachiever and workaholic, Jimmy Doolittle was a driven individual always in a hurry. Enough wrecked airplanes were left behind to make an insurance adjuster shudder. Following years of air racing, stunts, and serious work as a test pilot, Doolittle applied for and was granted tuition-paid enrollment at the prestigious Massachusetts Institute of Technology (MIT)—the nation's top-rated engineering school. The curriculum was aeronautical engineering.

Characteristically and consistent with past behavior, Doolittle threw himself toward dangerous tasks. Aircraft were taken aloft and then pushed to the edges of their capabilities—and sometimes beyond. Moreover, he willingly became a human guinea pig to probe the phenomenon of blackouts. Engineers define 1 "g" as the normal pull of gravity. Aircraft and those aboard can experience a spectrum of g-forces, ranging from negative g- (blood rushing to the head) and zero g- (or weightlessness) to multiple g-forces—depending on the maneuver. Doolittle took it upon himself to perform the tests. He concluded that blackout could be followed by death with more than ten or twelve seconds exceeding 4.5 g.[2]

Doolittle dabbled with instrument flying and was the first to take off and land while under a hood (view-limiting device). Another pilot with unobstructed vision was aboard to ensure their safety. The altimeter, invented by Paul Kollsman, was a significant breakthrough instrument. Improvements were also forthcoming in two-way voice radio communications even as airframes and engines improved with the passage of time.

The Army Air Corps of World War I consisted of two hundred thousand men and eight thousand aircraft. By 1925 it had shrunk to fewer than ten thousand men and fifteen hundred aircraft. Despite a dozen years of service as a commissioned officer, a profound list of aviation accomplishments, and a chest filled with ribbons, Doolittle remained at the bottom of the military pecking order as a lowly first lieutenant.

Sons James and John were born in 1920 and 1922, respectively.[3] Lack of promotion was frustrating. Lt. Jimmy Doolittle traded active duty for a reserve commission as a major[4] in 1930. The commitment was two weeks of military drill per year. Mr. and Mrs. Doolittle said goodbye to the many uniformed friends and the powerful social bonds that bring service people together. Employment at the Shell petroleum company awaited. An open-ended job description included air racing, stunts, working with industry, and collecting bigger paychecks.

Octane is a measure of an engine's ability to resist engine knock. The Army had already attempted to standardize gasoline for everything from motorcycles to aircraft at 87 octane. Doolittle organized and closely monitored testing of various grades of fuel at Wright Field, near Dayton, Ohio. The startling discovery was that increasing octane to 100 would increase power by up to 30 percent even in existing engines. It was then decided that all subsequent combat aircraft engines would operate on 100-octane fuel. By 1943, Shell was producing 15 million gallons of aviation gasoline per day. Standardized fuel was shared among bomber, pursuit, trainer, and transport aircraft as needed.

Some called it a "bumblebee"; others called it a "flying milk bottle." Only 17 feet long, with a chunky body and stubby wings, the Gee Bee Super Sportster had the cartoonish look of a toy airplane. Designed only for speed, the cutest little airplane was also the deadliest. Very few pilots could master it. Two of these were Jimmy Doolittle and Delmar Benjamin. Doolittle compared flying the unstable contraption to "balancing a pencil on your fingertip" even as he shattered a speed record at the 1932 Thompson Trophy race by whipping a Gee Bee around a racecourse at an average speed of 253.6 miles per hour.

Doolittle's accomplishments during the decade of the 1930s were many and significant. As an aviation celebrity and self-made man, Jimmy (along with many other World War I aviators) recognized the dire situation of a looming war. With a welcoming nod from General Hap Arnold, Doolittle's military career resumed with a recall to active duty in 1940, combined with a promotion to lieutenant colonel.

A Plan Is Hatched

The weeks following the Pearl Harbor attack found mission planners both at airplane factories and the War Department, with their protractors, slide rules, and maps laid out on big flat tables as bomb capacity, fuel loads, and the ranges of multiple types of aircraft were carefully evaluated. Tokyo was their target of choice. A pinprick attack on a hinterland Japanese base would not deliver much succor to families of those forever lost on December 7, 1941. Emotions remained raw, with the remains of deceased sailors lying unrecovered aboard USS *Arizona* and other Pearl Harbor hulks.

During late December an idea emerged in discussions between British and American flag officers. Navy captain Francis "Frog" Low, a World War I–era submariner, was on the staff of Navy vice admiral Ernest J. King (1878–1956). King was a hard-drinking, no-nonsense sailor, while also rated by historians as one the sharpest naval minds of that era. Low had seen Army bombers at Norfolk using an airfield marked for a Navy aircraft carrier.

Ernest King was more feared than loved, so Low waited for a private time to share his idea: "Could Japan be attacked by bombers launched from aircraft carriers?"

King responded, "What kind of airplanes did you have in mind?"

"How the hell do I know? I'm a submarine man," retorted Captain Low. The American public and President Franklin D. Roosevelt remained eager for retribution. Admiral King embraced the idea and shared it with Army generals George Marshall and Hap Arnold. As the antithesis of King, the easygoing and gregarious Hap Arnold eagerly jumped aboard the bandwagon. In the middle of the shakeout of other senior leaders rated as "deadwood," all three men were equally committed to keeping their jobs and winning the war.

Hap Arnold called upon Lt. Col. Jimmy Doolittle for advice. Doolittle sensed an opportunity for a patriotic adventure far greater than motorcycle riding, fistfights, or air races. Contrary to Hap's desire to preserve the life of this promising war planner, Doolittle decisively seized for himself the role of "hands-on" leader for this high-profile airborne mission.

	B-25 Mitchell	**B-26 Marauder**
Builder	North American Aviation, Inc.	Glenn L. Martin Company
First flight	August 19, 1940	November 25, 1940
Engines, two	Wright R-2600 Radial	Pratt & Whitney R-2800 Radial
Horsepower (each engine)	1,650	2,000
Propeller	three-blade Hamilton Standard	four-blade Curtiss
Top speed (mph)	328 → 272	323 → 287
Cost in 1944	$142,194	$192,427
Service ceiling	24,200 feet	19,800 feet
Landing gear	tricycle	tricycle
Empennage	twin tail	conventional
Wingspan	67 feet, 7 inches	67 feet, 6.7 inches
Built at	Inglewood and Kansas City	Baltimore and Omaha
Units produced	±9,984	5,288
Production ended	August 1945	March 1945

Every type of available Army Air Forces bomber was evaluated for use aboard aircraft carriers. Boeing B-17 and Consolidated B-24 were obviously far too large. Douglas B-18 Bolo and B-23 (derived from the DC-2 and DC-3 airliners) also had unacceptably long wings. The Martin B-26 wingspan was nearly identical to the North American B-25. Both could clear the island (an aircraft carrier's starboard-side vertical structure). Furthermore, the Marauder also had more-powerful Pratt & Whitney R-2800 radial engines.

All the Army bombers were deemed unsuitable for carrier landings. A water landing (ditching) adjacent to Navy ships was also quickly ruled out because land-based bombers were especially ill-suited for ditching—especially in the huge swells of the open ocean.

Doolittle rejected the Martin B-26 Marauder because of performance and safety concerns. The stability and superior flight safety record of the Mitchell bomber became the deciding factor. Frequent crashes bestowed the nickname of "Widow Maker" on the Martin Marauder.[5] Only the Mitchell emerged as suitable for aircraft carrier takeoffs. Proof came by launching B-25s from surfaces outlined with paint to emulate the flight deck of an aircraft carrier. The requirement boiled down to a range of 2,400 miles and a bombload of 2,000 pounds. The Mitchell bomber was the best choice.

Despite earlier crude experiments with hoses and buckets, reliable midair refueling was unavailable before 1950. As planning proceeded, the strategy evolved into a one-way mission starting aboard an aircraft carrier, bombing the heart of Japan, and then seeking a landing airfield somewhere. But where? Western Russia (Siberia) was the best choice as measured by distance. Consistent with Lend-Lease,[6] the airplanes would be donated to the Soviets in exchange for safe passage of the crews; however, at the end of 1941, Joseph Stalin was mired in a death struggle with Hitler's Wehrmacht, making the risk of another battlefront with Japan foolhardy.

What about landing in China rather than Siberia? Distance, fuel load, timing, and navigation all became more tenuous. Could a squadron of warplanes be delivered for a good cause? Yes, the American Volunteer Group (AVG, but better remembered as the "Flying Tigers") was already Air Corps affiliated and expanding into B-25 operations. However, the AVG headquarters in Chunking was working under contract to the Nationalist Chinese government, and that relationship was riddled with information leaks at every level. Distrust extended all the way to Generalissimo[7] Chiang Kai-shek (1887–1975) and his power-hungry spouse, the stunningly beautiful Madame Chiang Kai-shek[8] (1898–2003). Plans for landing somewhere in China needed to remain fuzzy, and that decision ultimately proved problematic.

Doolittle and the other mission planners fully understood that China was a huge, impoverished country mired in turmoil. Furthermore, it was US strategy to stoke the war in China because it kept a million Japanese troops engaged in battle and away from the other fronts. Online estimates put the wartime Chinese population at 517.5 million. Like a predator devouring live prey, the Japanese invasion was tearing away at the east coast of China. The World War II savagery of Japanese troops when on offense is well documented elsewhere and requires no retelling here. An estimated 19.5 million[9] Chinese perished in fighting between 1939 and 1945. The invaders were gaining ground by gobbling up real estate, while bestowing death (or worse fates) upon hordes of innocent Chinese.

Civil war beset other areas of China. The Nationalists, under Chiang Kai-shek, clung to the path of a free democracy, while the Communists, led by Mao Zedong (1893–1976), were collectivists. Meanwhile, various guerrilla factions roamed the countryside. Some were well-intentioned vigilantes while others were criminal thugs who robbed, pillaged, and extorted. Beset with this chaos, an estimated four million Chinese military members[10] died, while an additional sixteen million civilians perished in China during World War II.

The B-25 was one of the Air Corps' newest, fastest, and most lethal warplanes during the early months of World War II. The 17th Bomb Group was headquartered at Pendleton, Oregon, with operating locations at other Pacific Northwest airfields.[11] The 17th consisted of B-25 aircraft and their crews, organized into well-functioning squadrons. The cream of the crop became earmarked for a mysterious and undefined mission. Even more rigorous training commenced. About three months were spent in preparations with the crews, consisting of mechanics, technicians, armorers, et al. being trained together. Time was spent on cross-country trips, night flying, and overwater sorties to permit pilots and navigators to become accustomed to flying without visual or radio references or land markers. Low-altitude approaches, rapid bombing, and evasive actions were repeatedly rehearsed.

Two dozen B-25s with their crews departed Pendleton and headed east. The first wintertime stop was at Mid-Continent Airlines in icy Minneapolis. As skilled civilian technicians swarmed over the airplanes, aircrew members were called into a secret meeting in a hotel conference room. That is where general mention of the true mission was first broached.

Military victory often depends on surprise, deceit, and misinformation. As normal, a false cover story for the Minneapolis stopover was concocted: "More range was needed so these B-25s could fly anti-submarine patrol in the Atlantic." Therefore, a 160-gallon rubber fuel tank was installed above the bomb bay. It would temporarily block the void over the wing spars, which was the only in-flight passageway between forward and aft fuselage. The mechanical changes to the planes were many and ingenious. Modifications were intended to conserve weight and space for essential items. After careful deliberation, some parts were added while others were removed. Deicers and anti-icers were installed. Liaison radio sets were removed. To avoid fire hazard, no pyrotechnics were carried, although two conventional landing flares were stored immediately aft of the rear bulkhead. Self-sealing fuel tanks, intended to close about and seal bullet holes, were then a recent innovation.

A bomb was then defined by the Ordnance Department as "a missile intended to be dropped by an airplane." Air Corps dogma regarding aerial bombardment was already established before World War II erupted. Interwar doctrine was to use conventional bombing tactics at 20,000 feet to avoid enemy AAA (antiaircraft artillery) fire,[12] called flak. The tight box formations offered overlapping machine gun protection from swarming interceptor aircraft. The term "precision bombing" was a misnomer. The variance between bull's-eye and where the bomb hits is called "circular error of probability" (or CEP). The CEP from 20,000 feet was significant—especially against targets with a small footprint—such as a bridge or radio antenna.

Doolittle's mission planners rightfully rejected the "European mindset" of daytime raids in tight formations at high altitude. Creative thinking yielded a better plan for a small, fast, and nimble commando-style attack. Lacking escort and to confuse witnesses, they would spread out and penetrate the urban areas at rooftop altitude. The B-25 carried only a small load of 2,000 pounds (as compared to a B-17 payload of 5,000 to 8,000 pounds). There were no bombs to waste. Low-level bombing, even with a crudely fabricated bombsight, was more accurate and yielded less collateral damage (unintended carnage) than the high-level method, which was complicated by clouds, cold, lack of oxygen, and winds aloft. The Raiders would "pop up" only enough to avoid shrapnel damage from their own bombs, then make a quick escape. The strategy was brilliant, and it worked.

The winged armada next touched down at Columbia, South Carolina. Word of the true mission was further broached to the crews. The danger was becoming obvious, but to a man they all signed on—even the married ones. The next stop was Eglin Field on Florida's panhandle. In fact, Eglin Air Force base, which now measures 464,000 acres, is a collection of scattered airfields sufficiently distant from each other, meaning that operations at one field are invisible to the other locations.

Army pilots were conditioned to make smooth takeoffs from long runways. Speed builds until the velocity needed for rotation and initial climb is attained. Conversely, unassisted flight deck takeoffs demanded a short 500-foot run;

therefore, ingrained cockpit habits required discarding and relearning. Instead, heavily laden planes were jerked aloft just above stall speed.

As training at Eglin continued, Doolittle flew west to California for private meetings with Admiral William Halsey.[13] Over dinner and drinks, Doolittle expressed his absolute fealty to Navy demands anytime while shipboard. If necessary, the B-25s would be dumped overboard in case Navy aircraft from the hangar deck were needed to fend off an enemy attack.

Two aircraft carriers were committed to the Doolittle Raid. USS *Hornet* (CV-8) was freshly arrived in the Pacific via the Panama Canal from the Newport News Shipbuilding Company. It hosted Doolittle, his aviators, spare crew members, support staff, and sixteen B-25 medium bombers. USS *Enterprise* (CV-6) would escort and provide air cover. *Enterprise* was spared from the Pearl Harbor debacle because the "Big E" (as it was later called) happened to be at sea on December 7.

It was a mere five months after Japanese torpedoes demonstrated the capacity to inflict gaping holes into the heavily armored battleships tethered to Harbor Island moorage. America did not fare well during the first weeks of the war with Japan. Doolittle's autobiography asserts that Japanese intelligence gathered subtle hints indicating an armada (the Nipponese suspected two or three aircraft carriers) was steaming toward Japan in April 1942.

Unknown to US naval intelligence, Honshu (the primary Japanese home island) was encircled by picket boats constantly on alert for any unwelcome intrusions. Lookouts on both sides, with binoculars in hand, warily scanned the wave tops to the horizon in search of telltale signs of trouble.

CHAPTER 3

WHITE JOINS THE RAIDERS

I WAS A BRAND-NEW AME (aviation medical examiner) fresh out of the School of Aviation Medicine at Randolph Field, Texas.[1] Patriots were smarting under the series of reverses which the United States had suffered during those first dark months of the war; consequently, when I heard of the opportunity, I excitedly wired my skipper, Maj. Jack Hilger, to ask if he could possibly, repeat "possibly," squeeze me in somewhere—even though no medical officer had been contemplated for the mission. I got my orders the next day and flew down to Eglin Field, Florida, with Capt. Edward "Ski" York.[2] The long transcontinental flight gave me time to admire the vast beauty of America from aloft while also celebrating my thirty-third birthday on March 29, 1942.

We were assigned billets in a couple of wooden barracks and immediately started on a course of intensive training to prepare for our task. The mission: ferry some airplanes to a foreign country and there would be "a chance of some action"—a considerable understatement, as it turned out. The conjecture that circulated as to our real objective was weird and wonderful. It was rather surprising how close to the truth some of the rumors were. We were known as "Special Project Detachment No. 1," and everything about us was very hush-hush. We were warned about the utmost secrecy of everything we heard or saw. Always vigilant, our duty was to report to authorities anybody who seemed unduly curious about our activities.

I will never forget how excited we all were when we heard that Lt. Col. James H. Doolittle was going to be our commanding officer. Jaws dropped and some of the men audibly gasped when Doolittle confidently first strode onto the stage. He completely won our hearts and minds at our first meeting with his sincerity, friendliness, and enthusiasm. Very few of us ever had cause to regret our association with him. From that day on, everyone called him "Jimmy."[3] Jimmy never hesitated to go to bat for anyone he thought deserving. Doolittle always gave me the closest cooperation—even dispatching an aircraft to Washington, DC, to obtain some vaccines on my requisition list directly from the surgeon general.

Our training at Eglin Field was much as depicted in the movie *Thirty Seconds over Tokyo*, short takeoffs, low-level flying (and I do mean low; we'd have to gain altitude to avoid a haystack), navigation, bombing, and gunnery. In addition to our specialty, each of us was trained to do several other jobs. In case of casualty before our mission was completed, I learned to bomb and navigate. I could already fly, having had a private pilot's license before the war, and I qualified in aerial gunnery with the .50-caliber Browning machine guns with the second-highest score in the detachment, a source of considerable satisfaction to me. We trained more crews than we planned to use, and the competition among them to be chosen was very keen. Jimmy gave us all several chances to back out; he never minimized the dangers and always said, "I don't want anybody with me who isn't 100 percent anxious to go."

My medical preparations consisted chiefly of inoculating the aircrew members with every type of vaccine available. Besides the usual typhoid, tetanus, smallpox, and yellow fever, they received protection from typhus, cholera, pneumonia, and bubonic plague. Most took it gracefully, aside from a few remarks about being human guinea pigs resembling pincushions. One chap swore he'd bleed serum if he were ever wounded, since he was certain there was no room for blood in his veins. Another wanted to know when I was going to give him his latex shots—he wanted to be self-sealing like the fuel tanks. An army thrives on paperwork. Each inoculation was annotated in the bearer's small paper booklet we called a "shot record."

I assembled a small kit of surgical instruments, essential drugs, and dressings to take along. Weight considerations limited what I could take, as every ounce counted. Clothing and other personal equipment was limited to 50 pounds.

We began to suspect that something extraordinary was afoot when the intensity of our preparations became evident. Internal speculation surged when US Navy lieutenant S. G. "Hank" Miller reported as liaison officer. The next clue was information that the mission was to bomb "an enemy capital." By connecting the dots, the conclusion was by then inescapable—a carrier strike against Tokyo. During this time, news commentators were demanding bombing of the Japanese home islands. We became alarmed they were leaking our plans.

"Hank" Miller delivered several useful lectures on naval etiquette and told us what to expect while underway. This was in addition to his primary job of teaching the pilots to get their planes off in the shortest possible space. Lt. Miller cautioned us never to call the ship a boat. "Ships carry boats, you know." He taught us how to salute first the quarterdeck and then the officer of the deck when boarding, as well as the proper way to crisply orate the verbal salutations: "Lieutenant So-and-So reporting on board in compliance with orders!" We were told how to take a shower without wasting water; how to tell port (left) from starboard (right); that floors were hereafter to be known as "decks" and walls as "bulkheads." One never went upstairs, one always went "topside." Ask for the "head" when seeking the toilet. All this was not as new to me as it was to most of the others, as I have boated most of my life and had been on board many Navy vessels—including the gallant aircraft carrier *Lexington* (CV-2).

We had the closest possible cooperation from the Navy, who were in general much more generous with their supplies than the various Army installations with which I interacted. It was a continual battle to get medical supplies and equipment. The fact that we were on a secret mission prevented my filing the routine type of requisitions. Most of the time I was reduced to circumventing the prescribed system.

Training and Preparations

Our planes were modern B-25B Mitchell medium bombers from North American Aviation, Inc. (NAA), of Los Angeles. Each was gone over from nose to tail, deicers installed, and extra gas tanks had been added to deliver the needed range. The motors and all the other equipment were inspected by field service experts. Everything was tuned to the ultimate peak of efficiency.

The Norden bombsight was a mechanical contraption unable to deliver precision bombing at low altitudes. Furthermore, it was classified as "top secret" and considered too valuable to fall into enemy hands on a high-risk mission. The planes were instead retrofitted with simpler low-level bombsights fabricated of scrap aluminum designed by Capt. Charles Greening (pilot number 11). Greening was also a talented painter.

I was given my choice of assignments aboard two airplanes and chose number 15, the one piloted by Lt. Donald G. Smith. I did not realize it then, but that decision made the difference between life and death, because the other airplane (number 16), piloted by Lt. Bill Farrow, was found by the Japanese in China. Its crew was betrayed by a corrupt local official and Farrow was one of three men executed. The fancy names and pictures (nose art) which adorned the sides of American fighting planes of the era were randomly applied. Our plane bore the explosive initials TNT, an idea derived from my college chemistry studies. Some of the planes were named, while others were not.

After about six weeks, we finished the Florida training and flew cross country to Sacramento Air Depot, California, with stops at Kelly Field, Texas, and March Field, California. I was able to spend one night with my wife and children in Redlands but of course couldn't tell them anything about the mission I was on—or even that there was a good chance that I'd never see them again. They thought I was on a routine cross-country flight. It was wonderful to see them, even for a few hours. It reminded me of what we were fighting for.

At Sacramento, new replacement three-bladed variable-pitch Hamilton Standard propellers (measuring 12 feet, 6 inches in diameter) were installed on our planes along with some other repairs. Practice takeoffs were continued. We next flew to the Alameda Airport, Oakland, on March 31, 1942—where USS *Hornet* (CV-8) was seen for the first time. As a new and modern aircraft carrier, *Hornet* looked much bigger tied up at the dock than it did days later, when it was time for takeoff. It was becoming evident in the wake of the Pearl Harbor attack that winning modern wars demanded not only navy and army might but also airpower.

Life on the Home Front

During World War I, the United States took its first major plunge into deploying military forces overseas and sustaining them. As it turned out, Uncle Sam demonstrated an unmatched aptitude for logistics over very long distances and a knack for fighting effectively while abroad. Hostilities ended in November 1918, and most of the troops returned during 1919. However, the horrors of trench warfare, poison gas, and suicidal mass charges into machine guns were now unacceptable to mothers and fathers. More specifically, there was no public appetite for American participation in another overseas land war.

While Chinese peasants were stuck in a grim medieval style of subsistence, life in America was filled with excitement and technical advancement; however, the good times slowed when the stock market crashed in October 1929. Unlike previous financial panics, this time a tenacious Great Depression settled in. Government spending priorities decimated the US military. The year 1939 found the US Army ranked number 19 in the world—or just behind Portugal. The Army operated the CCC (Civilian Conservation Corps) camps, a program whereby underemployed young men could work in wilderness areas with a designated stipend to assist other family members. Thousands of young men were exposed to drill sergeants and a quasi-military lifestyle, which later eased their transition into the armed forces.

America's investment in troops and military hardware during the 1930s remained woefully inadequate. The Axis powers (Germany, Italy, and Japan) established both qualitative and quantitative advantage. By 1939, with war well underway in Asia and commencing in Europe, President Franklin D. Roosevelt finally awoke to the crisis and then adroitly prepared the nation for battle despite half-hearted political support from the public and their elected representatives.

During the summer of 1940, the US Navy moved the Pacific Fleet forward from San Diego to Pearl Harbor in a futile attempt to blunt the looming Japanese threat. People sensed something was amiss and conflict with Japan was imminent; however, nobody knew what event would trigger the melee. Was seizing one or more of the small islands like Guam, Midway, or Wake in the offing? Would an open-sea shoot-out between massed battleships clear the air? Many expected an invasion of the American-held Philippines. The well-executed sneak attack upon Pearl Harbor on December 7, 1941, resolved the uncertainty.

The Pearl Harbor debacle was a life-altering event for every rational US citizen alive at that time. Everything changed as mass hysteria ensued. A militia spontaneously emerged to defend the brand-new B-25 factory still under construction at Kansas City's Fairfax Airport. Panic and hysteria gripped the nation. Everybody everywhere was braced for an invasion. Paranoid and irrational ideas took root. Would the despised Nazis take everything east of the Mississippi? Would the West fall to the dreaded Japanese horde? Coastal residents cleaned and lubricated their deer-hunting rifles and shotguns. Cartoonish xenophobic stereotypes emerged of the now-vilified rice eaters, depicted with buckteeth, slant eyes, yellow skin, myopia, and the inability to shoot straight.

Cooler heads prevailed. The American fighting spirit was now unified as never before. Further, that burning emotion was sustained for the nearly four years necessary to unseat the Fascist militarists of both Europe and Asia. Young people (mostly males) stepped forward to take the oath of enlistment even as local Selective Service draft boards tracked down and rooted out their less eager neighbors. Enlistment paperwork stipulated a term of service equal to victory plus six months.

The vast agricultural and industrial might of America shifted from idle into overdrive. It took until the autumn of 1943 before full-throttle wartime footing was finally achieved. America became not only the world's breadbasket but also a cornucopia of weaponry and other industrial production which was the Allied nations' lifeline.

Evert D. Carter (1924–2024) was a young man who followed the news. With a family legacy that included Civil War veterans and a father who was a World War I cavalry soldier, young Evert was anxious to experience military service for himself. Carter's parents were blue-collar people. Family life was shared with a younger sister. Hormones surging in his teenage body fueled emotions that made him eager to enlist and join the fray. His comments provide insight into the American culture and the typical psyche as the 1940s settled in:

Our family moved from the hinterland to the big city of Portland, Oregon. Portland was also known as the Rose City because of beautiful rose gardens. Electric trolleys, some of them ancient, trundled up and down the streets with a constant "clang, clang" of their bells. For a nickel you could ride the trolley to any place in town. At the end of the line, everybody would jump out and help reverse the trolley car on the turntable.

A job during the Great Depression was as rare as a mud puddle in the desert on a sunny day; however, the economy suddenly shifted with the advent of war in Europe. Ships and other wartime supplies were now in great demand. For a young, unencumbered teenager like me, it was easy to make quick decisions regarding employment based upon whim or passing emotion.

December 7, 1941, was the day of the Pearl Harbor attack—when I again changed my adolescent mind. My ire toward the Germans faded from the foreground. Now, I despised the Japanese attackers enough to want to kill them. This wish was ultimately granted—but I was still too young for military service with the Army on that fateful day. The Navy may have been enlisting younger teenagers—but not the Army.

The American resolve for unconditional surrender was irrevocably sealed by the dastardly sneak attack on Pearl Harbor. Later, I learned firsthand that the Imperial forces had won no friends anywhere in Asia with their crushing conquest of large tracts of real estate and subsequent brutal treatment of the innocent people who occupied it. Japanese military forces were universally despised. Any peoples taken by them were subject to enslavement, confiscation of food and wealth, brutal treatment, starvation, disease, and even execution for the smallest of infractions.

It was in April of 1942 when Lt. Col. Jimmy Doolittle's Raiders brazenly flew the B-25 Mitchell warplanes on a bombing raid over Tokyo. I was seated in a city transit bus while making my way to work when a shipyard worker climbed aboard at a stop and shared the startling news. Everybody on the bus quickly became euphoric. We all clapped our hands, hollered, and backslapped each other. Strangers became friends under the circumstance of a shared celebration. We were all directly or indirectly working for the war effort and proud of it. The raid was a morale booster that I will never forget. We were motivated to work harder, and our spirits were lifted because it was the first evidence that Uncle Sam could mount a surprise attack deep into enemy territory.

Evert D. Carter entered the Army shortly thereafter. Unlike subsequent wars, World War II enjoyed overwhelming public support. Only knaves would speak out against the "good war" either during or after. Industry quickly absorbed every capable adult still unemployed after the Great Depression.

While the public demanded swift action against the now-reviled Japanese, British prime minister Churchill and American president Roosevelt instead convened the Arcadia Conference in Washington, DC, from December 1941 to January 1942. A strategy called "Germany First" was adopted where the Allies committed to focus on the European theater of operations (ETO) first, with the Asian front (Japan) secondary.

CHAPTER 4

LIFE AT SEA

Alameda Naval Station, End of March 1942

We were given rooms in the Navy Bachelor Officer's Quarters (BOQ), a military "hotel" which was palatial as compared with the Army counterparts to which we had become accustomed. The change of venue also came with wonderful meal service.

The land phase of "Special Aviation Project No. 1" was now complete. Sixteen of the twenty-two assigned B-25s which made it to California were selected. The following day we watched these airplanes being lifted onto the *Hornet's* deck by dockside boom cranes. They were lined up facing forward along both sides with interlaced wings and referred to in takeoff order from one (Doolittle) to sixteen (Farrow). World War II carriers had wooden decks for ease of repair in case of crash or fire. Sixteen medium bombers really crowded the available area. The B-25s are much too large to fit onto an elevator, even if the hangar deck hadn't already been packed with the carrier's normal complement of seventy-two fighting planes. Those airplanes, with wings folded, fit together like the pieces of a jigsaw puzzle and were securely lashed down.

We then formed into long lines and proudly boarded single file—carefully remembering our coaching—and rendered the requisite hand salutes crisply. I think the officer of the deck was surprised (and somewhat disappointed) that we already knew the proper protocols. Under sealed orders, seventy US Army officers and sixty-four enlisted men boarded. Our unprecedented group included spare crew members and the technicians necessary to maintain a squadron-sized unit of Army bombers at sea.[1]

As the seventh US Navy vessel named USS *Hornet*, CV-8 enjoyed a short but accomplished life. Built at the Newport News Shipbuilding Company, it was commissioned on October 20, 1941. Yorktown-class vessels measured 824 feet long, 83 feet abeam. The design speed of 32.5 knots (37.4 mph) was achieved by four shafts, geared steam turbines, and nine Babcock & Wilcox boilers producing 120,000 shaft horsepower. The normal complement was an aviation wing with warplanes plus 2,217 officers and men.

The Navy very cleverly allowed a rumor ("scuttlebutt" in sailor's lingo) to leak that big Army planes (with crews) were being ferried to Hawaii. The reality was that other B-25s, with optional 600-gallon bomb-bay fuel tanks installed, were already secretly making the same sojourn by air; however, the ruse was credible and concealed our real intentions with a viable explanation of the presence of very visible Army planes riding on a Navy flattop. One unexpected repercussion arose. A field service representative for Grumman, a company which makes planes for the Navy, got wind, assumed a nice free trip to Hawaii, and requested passage. Of course, he was rebuffed, but having connections, it became a question of taking him along or spilling the beans, so he also came aboard.

I went ashore for a final restaurant meal. The April Fool's Joke was on me. The fish must have been spoiled because I was sick on departure day. In any case, we put to sea the morning of April 2, 1942, and exited inland protected waters by passing under the Golden Gate Bridge in convoy with the cruisers USS *Vincennes* and *Nashville*, four destroyers, and the tanker USS *Cimarron* (AO-22). The *Cimarron* captured our eye because she had regular combat-type fire control and as many guns[2] as a destroyer. When we were out of sight of land, shipboard speakers carried Capt. Marc Mitscher's (1887–1947) booming voice telling everyone that we were on our way to bomb Japan. You've never seen a longer face on a human being. You'd think it was Grumman's man who ate the spoiled fish!

It took several days for us "landlubbers" to navigate the myriad passages, ladders, and watertight doors which divide the interior of a big fighting ship into a veritable rabbit warren. We never did get to the point where we were certain when we stepped through one of the dogged-down access hatches whether we would wind up in the admiral's cabin, a fuel tank, or the Pacific Ocean!

Our quarters aboard *Hornet* were eclectic and sometimes crowded. Some aircrew members were quartered in the captain's and the admiral's cabins (on cots), the others being scattered throughout the ship in bunking spaces with Navy personnel, or on cots set up in the corridors. I had a cabin all to myself down in what we laughingly called "torpedo junction." A first lieutenant really rated in those days— but I had to move when one of the Navy fliers came down with measles!

Onboard Preparations

The stated purpose of the Tokyo raid was to inflict both material and psychological damage upon the enemy. It was anticipated that material damage and the retarding of production could be obtained by the destruction of specific targets in the industrial centers of Japan. Further, it was expected the attack would result in recalling to the home islands defense fighter aircraft (Zeros), troops, and other combat equipment. Finally, the psychological damage—maybe an attack would inculcate a fear complex (phobias) among the Japanese people.

Capt. Marc Mitscher generously surrendered his quarters and resided in his sea cabin adjacent to the bridge—a vigilant skipper always does so when action is imminent. His suite included a conference room. It was one of the few places aboard where Lt. Col. Doolittle could conduct private meetings with his crew members.

Doolittle met with his aircrews every day, and we ate together in the wardroom. Primary and secondary targets were selected in the city of Tokyo and southward, with a specific course and coverage for each pilot. It was planned to spread the flight over a 50-mile front to provide the greatest coverage, create the impression of a larger force than existed, and to dilute the expected ground fire. It was decided that nonmilitary sites should be avoided.

On one occasion, Doolittle overheard a couple of the men talking about bombing the emperor's palace, the Temple of Heaven. He promptly intervened, "You are to bomb military targets only. There is nothing that would unify the Japanese nation more than to bomb the emperor's home. It is not a military target! You are to avoid civilian buildings, including hospitals, schools, or homes."

He then reminded us of his visit to London in 1940. The Germans bombed Buckingham Palace, and it cemented British resolve. Surely, an attack upon a religious shrine and upon the spiritual leader would foment further Japanese unity—an outcome unworthy of risking our lives.

The crews were briefed about the type of bombs and bombloads we would be carrying. Some aircraft carried type M-43 500-pound demolition bombs packed with 50 percent TNT and 50 percent amatol[3] with a 1/10 second nose fuse and a 1/40 second tail fuse. The other option was a type M-54 incendiary cluster, also weighing 500 pounds. Each aircraft carried four bombs which were mixed or matched depending on the intended primary target. For instance, at a petroleum depot, a demolition bomb would release the liquid fuel, thus making it more vulnerable to ignition by an incendiary bomb.

"You will drop the demolition bombs in the shortest space of time," he said, "preferably in a straight line, where they will do the most damage. The incendiary clusters should be dropped as near the others as possible in an area that looks like it will burn. If you can start a fire in a Japanese city, their buildings are so flammable they'll have great difficulty putting it out. Avoid hitting stone, concrete, and steel structures, because you can't do enough damage to them."

One pilot asked if they should deliberately head for residential areas to drop their incendiaries. Doolittle said, "Definitely not. You are to look for and aim at military targets only, such as war factories, shipbuilding facilities, power plants, and the like. There is absolutely nothing to be gained by attacking residential areas."

The admonition regarding bombing only military targets was reiterated in subsequent sessions. Doolittle realized his raid bore global media and public opinion ramifications. Japan attacked only military targets at Pearl Harbor. America reciprocated when Doolittle's crews were also ordered to select only military targets,[4] because the world's press was watching. The Pacific conflict between the US and Japan began as a gentlemanly joust; however, chivalry evaporated with rapid tit-for-tat escalations of violence.

When scuttlebutt emerged about a couple of our pilots cutting cards to see which would bomb the Imperial Palace, a fit of anger instantly emerged. It was of the same hot temper that made youthful Jimmy Doolittle into a street brawler and fistfighter. He thundered, "Dammit! It is not worth a plane factory, a shipyard, or an oil refinery—so, leave it alone!"[5]

Hank Miller continued his technical briefings regarding naval flight operations. We also had lectures by Lt. Cmdr. Stephen Jurika—with recent experience as the naval attaché in Tokyo for two years. The Philippine-born Jurika shared a great deal of firsthand information about Japan and the Japanese. "The Chinese know Americans as friends and would probably help," he said. "*Lushu hoo metwa fugi*" means 'I am an American,'" he continued. If the Americans were shot down over Japan, the news was not so good. In contrast to the Germans,[6] capture by the Japanese was indeed grim. It meant "they would be, first of all, paraded through the streets, then tried by some kangaroo court, and probably beheaded."

How to tell a Chinese from a Japanese? According to Jurika, "The big toe of a Japanese is splayed out from the other toes by years of wearing thongs. Chinese toes are close together because the Chinese wear clogs." Then, Capt. Apollo Soucek gave us some tips on what we could expect of enemy air and ground opposition, along with the best tactics to use against each.

Most of our time was spent going over maps, familiarizing ourselves with the drawings and photographs of our objectives, and their approaches. It was very reassuring to realize how comprehensive our information was. Everybody had heard the Japanese would never allow any foreigner anywhere near their essential areas, especially anyone with a camera. Despite this, there were many good photographs and drawings of the vital factories and munition storehouses which were our targets. Briefings were so well presented that when we saw our targets for the first time, most of us had the impression of revisiting familiar areas. I had no difficulty in recognizing streets and areas in Kobe and could even identify some of the buildings.

CHAPTER 5

RAGE UNLEASHED

A gigantic fleet has amassed in Pearl Harbor. This fleet will be
utterly crushed with one blow at the very beginning of hostilities.
Heaven will bear witness to the righteousness of our struggle.

—Rear Admiral Ito, Imperial Japanese Navy, November 1941

THE PEARL HARBOR DEBACLE yields questions which beg for answers. First, what inspired the Japanese (ca. 1941) to loathe the Western nations? Moreover, what triggered the Fascist leaders of the empire to unleash their pent-up rage with a well-planned and massive aerial assault at Pearl Harbor on December 7, 1941? With six aircraft carriers and 353 aircraft, a sneak attack of this magnitude remains unprecedented in modern warfare.

Like a spring gradually overwound, the many perceived insults accrued incrementally over centuries. Historically in Japan, there's been an undertone of resentment against "outsiders" that can be radicalized or mobilized under certain conditions. The seeds of resentment within the Japanese were strewn starting in medieval times, when wealthy European monarchs underwrote explorers probing unmapped continents in their quest for wealth and power. The British, Dutch, French, and Spanish were master colonialists who were then emulated by other nations.

The colonial era was already facing global retreat when Japan undertook its first pair of colonies: Taiwan (1895 to 1945) and Korea starting about 1910. The Nipponese soon hungered for more holdings. They held a portion of China (1932–1945) called Manchukuo. By September 2, 1945 (day of surrender), the initial pair of colonies ended with opposite outcomes: The Koreans came to despise Japanese rule, and this animosity persisted. Separately, the Taiwanese held their experience with the Japanese in high regard.

It was Portuguese explorers who found themselves driven to anchor aboard a Chinese junk by a storm at the island of Tanegashima in 1543. The lord of the island, named Tanegashima Tokitaka (1528–1579), purchased two matchlock weapons from the traders. A swordsmith, Taita, was put to work copying the matchlocks. The Portuguese returned a year later with a blacksmith who assisted the Indigenous people with the apparently tricky task of drilling the barrel so a screw could be inserted. With this bit of external coaching and some internal improvements, the Japanese within ten years were estimated to have produced three hundred thousand of their own firearms—which then found use in frequent bloody clashes between feudal warlords.

During the Sengoku period (late 1500s), the Portuguese schemed to establish a Japanese toehold. The spark of cross-cultural flirtation sputtered for a few years but never took flame. The relationship soured. The small cadre of Portuguese who had already settled in as merchants, diplomats, or missionaries were rebranded as "barbarians" and rounded up for either execution or expulsion. The samurai-sword-based culture was reinstated. A 250-year Japanese isolation followed this first unsatisfactory encounter with Westerners.

Some scholars assert the samurai moral code of ethics called "bushido" inculcated within the Nipponese a self-perceived sense of superiority over other Asian peoples. The self-imposed isolation of Japan ended in 1853–1854, when President Millard Fillmore ordered Commodore Perry, with his "great white fleet" of warships, into Tokyo Bay. China had become a major trading partner with the United States. The goal was to build similar economic ties with Japan even as certain European powers patiently probed about the periphery with their own overtures.

Perry delivered the ultimatum. Stated in simple terms: "Open your country to trade or be ruled. You have one year to decide." The West's perception of political unity within Japan was a myth. The Tokugawa held a precarious margin, and Perry's strong-armed tactics left a perception the ruling Tokugawa was weak and suffering eroding political control. This was sufficient to spark the Meiji Restoration and then civil strife called the Boshin War. The Japanese realized self-imposed isolation combined with ignoring technology left them without means to fend off recurring waves of the hated barbarians.[1] Japan signed lopsided treaties (called Ansei Treaties).

It was during the Meiji Restoration of the late 1800s when Japan embraced industrialization. The Japanese came to expect and demand parity with the Western powers. As long-term thinkers, their new goal was to beat the Westerners at their own game. They would adopt Western technology and then hone it like a sword until their version outshined the barbarians'.

The global colonial model continued crumbling by the time of the Spanish-American War in 1898. War erupted after the battleship USS *Maine* exploded[2] in Havana Harbor on February 15, 1898, under mysterious circumstances. The Japanese watched with more than a passing interest the lopsided outcome. Upon settlement of the brief spat, a vast amount of colonial real estate shifted from Spanish purview into the American orbit. Like the recipient of a litter of stray kittens, the US found itself the reluctant custodian and protector of orphaned colonies to include Hawaii, Philippines, Guam, other random Pacific Islands, Cuba, and elsewhere.

Japanese self-confidence soared after the heady defeat of the Tsarist forces during the Russo-Japanese War of 1904–05. Japan proudly established a couple of colonies of their own: South Korea and Taiwan. However, darkness was descending over the reclusive nation. Nationalism was growing in parallel with the growing human population in a homeland lacking many of the essential resources. Living space was constrained by mountainous areas unsuited for either agriculture or habitation. Wood, petroleum, and almost every other raw material were imported. The export economy relied upon textiles and cloth.

The year 1900 found Great Britain to be the world's superpower as measured by political clout, military might, and wealth. Japan joined with England and the other Allied nations when it sided against Germany during World War I. The League of Nations was established immediately thereafter. As a charter member, Japan eagerly sought international respect and expected parity with the Western powers. The first draft of "Racial Equality Proposal" of 1919 was presented to the League of Nations in Paris on February 13, 1919.

The proposal carried the popular vote; however, Australia balked in deference to their "whites only" immigration policy. Thereupon, it fell to Woodrow Wilson of the United States to quash the proposal. The Japanese were outraged. Hatred of Westerners (scorned as "*gaijin*") continued to simmer, with Great Britain perceived as a bigger culprit than the United States. Japan had already mastered maritime skills needed for fishing and coastal commerce. Their naval armada ultimately grew beyond coastal patrol boats to include submarines, battleships, and aircraft carriers.

The Fascist leaders of Japan scanned the horizon and observed weakness and opportunity. Large parts of China were annexed starting in 1931. The Japanese were brutal to their outmatched foes, and the world press took note. Had not the US Army cavalry been equally unkind to the natives of North America during the 1870s? Also, that same army under General John J. Pershing ruthlessly crushed insurgency in the Philippines, with Japanese in plain sight to witness the atrocities. The double standard of world opinion was obvious—at least to the Japanese.

The Japanese grew their real estate holdings without serious challenge. China was beset with poverty and a civil war. The British-affiliated colonies (Singapore, Hong Kong, Burma, and even India) appeared vulnerable. The French were also distracted by the Wehrmacht (German military)—which left Vietnam, Laos, and Cambodia equally at risk. With a long transpacific resupply line, the United States' toehold on the Philippines was tenuous. Even Papua New Guinea and the underpopulated desert continent of Australia looked like easy pickings.

Members of the Netherlands East Indies (NEI) air force flew themselves to safety in Australia. Those Dutch colonialists left behind (both military and civilian) became some of the slave laborers essential to the Japanese economy. Food, petroleum, wood, rubber, various metals, and every other resource was commandeered (stolen) as needed to sustain a massive military force while also meeting home-island needs. Like Japan, Siam (now Thailand) had successfully fended off the colonialists. Rather than fight, the Thai (meaning "free people") king granted the Japanese unhindered passage through his nation.

In general, the elite of Japan despised Westerners. They demanded some long-overdue respect for the empire's culture and power; however, the Nippon military closely studied and emulated Western actions. If the British Royal Navy and the US invested in aircraft carriers, battleships, and submarines, then Japan did the same. Ditto for army tanks, warplanes, and other war-fighting hardware. The Nipponese military fielded a potent army, a top-notch blue-water navy, and both operated world-class aircraft of their era. The alliance between Hitler's Nazi Germany, Mussolini's Fascist Italy, and Hirohito's Japan was documented with the Tripartite Pact, dated September 27, 1940; however, the Axis agreement never yielded any military operational collaboration worthy of mention. Hitler ordered delivery of some advanced technology (via submarines) to Japan late in the war, but it was too late to make a difference.

Japan set about to fill the power vacuum in Asia by seizing most everything within their reach. With seasoned, disciplined, and highly trained troops, Nipponese military assaults were swift and victorious. Each action was meticulously planned, decisively executed, and backed by overwhelming might.

Strained relations with the United States remained even as negotiations continued. The American list of demands was long and included a complete retreat from China. A festering sore point was the sinking of the gunboat USS *Panay*[3] by Nipponese aircraft while patrolling the Yangtze River on December 12, 1937. Three US Navy men died and another forty-three were injured.

Tensions between the US and Japan escalated into uncharted territory during mid-1941. All Japanese assets in the United States were frozen effective July 26, 1941. An embargo on the export of gasoline was placed on August 1, 1941. According to Fuchida and Okumiya in their authoritative 1955 book, *Midway,* severing the petroleum supply was the single event which guaranteed war.

Dwight Eisenhower and Jimmy Doolittle are high on the celebrated list of American battle planners. The mastermind behind the Pearl Harbor attack was adored with equal esteem by the Japanese militarists. While acting under orders, Admiral Isoroku Yamamoto mapped out not only the strategy but also the details. At age fifty-seven, he sported closely cropped gray hair while standing 5 foot 3 and weighing 130 pounds. Yamamoto gained understanding and appreciation of the raw industrial potential of the United States during two visits—the first in 1919 and again in 1926. He knew of the abundant minerals, vast petroleum reserves, and the nation's awesome military potential. Even while engaged in detailed planning of the Pearl Harbor attack, Yamamoto harbored qualms. He wrote to a friend on October 31, 1941, he would be leading the Imperial Navy in a war that was "entirely against my private opinion."

The fleet of six Japanese aircraft carriers along with a plethora of escorting warships crept within 230 miles of the north shore of Oahu. Like a predator waiting to pounce, the treacherous fleet lingered there but remained undetected. The Japanese plan to deliver a "last instant" declaration of war in Washington, DC, went awry because of bungling within the Foreign Ministry. The pilots then sitting off Oahu were rigorously trained, hardened by combat missions in China, and well rehearsed in the attack scenario. Their 353 aircraft launched in multiple waves on Sunday morning, December 7, 1941. The radio command "Tora, Tora, Tora!" was their final coded authority to consummate the evil deed. The first wave arrived over their targets at 07:55 hours (local). Many of the attack planes were laden with torpedoes especially modified for airdrop into the shallow waters of Pearl Harbor. Many of these successfully found their way into the hull of a warship.

The comedy of errors, bad luck, and ineptitude were already well underway. Given the tenuous political relationship between the US and Japan, the defensive measures in effect at Oahu were woefully inadequate on that fateful Sunday morning. In the end, Adm. Husband E. Kimmel (four-star Navy status) and Maj. Gen. Walter Short (two-star Army status) were rightfully stripped of not only their jobs but also their reputations.[4]

An early-morning encounter with a midget submarine was reported but discounted. Radar was then an infant technology that was barely understood and not yet fully trusted. Operators observed incoming aircraft, but a superior officer incorrectly attributed the radar blips to the expected arrival of a dozen Boeing B-17s from the mainland. There had been music and parties the prior evening, and many military men were either still asleep or just awakening as the initial bombs exploded.

Eyewitness to Rage Unleashed

Sixteen-year-old Abraham M. S. Goo[5] became an accidental eyewitness to the Pearl Harbor attack by happenstance. Abe was born on Oahu in May 1925 as one of eleven children to parents of Chinese ancestry. His father earned a Depression-era living by carving wooden bowls and other items from native wood for sale to tourists as souvenirs. The youngsters gathered at the nearby school playground for their regular Sunday morning scrimmage. But this day was different. Something was amiss. As bombs began falling, young Abe Goo quickly grasped the meaning of the scarlet disks on the "unidentified" airplanes swooping low overhead. Then, explosive flashes, puffs of smoke, and sharp reports were increasing overhead as antiaircraft artillery (AAA) struggled to deter the low-flying attackers.

A late-arriving boy ran onto the field and shrieked, "There is a headless woman lying in the street." Instinctively, Abe and the other wide-eyed youngsters dashed toward their homes, took shelter, and turned on the family radio. The radio announcer advised, "Stay indoors. A military attack is underway." Abe estimated about thirty civilians in Honolulu were killed. Other sources state forty-nine deaths—but this number includes firemen and civilians working on the military bases of Pearl Harbor, Ford Island, and Hickam Field.

The attack on Pearl Harbor was an opportunity for the brave to shine—unlike those who would cower under such devastating circumstances. Military officials initially blamed Japanese attackers for the civilian fatalities in Honolulu; however, more-careful analysis later proved unskilled and undertrained sailors had taken over vacated AAA (antiaircraft artillery) guns and fired them indiscriminately. An antiaircraft shell is a metal casing packed with high explosives. The National Park Service web page states: "Perhaps the most tragic civilian casualties come from those killed by 'friendly fire.' Many of the

5-inch anti-aircraft rounds fired at the Japanese aircraft did not detonate properly and landed in civilian areas around Pearl Harbor, exploding on contact with the ground."[6]

Although unseen by the teenagers, Lt. Frank P. Bostrom piloted one of the dozen Boeing B-17s inbound from Hamilton Airfield near San Francisco. Departing on December 6 and flying overnight, the badly timed formation arrived concurrent with the Nipponese attack. The Boeing B-17 was named "Flying Fortress" because it bristled with guns pointing in every direction. Consistent with peacetime protocols, ammunition and gunners were left behind in a weight-savings trade-off that crammed more precious avgas aboard. To minimize drag, the lethal Browning machine guns remained packed away in their wooden crates. With limited options and low on fuel, it was every man for himself.

Bostrom could do little more than try to escape, so he played tag around Oahu with Japanese fighters even as some US Navy ships blasted AA at the B-17s from below. With fuel tanks nearly dry, Bostrom bounced the cartoonishly fat tires onto the turf and skidded to a halt on a grassy fairway at Kahuku[7] golf course. It was a safe landing. Given battle damage on two engines, the airplane was officially declared "repairable." Only a few Curtiss P-40 Warhawk fighters rose to join the fray on that fateful day.

The Japanese attack damaged or destroyed thirty-one US Navy ships. Eight of these were older battleships which were past their prime and of diminished utility. The number of aircraft damaged and destroyed exceeded three hundred. Their loss was painful. Ships and airplanes were neither easily nor quickly replaced. It took two more years (1941–43) for American industry to achieve full-rate production. A new battle cry[8] was coined, "Remember Pearl Harbor!" Consistent with the "Germany First" policy, payback to the Nipponese came slowly at first but grew into an overwhelming tsunami of violence during 1944 and 1945 (up to the Japanese capitulation).

Fortunately, the precious few US Navy aircraft carriers had been out to sea and spared from the Nipponese bombs and torpedoes. The attackers also missed the repair facilities and totally ignored the huge fuel tanks containing 4.5 million gallons of petroleum. That strategic reserve kept the early war in the Pacific (Doolittle Raiders, Battle of Midway, etc.) fully fueled.

A state of confusion, misinformation, and occasional panic engulfed the islands. Initial reports of enemy landings, fifth-column actions, and sabotage were credible and frequent at first but later debunked. Martial law prevailed as machine gun nests encircled by sandbags were established at vital street intersections. Ford Island, Hickam Field, and Pearl Harbor were all in a state of shambles. Buildings were destroyed, ships sunk, and the charred remains of shattered aircraft littered the tarmac.

Recovery and restoration were formidable undertakings. Frantic rescue efforts were mounted to save sailors trapped in the hulls of capsized ships. Many of them perished by suffocation. The sunken hull of the fully fueled USS *Arizona* is a tomb that seeps oil (characterized as symbolic tears) to this day.

California was 2,400 distant miles to the east. Ships moved slowly and transpacific flight was in its infancy. Assistance from the mainland trickled into Hawaii slowly. Distrust of Japanese Americans on Oahu did not extend to citizens of Chinese ancestry. Abe and the other boys were temporarily excused from high school and encouraged to participate in the cleanup. There was much to do. As patriotic youngsters, they worked diligently and did their best.

Goo was drafted into the US Army at age eighteen, immediately upon high school graduation in 1943. Basic training was in Hawaii. He advanced to serve in the Pacific region as an airborne radio operator. On one Curtiss C-46 mission, their cargo was Coca-Cola from Auckland, New Zealand. On arrival at Guadalcanal, the garrison commander grumbled that his troops needed "real" food. Hungry himself but wise in survival on the Pacific islands, Abe shouldered the airplane's M-1 carbine, aimed carefully upward, and shot a coconut out of a tree. Abe further confided that he feared for his life while remaining overnight on Guadalcanal. He explained a person of Chinese descent could easily be misidentified as Japanese. After dining on raw coconut meat washed down with bottle of Coke, the Asian American teenager locked himself into his assigned airplane, cowered in solitude, and then fell into a fitful sleep with the aircraft's M-1 carbine rifle loaded and clutched tightly at his side.

CHAPTER 6

BOMBERS AWAY!

Dr. White Aboard USS *Hornet*, April 1942

The weather was rough and cold from the start. The armada zigzagged both day and night to elude lurking enemy submarines. Absolute radio silence was maintained. We were not allowed to play uncertified (not tested for radiation) radios or phonographs. The use of electric razors was absolutely forbidden. Initially, there were a few cases of seasickness, but we soon got our sea legs and gradually became accustomed to life on the ship.

The ship went to "general quarters" at dawn and dusk. Even now, when I hear that bugle call either in a movie about the navy or on the radio, my blood pressure goes up 20 points! Dawn and dusk are the two most dangerous hours during the day for ambush by submarines or airplanes and demanded extra vigilance. At those times we'd man our airplanes with life jackets and gas masks at the ready. Our navigators always knew the location and distance of the nearest friendly land mass. We were ready to take off if attacked before coming within range of Japan. In the event of an attack with no friendly land within range, our planes would be pushed over the side to clear the decks for *Hornet*'s normal air wing.

A day at sea normally started about 04:30 hours with "general quarters," which would usually last about an hour, then "secure from general quarters" would sound and mess followed. The wardroom of *Hornet* was large, but even so, we had to eat in relays. Because the food was excellent, we never minded waiting for it.

The days were packed with activity: going over our maps, checking our personal equipment, practice gunnery, and navigation. Braving a cold and wet environment rich in corrosive salt spray, the pilots and crews made regular trips to the slippery wooden flight deck to check on their bombers. It was a never-ending job to keep the planes in tip-top shape. Batteries needed charging, guns were cleaned, and tire pressures were checked. For mental reassurance, takeoff distances would be paced off. Manual effort was expended to rotate the propellers daily. This was to eliminate pooling of oil in the lower cylinders. The twin 1,600-horsepower Wright radial engines were started every day to keep everything battle ready.

Pilot Donald Smith then prepared the right engine for starting. The left engine would follow. Every action is dictated by a checklist:

Ignition switch: on

Right booster switch: on

Energize: 20 seconds when starting from battery power

Prime: for two seconds

Engage: hold down the energizer, primer, and engaging switch until
    the engine starts

By the fifth revolution, the engine came alive by coughing and gasping as a thick plume of black smoke spewed forth from the exhaust manifold. Move the mixture control to—FULL RICH. The Wright R-2600 Double Wasp engines were radials (air-cooled, with two rows totaling fourteen pistons arranged in a circle) and were notorious for running rough when cold. It took several minutes for them to warm up and smooth out. In the meantime, Smitty kept the rpm at 1,200 and closely monitored the cylinder head temperatures. "Round engine" pilots often reminisce about the "burnt oil smell" and snap, crackle, and pop noises when starting the R-2600 motors.

On certain days I'd give my assigned patients their last shots and generally keep tabs on their physical condition. Several extra aircrews were aboard, and their primary hope was that one of the "chosen" would break a leg or a neck or develop some exotic and preferably fatal disease! They were always going around and asking people if they felt well [*sic*], and were disappointed when they did. Even at this late stage, Jimmy Doolittle gave anybody who wished the chance to back out without having any stigma of cowardice attached to him—but nobody accepted that offer.

Feeding bomber crews with a hearty high-protein breakfast before long missions evolved because of a dearth of proper toilet facilities aboard some planes. This tradition continued into the Cold War. A meal built around steak and eggs was the menu of choice to reduce fiber and bulk while also minimizing the amount of intestinal gas encountered at altitudes far higher than we expected to fly. The B-25 had a toilet seat with a catch basin beneath. This minimal facility was installed in the very rear of the aft fuselage and without partitions or curtains for privacy. Those who used it were also expected to clean it upon landing. Dehydration was another risk on long flights—so visiting the coffee and water jugs was encouraged. In an unpressurized aircraft, bladder relief came in the form of a funnel attached to a tube which vented out the bottom of the airplane.

The routine aboard *Hornet* was a never-ending source of interest for us landlubbers. Any spare time would be spent touring the ship, inspecting the engine rooms, the cold storage lockers, the hangar deck with its myriad of planes, and all the shops necessary to maintain them. In the late afternoon, there would be a "general quarters" drill again.

Evenings consisted of Hollywood movies and a visit to the ship's ice cream station. Others participated in spectacular card and craps games with the sailors and were soon relieved of their money. It was rumored that, contrary to strict regulations, some of the Army men had brought liquor aboard the ship, which increased their popularity with the sailors. Just plain loafing and shooting the breeze sufficed for others. On April 5, some of the airmen attended Easter service in the main mess hall.

With the help of Navy medics, the immunization of my aircrews was completed. Each was issued an individual kit which contained a morphine syrette, a first-aid dressing, and sulfanilamide tablets—in case he was wounded, 60 grains of quinine to take as prophylaxis against malaria, a small bottle of tincture of iodine to serve as water sterilizer as well as disinfectant, some caffeine tablets as stimulant for the long grind to the China coast, and a pint bottle of whiskey for relaxation after it was over.

When it was my turn to speak, I gave the group a series of lectures on personal hygiene and sanitation while in primitive circumstances. Particularly stressed was the need to drink only "chow-water" (boiled or sterilized water) and avoiding raw or uncooked foods. No matter how slight, any wound should be treated immediately. I also told them some of the interesting conditions they could acquire from intimate contact with the native populations. Included in each kit which I had given the men was a venereal prophylaxis outfit (condom).

The twelfth of April was an eventful day. The ship went to "general quarters" as usual in the morning but did not secure as usual after an hour was up. Relief came in relays for breakfast. Shortly after breakfast the alarm bells rang, and word was quickly passed that an airplane had been picked up on the radar screen. After a few moments we could see it coming in toward us fast and low; believe me, the tension mounted fast, but at the last moment before antiaircraft fire commenced, it flashed the recognition signal and was recognized as a Navy plane. She flew low over our flight deck and dropped a message. A little while later we rendezvoused with the carrier USS *Enterprise* (CV-6) and escorts. The joining of the two parts of Task Force 16 near Midway Island was a considerable feat of navigation and timing because radio silence was constantly maintained.

The mission of *Enterprise* was to provide air cover while *Hornet* launched Jimmy Doolittle and his Raiders. We now made quite an impressive sight as we set course toward Japan, the two carriers in the center, the cruisers ahead and astern, and on each side and all around, the scurrying screen of destroyers. These Navy destroyers were always coming and going on various duties, occasionally rushing off to investigate some suspicious sight or sound and then racing back to their stations. On several occasions we felt the thud of depth charges.

The underway refueling technique, developed by our Navy, is one of the many reasons that our fleets were able to operate continuously in the Japanese home waters without the need to find a friendly port in which to refuel. The sea was very rough, and it took three tries to refuel USS *Hornet*. On the first try a line parted (a dainty thing, 10 inches in diameter). On the second try a hose line burst and soused the tanker with thick black oil before the pumps could be stopped. The third try was the charm, and finally—all went well. A seaman was washed overboard from the refueling USS *Cimarron*; however, the Navy looks after its own and he was later picked up unharmed by an escorting destroyer.

As the days dragged on, the crews were having difficulties with their planes. Tie-down ropes loosened, and the airplanes banged in their chocks with each rise and fall of the deck. There were generator failures, spark plug changes were required, gas tanks leaked, and hydraulic troubles plagued almost every airplane. *Hornet*'s maintenance men worked with our own mechanics, and every mechanical problem was addressed.

Gunners expressed the need to stay proficient at their craft; therefore, kites were flown from the ship and used as targets for the rotating twin .50-caliber machine guns in the top turret. Also trained to perform as a top gunner, I knew there were 700 to 900 rounds of .50-caliber ammunition in the proportion of one tracer, two armor piercing, and three explosive bullets. Tail guns, waist guns, and the bottom turret had all been sacrificed to save weight and reduce drag. A broom handle painted black was the substitute for the tail gun. The same amount of .30-caliber ammo was carried. Our navigators used their sextants to make daytime solar observations, and nighttime star sightings to plot our location while at sea. The results were compared with the ship's navigator.

On the morning of April 13, we were at "general quarters" when the public address system suddenly announced, "We have just crossed the International Date Line; it is now April 14th," an amusing experience.

On this day another situation arose which was not amusing. The right engine of number 15 developed a loud knock during the routine run-up. That was bad news. Our own crew chiefs (mechanics) and the ship's engineering department went into a huddle. Our own crew member, Ed Saylor, was mechanically inclined and in the middle of the repair. The choices were binary: either fix the engine or the airplane would be pushed overboard. Certain Navy planes also used Wright radial engines—so tools and expertise to attempt a repair were available. Using skills akin to surgery, they finally took the motor off and down to *Hornet*'s shops. A pin had dropped out of a gear in the second stage of the two-stage blower and by the grace of God had not gotten caught between the teeth of the other gears—or it would have been damaged beyond repair. The mechanical problem was fixed by highly skilled people working collaboratively. Soon we heard the motor singing as sweetly as ever. Here again was the long arm of coincidence—for if the motor couldn't have been repaired, I would have been reassigned to Farrow's airplane.

Underway aboard USS *Hornet,* Northern Pacific, April 17, 1942

Our planes aboard *Hornet* were now fueled, bombs fused and latched into their shackles, and machine gun ammunition cans filled. I repacked my bag for the umpteenth time, trying to get what I would need into still less space and weight. Most of the planes were carrying three 500-pound standard demolition bombs and a cluster of 128 4-pound thermite incendiary bombs. The explosive mixture in the demolition bombs had been enhanced with amatol, so they had the destructive punch of a bomb of twice their weight; however, my plane was assigned to carry four incendiary clusters instead of demolition bombs.

The original plan of battle was for Doolittle to take off alone about three hours before sunset on April 18 and for him to reach Tokyo about dusk, while there was still enough fading daylight to see his objectives. He was to then ignite into flames the destination with his incendiaries while the rest of us were taking off at dusk would reach Japan after dark, in hopes to find our targets by the fires he had ignited. We would do our bombing and then fly on to China, reaching the coast about dawn on April 19. There we expected to recognize landmarks and fly on to the bases the Chinese prepared for our arrival, gas up, and fly on to Chunking. We had arranged for a plane to make periodic rounds of the airdromes from Chungking to pick up any crews who had crashed, landed elsewhere, or otherwise reached the airdromes on foot. However, as is so often the case, "the best-laid plans" collided with Murphy's law—whatever can go wrong—did go wrong.

On the morning of April 17, 1942, Task Force 16 left the tankers and destroyers behind. The two carriers, accompanied by four cruisers, began the high-speed run in toward the Japanese home island of Honshu. We were surprised to learn the lumbering aircraft carriers were fast and could outrun their escorts. The destroyers and oilers were left behind because the oilers lacked sufficient speed, while the destroyers lacked the fuel capacity for an extreme speed dash of that duration, and so they became detached.

Two parallel white lines were freshly painted on the deck. They defined the pathways for the nosewheel and main gear necessary for an unobstructed takeoff trajectory. There was also a ceremony on the flight deck as the bombs were pulled from their storage lockers far below and brought into view for loading. Some received crew-inspired chalked messages, including "I don't want to set the world on fire—just Tokyo" or "You'll get a BANG out of this!" Jurika and others contributed medals awarded by the Japanese, and these were attached by wire to bomb tail fins. Daniel Quigley, a former sailor living in Pennsylvania, wrote to the War Department, "I herewith enclose the [medal] awarded to me and trust that it will eventually find its way back in company with a bomb that will rock the throne of the 'Son of Heaven' in the Kojimachi Ku district in Tokyo."[1]

It was wildly rough, with a dull-gray overcast sky, and the sight of those lean gray cruisers and the huge carriers knifing through the swells was inspiring. The extent of the preparations and the sheer cost of our enterprise began to sink in. We went through an agony of last-minute preparations, then turned in for our last night's sleep as guests of the Navy. Sleep, if any, came with difficulty.

The morning of April 18 dawned windy with wild squalls as we threw our toilet articles into our bags and went to "general quarters" for the last time. We were relieved in relays for breakfast, then assembled in our ready room to get the last-minute information as to our position, the weather, the distance and bearing of the nearest land, Point Inubosaki, on the mainland of Honshu. We were just settling in for another long day of waiting when we received our first indication that something was amiss. The public address system suddenly blared out: "Stand by for a high-speed turn!" A fast ship sometimes tilts alarmingly when taking sharp turns at speed. After that buildup, the turn itself was rather an anticlimax. Next came the order "Army fliers, man your planes; Army fliers, man your planes, man your planes!" As we tumbled out of our ready rooms and raced for our winged chariots, we knew that something was seriously awry. We were then some 250 miles farther at sea, and some ten hours ahead of our scheduled takeoff place and time. A gale of more than 40 knots (46 mph) churned the sea with 30-foot crests. Heavy swells caused the ship to pitch violently, put spray over the bow, wetted the flight deck, and drenched the deck crews.

Once topside, nothing amiss was immediately apparent, so I settled myself far back on the deck under the wing of "TNT" (our airplane) and awaited developments. They weren't long in coming. The cruiser USS *Nashville* on our port beam suddenly turned, swung her guns out, and let go of a broadside. The thunderclap which followed nearly took my hat off, but the visage was so interesting that its implications did not immediately resonate in my mind. The sight of a heavy cruiser firing broadside after broadside was inspiring. The huge ship is wreathed in smoke and flame. Suddenly I realized that this wasn't target practice. An enemy ship was under fire, and it might start shooting back at any instant. I got scared then and remained frightened for the next two weeks. We could not see at first what *Nashville* was firing at, but soon saw a small ship rising and falling in the tall waves amid the shell splashes. Abruptly there was a puff of black smoke from a direct hit, and then the target disappeared. The small boat had been sunk in minutes by the most beautiful exhibition of marksmanship I have ever witnessed.

Attack aircraft from USS *Enterprise* orbiting in lookout positions overhead also joined the fray by dive-bombing. The small craft, one of many in a protective chain surrounding the Japanese main island of Honshu, was constantly in motion and often hidden in the troughs between towering waves. USS *Nashville* expended over 900 rounds in the quest to sink this threat to the bottom. But we sensed our mission was hopelessly compromised.

Task Force 16 encountered a small Japanese patrol vessel, about 110 feet long. In the moments before patrol boat no. 23 (*Nitto Maru*), was sunk, she got off radio messages which we picked up but naturally couldn't read. We assumed that the jig was up. The Japanese by now surely knew our position, strength, and probable intentions—so our plans had to be revised. The Navy was naturally loath to take us any farther toward Tokyo, since they surely and quickly would meet heavy air and surface forces. Unlike the Americans at Pearl Harbor, the Nipponese had established a defensive perimeter at sea, and it worked.[2]

Lt. Col. Jimmy Doolittle went into conference with Marc Mitscher and via blinker with Admiral William "Bull" Halsey (1882–1959) aboard USS

Enterprise (CV-6). As is traditional, the fate of young men is placed into the hands of the older men—the seasoned gamblers entrusted to wager men and equipment against the despised enemy. The war was still young in April 1942. American industry had yet to surge. Aircraft carriers, B-25 bombers, and qualified aircrews were all precious in the months following Pearl Harbor. Nobody wanted them squandered—yet, after a string of defeats, the America public demanded retribution.

In contrast to Japanese leadership, which were inclined toward handwringing, dithering, and huddling in search of consensus during the fast-changing circumstances of modern battle, American flag officers were decisive. A decision, right or wrong, was forthcoming, and its execution would be swift. At 08:00 hours a message was flashed from *Enterprise* to *Hornet*:

LAUNCH PLANES X TO COL. DOOLITTLE AND GALLANT COMMAND GOOD LUCK AND GOD BLESS YOU—HALSEY.

It was decided then and there that rather than call the whole raid off and return ignominiously to the United States, the mission would continue. We would take off and gamble on our chances of reaching first Tokyo and then the Chinese coast. We were over 700 miles east of Inubosaki, an important navigational reference point, and some nine hours ahead of schedule. We had to figure some way to carry enough 105-octane aviation gasoline to make up the 250 extra miles we now had to fly. Our gas consumption was figured nearly to the last drop, so we loaded 5-gallon tins of fuel into the airplanes until there was barely room enough for us to squeeze in. This brought our gross weight up to over 31,000 pounds—a record load for B-25s at that time.

A Catholic chaplain was on hand to console anybody in need of spiritual comfort. It didn't do our peace of mind any good, especially when considering the shortness of our runway, the wildly pitching deck, and the hungry gray water surging below.

The carrier turned into the wind and began to put on speed. Wind over the deck ("apparent wind" to sailors) made it possible for the wings to generate sufficient lift even after a truncated deck run. The associated physics had been previously validated by aeronautical engineers using wind tunnels and slide rules. Our lives were in their hands. The B-25, a land-based bomber, was not designed for catapult assistance. One of the cruisers fell into the guard position astern, a further reminder that some of us might not make it. We had been warned to jink right or left immediately after takeoff. It would be impossible for a carrier to stop or turn in time to avoid a floundering plane with crew still aboard.

The public address speakers blared, "Stand clear of propellers," and then, "Start your motors." Jimmy fired up both his engines, and shortly afterward the second and third planes did the same. Two white lines painted on the deck denoted the proper place for the nose and left main tires, which would allow the right wingtip to clear the island.

Doolittle had some 50 feet less runway than the rest of us due to the crowding of the deck. Everybody held their breath as he began to rev up in response to the signals of the lead deckhand (called the "starter"). Finally, the sound of the motors seemed to satisfy, and choosing a moment when the deck was almost level, the starter gave Jimmy the takeoff signal. Jimmy released the brakes, and his plane began to move, nightmarishly slowly at first, but gradually faster and faster. The nosewheel came up, then at the last possible instant the big main wheels left the deck. She sagged, then lifted, and then we knew they were safe. The shout that went up should have been heard in Tokyo. We were all yelling and pounding each other on the back. I don't think there was a quiet pair of vocal cords in the entire flotilla. Jimmy circled and came over the carrier to verify his compass bearing[3] and then settled onto a vector toward Tokyo.

One by one the other planes roared down the heaving deck and staggered into the air, wobbling akin to a drunken sailor. There were some very close calls. One plane, I think it was Larsen's, went right over the bow of the carrier and dropped out of sight. We all thought for sure that he'd "bought the farm" (crashed), but the next time the bow dipped into a trough, there he was, clipping along just above the crests. Another plane veered suddenly and took off over the side, but, here too, it hung in the air—though our hearts were in our throats for the moment. The sea had been building up all the time, and now USS *Hornet* was pitching and rolling like a destroyer. It was difficult to stand on the deck, let alone launch an overloaded bomber.

Finally, it came our turn to start engines and grope our way up the slippery deck to the takeoff position. A bunch of navy handlers with ropes did their best to help steady us, but there were some bad moments when the pitching deck would send us sliding one way or another. We reached the takeoff spot, and both throttles were advanced to the firewall. As the fifteenth plane in line for takeoff, nearly an hour had elapsed since Lt. Col. Doolittle departed.

The signal to commence takeoff on the tiny runway came at 09:15 hours. Everybody was mentally pushing and lifting as hard as we could. When about two-thirds of the way down the deck, *Hornet* hit a steep wave, tossed us into the air, and we hung there shuddering just above stall speed for a couple of heartbeats, and then the gallant "TNT" proved her worth by picking up speed and beginning to climb. Wide-eyed, we all looked at each other as though seeing each other for the first time, and then relaxing. We listened anxiously to the number two engine, but both the Wright R-2600 radials were running beautifully.

Officially I was listed as surgeon, but unofficially I acted as relief gunner and photographer.[4] The pilot normally sits in the left seat and is also the aircraft commander. Even if outranked by other crew members,[5] the pilot is in charge and makes inflight decisions. The copilot occupies the right cockpit seat. An act of Congress eliminated (by promotion to officer) the small number of enlisted pilots early in World War II.

Farrow's plane, which took off after ours, was cursed from the start. While taxiing up to the takeoff position, Jack Hilger's plane slid into it during a particularly vicious roll and smashed some of the Plexiglas in the nose with its tail; then when Farrow was moving up for takeoff, one of the Navy deckhands[6] slipped and fell into the whirling propeller blades and lost an arm. Despite these setbacks, he doggedly persisted in his assigned mission, only to fall into enemy hands upon parachuting into China. One of his crew was bayonetted while resisting capture, and the Japanese boasted of torturing and finally executing[7] the others for "indiscriminate bombing."

The feat of launching the entire squadron safely was a succession of sixteen miracles. Once aloft, retraction of wheels and flaps was quickly accomplished to reduce drag. Throttles were then jiggered to achieve the most fuel-efficient cruise speed. We had thirty minutes of grace in which to return to the ships in the event of serious motor or other trouble. Landing an airplane in the water is called "ditching." We were to ditch into the water alongside one of the cruisers and they would do their best to rescue us, but after that time they would shoot at any plane they saw, friend or foe.

Its deck now cleared, USS *Hornet* readied for combat by bringing her own seventy-two airplanes up the three elevators and onto the flight deck even as Task Force 16 retreated at full speed destined for Pearl Harbor. Intercepted broadcasts, both in Japanese and English, confirmed at 14:46 hours the success of the raids. Exactly one week to the hour after launching the B-25s, *Hornet* sailed into Pearl Harbor. *Hornet*'s role in the Tokyo raid was kept an official secret for a full year.

After a half hour aloft, it was time to settle in for the long grind to Japan. We trailed Jack Hilger. Efficient engine operation is achieved by monitoring rpm and manifold pressure, and keeping the twin engines synchronized. Slow and gentle throttle control movements are better than constant jockeying. Control surfaces also merit attention. A properly trimmed B-25 will hold heading, course, and altitude for some time without pilot intervention.

The tasks at hand were physically and mentally grueling. A hand pump was used to evacuate the jerry cans. The strong fumes of fuel were everywhere.

Shifting weight internally demanded attention to the center of gravity. Empty gas cans were shed as we went. Every can was punctured in several places so it would sink promptly. We didn't want to provide the Japanese a trail of crumbs to follow back to *Hornet*. Only when the temporary fuel tank above the wing spars was empty and removed was it possible to again move between forward and aft fuselage.

Flying close to the water demanded constant vigilance. We flew low for multiple reasons: First, a camouflaged plane flying at low altitude is very hard to see, either from the air or the surface. Second, it was an economical cruising altitude. We really needed to economize by squeezing every drop of gasoline. And finally, the type of radar equipment the Japanese might utilize was unknown. While the technology of radar was in its infancy and poorly understood, it was suspected the Japanese coastline was protected by radar, since both the Germans and the Italians employed that technology. In any event, a bogey close to the water makes a poor image on the radar screen. Further, an inattentive operator might well mistake it for a tall wave, seabirds, or a drifting log.

CHAPTER 7

FLYING THE FRIENDLY SKIES

RATHER THAN SNOW-TOPPED MOUNTAINS, the first coastline the planes encountered was flatland, lying very low in the water in a slight haze that made it blend into the horizon. For nearly two hours we droned along without seeing any Japanese boats, then as we approached the land, a few mostly small steamers appeared—evidently on interisland runs. We flew close to several of these ships without causing any apparent alarm. The only notice they took was when some of the passengers waved handkerchiefs at us. At that time, the Japanese military operated a twin-tailed medium bomber[1] while we displayed the old Army Air Corps insignia—a red circle in the center of the white star in a blue field. Apparently, the local people saw two tails and the red dot but didn't look any further—completely overlooking the white star and the blue field. Only later did they report seeing the stars. Having been briefed to prepare for heavy antiaircraft fire (AA) and fighter attacks from the time they reached the coast, we were momentarily expecting the welcoming committee to arrive—guided by radio from the boats below, but to our ever-mounting amazement, we pressed on undisturbed.

Approaching the shoreline, we passed increasing numbers of small fishing boats or sampans, again without causing any apparent anxiety. The only person we frightened was a lone fisherman, who ducked and then jumped into the water as we roared low over his boat.

Thirteen planes were sent to Tokyo, Yokosuka, and Yokohama, practically one continuous city along the shores of Tokyo Bay; one attacker (Maj. John "Jack" Hilger) went to Nagoya, one plane (Farrow's) went to Osaka, while ours, headed for Kobe, an industrial city and Japanese naval base, about 350 miles south and west of Tokyo. As we flew past the mouth of Tokyo Bay, we could see Fuji in the distance, and the towering pillars of smoke from the arson fires our aerial armada had already ignited.

Doolittle reached Tokyo first. The city was immense, with eight million people. Unlike the water-constrained locations of San Francisco or Manhattan, which sit upon bedrock and grew vertically, Tokyo was an urban sprawl across the Kanto Plain more akin to Los Angeles, another low-rise but equally earthquake-prone metropolis. In the city itself, the airmen, flying at rooftop level, saw bicyclers and children looking up and waving. Citizens assumed the B-25s were a new type of Japanese aircraft. The military had conducted an air-raid drill that morning, and many assumed this was a continuation. The Japanese were expecting nothing more than a lovely spring day with cherry trees in blossom. Then the bombs began to fall. How could this be? The Japanese people had been told they were immune from attack.

At about 14:30 hours, Jack Hilger in number 14 waggled his wings and turned off toward Nagoya, going up and over a hill for a surprise arrival over their assigned city. Snow-capped Mount Fuji had been clearly visible and provided rock-solid confirmation that our navigation was spot on. It was the same Mount Fuji that Commodore Perry witnessed on his visit to Tokyo in 1853. Our airborne fleet was subdued in camouflaged colors. We continued forward and then turned to the left over the isthmus to Osaka and Kobe. There our first opposition was encountered as we zoomed over the beach, heading inland. Four small boys who were playing along the shore threw rocks at us as we skimmed a few feet over their heads.

Redoubled vigilance was needed because we were now completely alone. Intelligence briefers had stated that some eight hundred first-line Japanese fighter planes defended the home islands. As it was now over an hour since Tokyo had been bombed, surely some sort of alert message must exist? However, a true course was maintained as our unnoticed and unmolested mission continued.

It was April, and the Japanese landscape was very picturesque as the chilly weather of winter gave way to longer days and warmer temperatures of springtime. Plentiful rainfall combines with rich volcanic soil, yielding a lush paradise of junglelike plant growth. Fertilized by human manure, beneath us passed small farming hamlets, green fields and rice paddies terraced nearly to the tops of the hills. I had climbed back to the photographer's compartment and was frantically taking pictures of anything that might be a military objective. I had a hard time deciding whether to use my movie or still camera—so used them alternately, all the time keeping my weather eye out for the expected pursuit planes.

Several large military airfields were passed without a single airplane taking off to challenge our presence. The lack of opposition defied understanding. Either the Japanese defenders had not heard or had simply disregarded the radio warning from the sunken patrol boat—*Nitto Maru*. Tokyo residents were so certain they never could be bombed that they just didn't believe it even when the bombs were falling. Later, one of our pilots told me he had tuned in on the directional finder to AM frequency. One of the predecessors of Tokyo Rose, had been telling the world how wonderful it was to live in Japan, how beautiful the cherry blossoms were, and how good it was to know that they could never be bombed. Unfortunately for her thesis, her program was interrupted to announce that Tokyo was experiencing an air raid.

Upon [our] crossing a ridge, the smoky haze surrounding Osaka ("the Pittsburgh of Japan") was encountered. It was over ninety minutes since the bombing of Tokyo, and yet, there were no signs of an air-raid alert. Trains, trolley cars, and buses were still running on the streets. Pedestrians were out walking about as normal. We even passed a commercial airliner heading in the other direction. Our course was along the river which divides Osaka from Kobe. I was snapping pictures to both right and left. The area was packed with factories. On approach to Kobe, a sea breeze had deflected the smoke and provided a beautiful clear view of our target.

At 15:15 hours (Japan time), we picked up speed and altitude (to 1,500 feet) and dropped our bombs.[2] One cluster hit in a warehouse area, one in a freight yard, and the last two fell upon aircraft assembly plants. I was initially startled to look downward and see the air filled with whirling green-and-black sticks. It took several seconds before realizing these were our own incendiaries. While passing over a brand-new aircraft carrier being finished in a shipyard below, we heartily wished for some demolition bombs. The flattop would have made a perfect target. Sessler told me later that he couldn't have missed it blindfolded. When the "bombs away" call came, we dove down close to the water and got the heck out of there. It wasn't until then that the Japanese woke up enough to start shooting at us. Two guns fired about two rounds apiece, but I don't think they even stopped to fuse the shells; there were no bursts anywhere in our vicinity. We would have liked to have been able to stick around to see how well the Kobe Fire Department made out with the jobs we'd given them, but we had an appointment elsewhere!

Back in Tokyo, American ambassador Joseph Grew (and staff) were awaiting exchange for the Japanese diplomats in Washington, DC. The sound of bombs in the distance was heard, but nobody knew what was happening. People went to the roof to observe even as British diplomats celebrated with a toast. When the wife of a military officer exclaimed, "Those planes are American bombers, and I bet you Steven Jurika is aboard," she was close because Jurika had done the coaching back on the USS *Hornet.*

We headed out to sea again fast and low, past extensive fortified areas and airfields home to fighter planes—again, without drawing any fire. This was Pearl Harbor in reverse—but with a vengeance? Was the Japanese military so disorganized that they hadn't gotten around to alerting either their coastal defense forces or their interceptor aircraft? Once well out to sea, we throttled back and set course for China. Upon settling onto that course, I went back and relieved Sgt. Saylor in the turret so he could get something to eat and relax for a while.

I squeezed into the seat and wedged my shoulders between the breeches of the .50s. The Bendix-built turret was never designed to be operated by a large fellow like me. I concentrated on watching the land, fully expecting that pursuit would come from that direction. As it turned out, my attention was directed in the wrong direction when the opportunity came. At about 16:15 hours (Japanese time), we passed a couple of old Nakajima 97s doing gunnery practice on a raft. Pilot Smith called me on the intercom, "Two bogeys, Doc, upper-red; do you see them?"

Upper-red equals the left side of the plane, upper hemisphere. This code reduces confusion because the gunner normally faces aft, with the pilot looking forward. I whipped those guns around in an instant; however, the interceptors never got within range—with a top speed of only around 180 mph. Top speed on the early B-25s was 328 mph. A short run at maximum cruise left them hopelessly behind—but also ate into our fuel. I had them in the sights but didn't fire since we expected to need the ammunition later. At about 16:45 hours we passed a formation of three Japanese cruisers, apparently the same ones Ted Lawson writes about in his book, but here again no notice was taken of us.

At about 17:00 hours we passed through the Osumi Kaikyo, the strait between the lower tip of Japan and the Tokara group of islands. Again, we expected trouble in the form of pursuit planes from the many airfields in that region but were happily disappointed as nothing threatening developed. Shortly afterward we passed Kuroshima, a very picturesque island, composed of a volcano emitting smoke and steam. About this time, I sat down and had a good case of the "shakes." The trembling was an involuntary reaction to all the excitement and suspense. I knew we weren't out of the woods yet, but surely the worst must be over. Another thing I did then, why I don't know, was to take the film out of my camera and seal it in a tin, stick it in my pocket, and then promptly forget all about it.

Mid-April was a good time to be on this mission. The daily temperatures in China average somewhere between 62 and 74 degrees Fahrenheit, with the monsoon rains later in the year. Western Japan, China, and Korea are subjected to the extremes of either summertime heat or Siberian wintertime cold—depending on the calendar. In any case, the weather, which had been clear and lovely[3] while we were over Japan, now began to close in. We had a strong quartering tailwind all the way across the East China Sea. After leaving Kuroshima, we had no landmarks, and the overcast precluded taking sun lines to check how far we were being blown off course. As it happened, Howard Sessler did a grand job of navigation and we were dead on course, but we had no way of confirming that. The closer we got to China, the worse the weather became, until we were flying through rain squalls with visibility and ceiling rapidly approaching zero.

Multiple threats to our survival were emerging. Everybody aboard began obsessing over fuel. Each aircraft began the day with an identical 1,141 gallons. That amount of aviation gasoline could be stretched into a long ferry flight; however, range was sacrificed by dash speed and combat maneuvering over the target. At maximum gross weight and flying at sea level, using 1,475 rpm and 29" of mercury (Hg) manifold pressure, the gasoline consumption was about 85 gallons per hour. After releasing bombs and reducing the power to 1,300 rpm and 25" Hg manifold pressure, fuel burn improved to 63 gallons per hour at a leisurely 166 mph—or about 2.6 miles per gallon. Fuel efficiency improves on a curve as munitions are expended and the fuel load diminishes.

CHAPTER 8

WHAT HAPPENED TO THE OTHERS?

CONTRARY TO EXPLICIT ORDERS, plane number 8, commanded by Capt. Edward S. "Ski" York, opted to divert and instead fly to Siberia. The airplane, tail number 40-2242, landed safely at an airfield 40 miles north of Vladivostok. Despite an inoperative top turret, the crew successfully dropped their three demolition and one incendiary bombs on targets in Tokyo. The pilots reported the fuel shortage resulted from excessive gasoline consumption attributed to maladjusted carburetors. A political flap ensued. The US diplomats were caught flat-footed.

Dictator Joseph Stalin took the faux pas in stride even as US ambassador William Strandley scrambled to sort out the mess. Not wishing to invite Japanese attack, the Russians impounded the aviators and confiscated the airplane. Their treatment vacillated from drunken celebrations where vodka flowed freely to a prolonged stretch of isolation and malnourishment. Ultimately, desperate for any form of social interaction and useful activity, they volunteered to work in an airplane factory and were relocated near the Iranian border (then called Persia). As the Russians looked the other way, the crew arranged their own escape and made their way to freedom via the British embassy in Tehran.

Born in 1912, Edward York enlisted in the Army infantry in 1930. As a young soldier with potential, he earned an appointment to the elite Military Academy at West Point and entered pilot training thereafter. As seasoned captains, both York and David Jones held respected leadership positions in the 17th Bomb Group. Assuming the assertion of fuel shortage was truthful, the decision to divert probably preserved five lives. The chances of survival were slim after ditching into chilly open ocean in an area devoid of any friendly means of search and rescue.

The planning and accomplishment of the Doolittle Raid were built upon numerous deceptions. York and crew were late in joining the team yet moved ahead of other crews to garner the number 8 position on the flight deck. Conspiracy buffs assert the diversion was preplanned and known only to York (and possibly to navigator Lt. Nolan Herndon). Why? To test the Soviet reaction and gather intelligence. Being allied in the war against Hitler, maybe the Soviets would embrace the American visitors? Would the outcome be a warm meal, fuel, and a cheerful send-off to China for a reunion with the others? A safe destination in Siberia would certainly have been a godsend for future attacks on Japan. If it was a gamble, the test failed. Edward York and crew were impounded for fourteen months. The Doolittle Raid was unique and never repeated. Disobeying orders and creating a breach of decorum with a major wartime ally did not derail his postwar military career. York retired from the Air Force as a colonel in 1968.

After-action reporting is an internal military feedback loop that also provides grist for historians. The official account of number 15 (named "TNT") was summarized as follows:

Plane No. 40-2267 (Lt. Donald G. Smith). Before reaching the coast of Japan[,] picked up a radio station broadcasting a musical program. It continued over an hour and then suddenly went off the air. After ringing an alarm for forty-five seconds, a voice shouted three words. This took place about ten times before the station became silent.

Made a landfall north of its course at 13:50 hours. Swung south across Tokyo and Nagoya Bays, which were observed filled with small fishing craft.

Proceeded to Kobe[,] where four incendiary clusters were dropped along the waterfront. The first fell in the area west of the Uyenoshita Steel Works; No. 2 on the Kawasaki Dry Dock Yard; No. 3 in the area of small factories, machine shops and residences; and the fourth on the Kawasaki Aircraft Factory.

AA was light, and two planes sighted (97s) were soon outdistanced.

A large aircraft carrier was seen nearing completion, and several new factories were observed east of Kobe.

Each of the sixteen aircrews had unique stories to tell. Traditional "after-action" reports were prepared by Army Intelligence, "Informational Intelligence Summary (Special) No. 20, the Tokyo Raid, April 18, 1942." The report is marked "Confidential" and dated October 5, 1942.

Nearly every plane, on its approach to Japan, had reported the sighting of naval and merchant vessels, innumerable small fishing craft, and a number of patrol planes. Yet, the Japanese apparently were entirely unprepared for the attack. Either their dissemination of information was faulty, or the communication system had broken down completely.

As they [the planes] passed over the countryside, farmers in the field looked up and went back to work undisturbed, villagers waved from the streets, a baseball game continued its play, and in the distance, training planes took off and landed, apparently unaware of any danger present.

About twenty two-engined bombers were seen on the field and the same number of fighters warming up on the ramp, but few planes attempted interception, and those that did were not inclined to press home the attack. The pilots appeared inexperienced and their gunfire inaccurate.

The antiaircraft defense has been reported as consisting of either 37 mm or 40 mm, although description of the bursts and the absence of tracers would indicate that larger-caliber guns were in action. This supposition is supported by the fact no AA fire was reported below 1,500 feet. The altitude was accurate, but the bursts were generally behind—it is possible the gunners did not realize the speed of the B-25s.

There were a few barrage balloons in the Tokyo area in clusters of five or six, and in one case they diverted an attacking plane to the secondary target.

Ineffective camouflage was observed.

The overall picture is one of inadequate defense. The warning systems did not appear to function, interception by fighters was definitely cautious, and antiaircraft fire, responding slowly, did not reach the intensity one would expect for so important a city as Tokyo.

The flights were well executed, and in most cases, primary targets were reached, direct hits were made from low altitude, and explosions were followed by smoke and fires. The after-action report concluded, "Had it been known beforehand how complete was going to be the surprise and how weak the resistance, it would have been possible to concentrate all planes on such a target as the Mitsubishi Aircraft Factory."

The summary of Doolittle's sortie stated:

On the approach to Japan, passed a camouflaged naval vessel and saw multi-motored land plane.

Arrived north of Tokyo and turned south. Saw flying fields and many small bi-planes in the air—apparently trainers. Ten miles north of Tokyo encountered 9 fighters in three flights of three. They maneuvered for attack but did not close.

Proceeded to Tokyo and dropped four incendiaries in the congested area northeast and southwest of the Armory. Then lowered to housetops and slid over the western outskirts into a low haze.

The original plan was for Doolittle and crew to proceed alone to Tokyo, using their incendiaries to set raging fires. The others would be drawn to the flames and drop their own munitions. The following fifteen aircraft planned to arrive over China by daylight and seek a safe landing. The consequence of the encounter with the picket boat was at hand. Launching prematurely increased distance, which decreased fuel. Now, the squadron, with each plane flying separately and alone, was approaching China just as darkness fell.

The promised radio beacon and illuminated airfield markers were thwarted by distrust of the Chinese officials, fragile communications, and the demand for absolute secrecy. This was clearly the greatest failure of the mission and fatal to some aircrew members. All committed airframes were lost at a time when bombers were precious. The situation was dire because of approaching darkness, bad weather, and a landscape devoid of a safe place to land.

Hap Arnold's effort to secure landing bases in mainland China failed. The commander of the American forces in China and advisor to Chiang Kai-shek was Lt. Gen. Joseph "Vinegar Joe" Stilwell. Chiang balked at adopting the plan because he correctly feared massive Japanese retaliation against Chinese civilians. Stilwell reported to Washington, DC, [that] the fields would be ready with special equipment to broadcast a homing signal for the incoming B-25s, consisting of the number 57 repeated over and over. If the squadron arrived during darkness, they would be guided to safety by torches and bonfires. None of this happened. It was everybody for themself [*sic*].

Aircrew Survival Notes

With total darkness encroaching and unfamiliar rugged terrain below, one option was ditching into the water. Each crew member was issued their own personal flotation device, called a "Mae West." Additionally, each airplane was provisioned with a five-person life raft with an attached carbon dioxide bottle for instant inflation. Low-winged aircraft (Boeing B-17 or Douglas C-47) were better suited for emergency water landings. The B-25 had high wings, and that made ditching trickier. Bailing out with a parachute was another choice. Both options were invoked on the evening of April 18, 1942.

As a time-tested method to escape a balloon, parachutes were invented long before World War I; however, most World War I aviators were forbidden to wear them because commanders wrongly assumed pilots would jump instead of fighting. The silk parachute was a memory by 1942. Silk gave way to mass-produced ripstop nylon. Seat-style parachutes prevailed during the war; however, Doolittle, an experienced jumper himself, had the foresight to acquire the superior back-style parachutes for each of his B-25 crew members.

Advanced aircrew survival tools common during the Vietnam War were yet to be invented. These included rescue helicopters and handheld emergency radios. Parachute and water survival skills were not yet in the aviator's curriculum. Despite a dearth of formal training, Dr. White and associates hit it lucky on escape and evasion. For Jimmy Doolittle and others, the Army-issue Colt .45-caliber Model 1911 was standard issue.[1] Doolittle's autobiography makes mention of this weapon and further states that at age forty-five he had no intention of being taken alive as a Japanese prisoner of war (POW).

Fate of "Ruptured Duck" (Plane #7)

Ted Lawson and crew arrived at the Chinese coastline in a rain squall at sunset. The clouds opened and unobstructed beach (with neither rocks nor logs) appeared below. Ditch or bail out? He later confided in his memoir to having developed a fondness for their airplane named "Ruptured Duck." With an estimated 100 gallons of fuel remaining, rather than bail out[2] he opted to land on the beach. They would attempt takeoff the following morning and search for a nearby airfield.[3]

Except for Lawson, the crew removed their parachutes. Lawson lowered the landing gear and commenced a final approach. Precious altitude was lost when the engines sputtered. One (or more) wheel tires snagged the surf, thus forcing a violent nose-down crash into the water. A massive shudder ripped an entire engine from its mounts.

The result of an instant stop was an unmitigated disaster. Navigator Charles McClure had braced himself behind the two pilots. His weight and mass no doubt helped catapult the two seats and three officers out through the windscreen.

Lawson attributed his deeply torn leg muscles to a headset hook firmly attached to the left side of the windshield frame. Cpl. Thatcher, an agile nineteen-year-old from Montana, bounced about the interior like a rag doll but fared much better. He escaped the upside-down fuselage, which was rapidly filling with water. Lawson wrote:

I saw Thatcher do a strange thing. He was the only one who had saved his .45. Now he reached into his holster, got it out, and aimed it up over my head. I just watched him.

"Shall I shoot them, Lieutenant?" Thatcher asked me.

I rolled over, to look. Two men were standing on the top of the little cliff, staring down at us.

They were strong, squat-looking men, bundled up in some sort of coat that shone almost like a raincoat. They had on flat woven hats. We looked at them. I told Thatcher not to shoot. I don't know why I said it.

"Hey!" Davenport called.

Cautiously the men stepped down the embankment and walked over to us.

I tried to study their faces, but it was too dark.[4]

The four seriously injured airmen lay on the beach in the rain and darkness. Thatcher's son, Jeff, was quoted many years later: "Dad enlisted local villagers and guerrillas to guide them to safety. For the next five days, Dad, who was the only crew member able to walk, joined the Chinese in taking the injured crew members, who were carried on stretchers and sedan chairs. The entourage repeatedly barely managed to evade capture by Japanese troops searching furiously for them."[5]

David Thatcher earned for himself the esteemed Silver Star for the heroic effort to pull Ted Lawson and three others to safety. The nomination stated, "Thatcher kept his crewmates alive and 'kept the party going.' No sleep for the corporal and what little rainwater he could catch he gave to his officers. I do not know how to express the agony of that journey and the steadfastness and courage which Corporal Thatcher demonstrated in saving his four wounded comrades."[6]

Other Crews Bailed Out . . .

Lt. Col. Jimmy Doolittle used his scant remaining time aloft searching for the airfield at Chungchow by using instruments and dead reckoning. Having wrecked many airplanes, Doolittle was devoid of emotional attachment. When the fuel gauges neared empty, Doolittle ordered the crew to jump. He then engaged the autopilot and followed them out into the inky black void beneath the open forward hatch. Concerned about previously broken ankles, he kept his legs limp to absorb the shock. The landing came soon enough in a flooded rice paddy recently fertilized with "night soil" (human manure).

Doolittle pounded on the door of the nearest farmhouse but was ignored by the occupants. At daylight, he followed the path into a nearby village. Doolittle met a man and then followed him to the military headquarters, where an officer attempted to relieve him of his .45-caliber handgun. Doolittle resisted. Accompanied by a dozen soldiers, they hiked back to the farmhouse in search of the parachute—but it was nowhere to be found. The leader again demanded Doolittle's weapon; however, at the last instant, two soldiers emerged with the white-colored bundle (the parachute canopy) in hand. Doolittle was marched back to headquarters, ate, washed his uniform, and then was allowed to bathe. Despite laundering, the uniform fabric reeked of human excrement.

Doolittle was returned to his crashed plane that afternoon. Most of the removable parts were already pilfered. Jimmy hit the low point of this ordeal. He felt a total failure; however, flight mechanic Sgt. Paul J. Leonard was there to console him. Leonard stated Doolittle would get the Congressional Medal of Honor and a promotion, and Leonard was prophetic. Furthermore, Leonard wished to remain on Doolittle's team—and so it was. Doolittle's spirit was uplifted for the moment; however, at a later battle in North Africa, Jimmy witnessed Paul Leonard being blown into small bits by a German bomb. Doolittle later recalled seeing Leonard's severed hand with a wristwatch still attached to the stump. Doolittle forever grieved the loss of his loyal and trusted friend.

Doolittle was able to contact Washington, DC, by wire and received urgent orders to proceed there with haste via any means possible. He arrived at the War Department clad in an improvised uniform consisting of English-themed shorts and a pith helmet. Generals George Marshall and Hap Arnold seemed eager to greet Doolittle, but the trio was quickly herded into a waiting staff car. "But where are we going?" the diminutive Doolittle whispered meekly.

"To the Oval Office to see the president," responded the generals. Covertly flown in, Josephine was already waiting at the White House to be reunited with her husband.

CHAPTER 9

DITCHING AND CHINESE ASSISTANCE

IT WAS A DUSKY RAINY Saturday evening on April 18, 1942, as "TNT" (plane #15) approached the rocky coast of China. After about 2,250 miles and thirteen hours aloft, the force of nature called gravity was about to intervene. The decision to bail out and randomly drift into the darkness, crash-land, or ditch into the water was a gamble akin to spinning a roulette wheel. Gasoline was running low when a small group of islands was encountered. One of them[1] was circled in search of recognizable landmarks, but the gathering gloom and rain made it impossible to pick out any distinguishing features.

It became increasingly obvious that we would be on instruments before reaching the China coast, and since we weren't sure of our position, our pilot in command of "TNT" (Donald Smith) opted to ditch the plane while he could still see rather than risk flying blind over unknown terrain. This was after unsuccessful attempts to raise the radio station at Chuchow. The expected radio signal was to be a constant and repeating number 57, with the key held down for one minute and then off for one minute: however, the prescribed frequency was silent. Maybe the airfield was too distant, or inactive because we were nine hours ahead of schedule.

The interphone crackled, "Pilot to crew. Brace yourselves, I'm going to set down in the water!" I hastily doffed my parachute harness, checked the fastenings of my Mae West (life preserver), and clutched the emergency medical kit, while bracing myself against the forward bulkhead. It was reassuring to remember that I had tested the escape hatch of TNT to ensure I could squeeze by the lower turret tank and had found that I could make it okay. The actual shock of striking the water was an anticlimax after the suspense. In fact, there were two shocks, the first and smaller when the tail dug into the water and the second when the leading edges dug in. Luckier than Ted Lawson, Donald Smith performed a survivable ditching. Multiple light impacts with the water incrementally dissipated forward energy, thus reducing the chance of injury.

When I realized we were down and fully stopped, I found myself sitting in muddy water up to my shoulders, which was distinctly on the coolish side. I lost no time in getting the escape hatch out of the way and helping Sgt. Saylor. He scraped his ear on the fairing, and it was our only injury. I could tell by the way "TNT" rode in the water that the airplane was not immediately going to dive for the bottom. Sealed but empty fuel tanks were providing enough buoyancy for now. There was time, so I rummaged around inside the fuselage, looking for anything which might prove useful. Salvaged was my emergency kit, gun, and several other items which I passed outside. Pilot Don Smith, copilot Griffith Williams, and navigator Howard Sessler were getting worried about staying inside too long, so I squeezed out with my loot and helped load the dinghy. The others had salvaged some emergency rations, maps, and other items. "TNT" was starting to settle as we boarded the life raft and shoved off.

The five of us made quite a load, and it wasn't until then that I realized that none of the other landlubbers had any small-watercraft-handling skills. The freshly abandoned hulk was now taking on water faster and settling. The propeller, engines, and their heavy supporting structure tugged the nose inevitably downward toward its final watery grave. Like HMS *Titanic* in 1912, the empennage (tail section) rose vertically into the fading twilight sky. We barely avoided being slashed by the port rudder as it slid into the sea, and then suddenly we were alone in silence as the bubbles rising from below quickly dissipated. Our gallant steed had floated nearly nine minutes, and that gave us plenty of time to get clear. The loss of "TNT" felt terrible—like the passing of a family pet. If there is a Valhalla for warplanes, we knew "TNT" is enshrined in an honored place; however, we were in survival mode and there was no time for reflection.

Our location was about a half mile from a small island, the outline of which we could just make out through the dark and rain. We headed laboriously toward a break in the cliffs, which I expected would have a small beach at its foot. As we paddled, we noticed that one side of the raft seemed to be getting soft. It must have been ripped on jagged sheet metal. The leak could not be found in the darkness. The left side of the raft soon went limp, and then the goddamned thing suddenly turned turtle, spilling us and our precious supplies into the water. My surgical kit, gun, and most of the rest went to the bottom. We were able to salvage only the map and our emergency rations. Ed Saylor confessed, "I don't know how to swim." Sadly, none of our advanced training included swimming lessons. After floundering about a bit, we struggled back aboard and continued paddling toward shore. Saylor remained in the water and clung to a rope.[2] Howard Sessler decided that he had had enough of the raft and so struck out alone in his Mae West. He made better progress than our raft and was soon out of sight.

It quickly became evident that we weren't making much headway toward the chosen beach. I realized there must be a current, and changed course by heading toward a different point barely visible in the gloom. The change of course yielded better progress, but that damned raft turned over twice more. The second time I didn't have the energy to climb back on, so I popped (inflated) my vest and swam forward, towing the raft behind me. We finally made it ashore after the current had nearly swept us past the point and out to sea. We struggled through the surf and up nearly vertical rocky cliffs. We tried to salvage the raft since we didn't know if the island was inhabited or not, and might need it later, but our combined strength was not enough to lift the waterlogged dinghy. I finally tied it to a rock as best I could.

Atop the cliff, we found ourselves in a field of sorts and seeking some sort of shelter. We were a cold, wet, exhausted bunch, all naturally worried about ourselves and what happened to our navigator, Howard Sessler. There was a cold rain falling and a keen wind blowing which cut through our wet clothing like a knife. We tried huddling together in a small depression to get a little rest and mutual warmth but soon found it wasn't enough of a windbreak. There was one waterlogged flashlight, which gave a weak glow, and our total armament consisted of a sheath knife Sgt. Saylor was wearing and my pocketknife. There was no choice but to find suitable shelter—and quickly!

Our saltwater-soaked quartet set off across the island in the direction of a dim light one of us had momentarily spotted. [As we were] stumbling about in the dark and nearly falling over several cliffs, it was uncertain if the island was inhabited. Finally, a haystack and house with attached small goat pen was found. The unlit front door was barred against intruders. We beat on the door and shouted "Yushenmegua," which we had been told meant "I am an American"—but without result. Finally, we decided to curl up in the goat pen, which was dirty but dry and protected. It looked like the Ritz Carlton Hotel to us! We had hardly gotten settled when the owner of the house (Ma Liangshui[3]) came out with a lantern and finally gestured for us to enter.

It was a poor little hovel, with mud walls and floor and a thatched roof, but our host built a fire on the bare floor with rice straw. While our chilled bodies warmed, he roused his wife (Zhao Xiaobao) and mother to prepare some hot food for us. The stove was an ingenious contraption, consisting of two large copper bowls set in mud and stone. The grandmother sat behind it and fed rice straw (their only fuel) into the fire while the wife stood in front and cooked. There was no chimney, the smoke just came out into the room and filtered out through the thatched roof. The heat felt good, and soon we had some hot tea augmented with rice and dried shrimp for sustenance. I then became the object of the envy of the others, since I was eating with chopsticks while they had to use their fingers; however, they quickly caught on and were eating on a par with the natives after a few days.

The hot food and drink revived us enough to try some sort of communication with our saviors. By then, most of the village had crowded into the room. For most of these people it was the first time they had ever seen a white man, and their curiosity knew no bounds. We weren't too sure of the political affiliations of our benefactors, but their hospitality was unbridled. We tried to inform them of our identity by drawing pictures of flags and making gestures—but were making very little progress.

Worry set in regarding Howard Sessler, our missing navigator. So, I showed our host four fingers and then pointed to the four of us. He understood and did likewise, then I indicated a fifth finger to show that one of us was missing and made a searching gesture. Again, he understood and dispatched some of his friends to look for our missing compatriot. Finally, one of the people produced a paperbacked book, which was apparently some sort of almanac. In any event it had four English words across the top of each page, with their Chinese and Japanese equivalents. Thumbing through the pages frantically, I came upon the word for America and thus established that we were Americans (meguas).

They then told us that they were Chinese (Chunquas), and then the party really began! We told them that we had just come from bombing Tokyo, at which news their joy knew no bounds. They literally gave us the clothes off their backs to wear while ours dried. By means of our map we established where we were, and the Chinese told us that we had landed on Tan Do San, the only island in the whole group that did not have a permanent Japanese garrison.

We then explained to them that we must get to Free China as soon as possible, and that we wanted to go to Chungking to see Chiang Kai-shek ("Cheng-Ka-Sha" they called him). They in turn told us that there were two lighthouses close by, and that one was still in Chinese hands. They planned to take us there the following night, and there we would be picked up by a motor launch which made regular trips to a nearby Chinese town. The nearest Japanese base was at Shipu (Chang-shichen), and the local name for the Japanese was "Shipu-man." Our friends would have stayed up all night "talking," but at last we told our host that were very tired, so he shooed all the visitors out and directed us into the family bed.

A Chinese bed is strange to foreigners. It consists of a platform of bare wooden boards surrounded by an ornate framework. Wrapping yourself up in a big quilt called a "bee," a person lies down on the boards without benefit of springs, mattress, or pillow. We lay down two each way and despite the hardness of the bed were soon asleep. The last thing I remember that night was our copilot Griffith Williams saying sleepily that he was going to come back after the war and make a fortune selling the Chinese innerspring mattresses.

On April 19, we were awakened early the next morning by an influx of visitors, one of whom, more prosperously dressed, was evidently a person of some importance, since he was shown considerable deference by all the others. His nose was mostly eaten away by some disease, probably leprosy. He inspected us, our clothing, and our pitiful collection of belongings before departing. After a short while, our host returned and told us by signs that the "No-Nosed One" had gone off in a boat to do something about the "Shipu-men." This was interpreted to mean that we were betrayed and were naturally in a panic to get away before Japanese troops could catch us, so we put on our still-wet clothing and started off immediately after a quick breakfast of rice, garlic greens, dried shrimp, and tea.

The first person we met was our navigator, Howard Sessler, in tow of a Chinese fisherman. Much to our joy he was intact—having spent the night in a small cave about 2 miles from where we landed. After Sessler had had some breakfast, we all climbed to a high point on the island, where our host pointed out the nearby surrounding islands and the more distant mainland. He told us that there was a Japanese gunboat in the local waters, so it would be impossible for us to travel during the day. There was nothing to do but go back to the village and remain undercover in case an enemy plane flew by. When we got back to the village, there was the "No-Nosed One" with the news that the Nipponese had taken the other lighthouse during the night. We would have been taken captive if we had gone there the first night. Again, our plans had to undergo a complete revision. We spent the rest of the day undercover and napping while our uniforms dried.

We set out again at dusk. Five Chinese, including our host's best friend, took us down to a small junk in a cove below the village. On the way down, my feet slipped several times because of the wet, slimy soles of my shoes; the Chinese, however, interpreted this to be weakness on my part from our ordeal, and it was hard for me to stir for the next few days without having one of our friends render assistance by grabbing my arm. We bid our friends goodbye and were stowed in the bottom of the boat, covered with mats as the rickety craft was shoved off. It was another cold, drizzly night with no wind, so our friends had to scull the boat for about four hours before we reached another island. Several times other boats passed nearby, and we always kept very quiet until they were out of earshot. Once we heard motors and saw a searchlight in the distance. We got awfully cramped and uncomfortable lying still in the bilge of the little junk, so the fishermen gave us some crude raincoats made of tree bark, which covered our clothes if we were spotted. We then sat up and look around, although there wasn't much to see in the dark and drizzle.

About midnight, another, much-larger island appeared—and soon we're tied up at a small stone pier. Two of the Chinese took paper lanterns and led me down the pier to a small building. The others stayed in the boat. Anywhere we went, the Chinese always asked our ages. Being the eldest by several years, they assumed that I was the group's leader.[4] The building appeared to be an outpost of sorts. After a conference with the guards, we were permitted to pass and thereby began one of the weirdest journeys I have ever made.

We walked for over an hour along narrow trails, which wound in and out between rice paddies, often seeming to go around three sides of a rectangle of rice plants immersed in water, along the sides of steep little hills, and through deep crevices—all in pitch darkness, relieved only by the flickering light of two candles in the lanterns of my guides. It was misting, without a breath of wind. The only sound was the croaking of innumerable frogs and the scrape of our feet. The utter alienness of the surroundings made it seem as if were taking a stroll on another planet.

I was tired by the time we arrived at the farmhouse. I was admitted after another conference and met a stocky Chinese, who turned out to be the leader of the local guerrillas. He had been a cabin boy on the merchant ship SS *General Sherman* and therefore spoke some English—which was a godsend. He told me that one of our planes had crashed on his island. He sent that crew ashore into Free China only a few hours previously. He had some mementos the aviators had given him. Among them was a card with Davenport's name on it, so we knew it was Lawson's crew. "Charlie" (not his name; it was Jai Fu Chang) said they'd all been badly injured. He informed me (by gestures) of broken and cut arms and legs, and head injuries. I correctly assumed these were blunt-trauma injuries and the consequence of a crash landing. Naturally, I was eager to get quickly to the wounded to render proper medical assistance, but Chang said it was impossible to go further that night. We would go ashore the next night.

I sent a note back to the boat with one of Chang's men, saying that it was okay for them to join me. The next two hours were spent drinking tea and chatting with Chang. An older man, Kong Ah Fo, also joined the discussions. He had served aboard a British boat and spoke quite good English. Chang was very much interested in the story of our raid and wanted to know how much we'd been able to salvage from our plane. He was especially interested in machine guns and was very much disappointed that we'd been unable to salvage any. "Damn and fuck," said Chang when I told him that the Japanese had captured Singapore. I learned that five of our planes had flown over the island, and one had circled and dropped two flares. This must have been either Hallmark's or Farrow's plane, because none of the others mentioned had dropped flares.

I told Chang where we wanted to go. Further, when we got to our friends, we would fly over and drop him guns and ammunition. I did not yet appreciate the total extent of our disaster. When the other aircrew members arrived and had been introduced to Chang, we were all taken to another farmhouse, about a mile away, given mats and "bees," and left to ourselves. We curled up on the floor and fell asleep almost instantly.

The next day was April 20, and we remained undercover in the same building. We had been told that there was a Nipponese garrison on the island and that they were located only a short distance away. Chang called soon after sunup and brought some chickens for our dinner, and an educated Chinese girl with whom we had a lengthy conversation via pencil, paper, and dictionary—writing phonetically "L" for "R" and the like. We were having some trouble getting the names of the Chinese cities straight. Most of them have two monikers—one "old" and the another "new." Additionally, some had yet another local name. The pronunciation of these names varied in the different districts. Our maps had the names printed in English according to the British phonetic equivalents of Mandarin, while our friends spoke Chekiangese (the language of the Chinese coastal province of Chekiang); the confusion was considerable. Thus, the town we were seeking was labeled Chuchow-fu and was called "Chu-shien," and the alternate was labeled Chu-chow (Lishui) and was called locally "Leeshuay."

Dinner was delicious that day. Touring China by foot requires a lot of energy. Young and fit soldiers in combat can easily burn up to 6,000 calories per day. To me, the Chinese are the world's best cooks. By comparison, French cookery is flat and tasteless. After dinner, Chang told us that our next move must also be at night, since the invaders didn't stir much after dusk. When we asked him why, he merely laughed and patted his pistol. We found that all through occupied China, the Japanese (unless they were in great numbers) seldom ventured forth during the hours of darkness for fear of Chinese guerrillas.

Chang had detailed five of his men to guard us, including his "No. 1 boy." In pidgin English, "No. 1" means very best, or first class. Thus, someone's No. 1 boy is his first assistant, his most trusted servant, or lieutenant. It seemed to us that everybody we met in rural China had either a No. 1 boy nearby—or was proud of being the No. 1 boy of somebody important. Our escort was thus composed of the No. 1 boy, the No. 1 boy's No. 1 boy, and so on.

Our guard's armament consisted of the most amazing array of semiantique firearms that I've seen outside a museum; English, French, Belgian, and German pistols of many types, the most important part of each being a long red cord and tassel. They also had a few old rifles of the Snyder-Mauser type, and a collection of ammunition that was as nondescript as their weapons. Fully half of the cartridges wouldn't fit their guns, and I had my doubts that much of the remainder would fire. Whatever our feelings were about the arms of our escort, we never had a single doubt as to the personal valor of these men.

In the late afternoon we got word from our scouts that the Japanese were coming in our direction. They had evidently found the wreckage of Lawson's plane and were looking for its crew. We split up into small groups all going in different directions. Chang, another man, and I went out the back way over some hills. We all finally assembled again on the banks of a canal, where we found a boat waiting for us. Here we bid Chang and the girl goodbye and boarded the small, flat-bottomed skiff and took a long ride down the canal. All during the trip there was continual shouting going on between the boat and shore, and occasionally we would stop for heated discussions. Every so often we would stop by a farmhouse, and someone would run out to us with some hard-boiled eggs. We collected quite a store of these as we went on. Because of the consultations, we picked up a blue-robed chap at one stop who turned out to be a holy man of sorts. Finally, we concluded that shouting was the way [that] news was communicated. The famous Chinese "grapevine telegraph" was confirmed because of one interchange. We pulled into a narrow inlet and hid behind some shrubbery. Soon afterward there was some shouting in the distance, which gradually died away. One of our friends nodded in that direction and grinned, "Shipu-man" (Japanese soldier).

By this time, any retained sense of modesty had been overcome through sheer necessity. Sanitation is nonexistent in rural China, and we were such objects of interest and curiosity to the Chinese, most of whom had never seen a Caucasian before. Even the most-private acts were subjects for observation and discussion. Most of this we bore with as much good humor as possible because we were deeply indebted to these people. They intended no offense.

It was a lovely clear day, and we passed through some very pretty and interesting scenery. The extreme age of everything about us made a big impression—the carving on the ridgepoles of those houses which had tile roofs, the little wayside shrines, the carved stone of the sluice gates, the extensive canals and terraces, paths with the remnants of inlaid design on their stones. All these things pointed to an era of prosperity some centuries back; since then, very little had changed and little new had been built.

None of our companions spoke English, so we were now back to sign language, at which we were now becoming adept. We were also picking up a few Chinese words so could get our wants and needs expressed.

The end of the canal was reached at dusk. After getting out of the boat and walking about a mile, a kind of barracks was reached, wherein supper consisting of eggs, rice, shrimp, tea, and wine was served. This was our first experience with Chinese "water wine," and we nearly cauterized our gullets until we learned caution. It was clear, colorless, and somewhat syrupy in consistency and about 180 proof. Afterward we sat around while the others smoked, and then were alone again. The Chinese frequently shared their hand-rolled cigarettes for smoking. They were filled with a local tobacco, which might as well have been seaweed as far as I was concerned—since I don't smoke. After another 2 miles on foot, we reached the water again—whereupon another heated discussion ensued. We entered an abandoned house and waited for two hours— apparently for the moon to set.

As the moon went behind the hills we again sallied forth and boarded a small junk. After a short trip across a lake or inlet (I couldn't tell which in the dark), we disembarked and were once again on shank's mare.[5] We were having quite a bit of trouble with our feet. Walking in wet shoes and socks is not good for the pedal extremities; however, in attempting to dry out our shoes by the fire, the leather had been badly cracked. After a short distance we began to climb steeply and went over quite a high pass. I had to stop and puff several times but finally made it, and in a short time we were being shown into a small Taoist temple.

The visage of the old priest who ran the temple was one of the wildest looking I ever witnessed. He wore a long black gown and smoked a long Chinese pipe, which he also used as a staff. His hair was long and stringy, and he had one of those long, droopy mustaches you see on pictures of Dr. Fu Manchu! His features were finely chiseled, and there was no doubt in our minds whose side he was on. He and the blue-robed character burned some incense and said a few sacred words to their idols for us and then got out the jumping sticks.[6] They told our fortunes, the guerrilla's fortunes, and then "Chung-Ka-Sha's" fortune. From subsequent events the fortunes must have been good! Then we had some tea and eggs and curled up on the temple floor. Soon we were sound asleep, but this was a bitterly cold night, and we nearly froze.

The next day, April 21, 1942, was spent undercover inside the temple. Any notions about going outside to reconnoiter the surroundings were quashed by our guards when they shook their heads and then made motions of someone looking through binoculars. The meaning was simple. We might be seen by a Japanese sentry. The temple had evidently once been much larger and more ornate, but age and disrepair had reduced it to two rooms, although these were kept remarkably clean. We had our usual meals of tea, rice, garlic greens, and eggs. Meat was very scarce. We also broke out our canned emergency rations and gave the old priest and our guards some chocolate and crackers. They were much intrigued and reciprocated by giving us some sticky black Chinese candy.

About 15:00 hours, one of our guerrilla friends came running up the trail with word that some eighty-five Japanese soldiers were coming in our direction. We were in no position to make a stand, so we snatched up our few belongings and ran. We were taken a short distance down the trail and then entered a farmhouse. Here we sat while our guides and the owner of the house went into another of their hundred-decibel discussions, even as the Japanese troops got closer and closer. We were in a fine state of nerves when the argument ended, and the proprietor led us into a backroom and there, just like in a fairy tale, he pulled back a panel and a secret passage appeared. We crawled down this passage a short distance and wound up in a small cave carved into the side of the hill. The cave had evidently been dug for just such a purpose, for it had a higher bench-like platform at the back, which our friends then piled with mats and motioned us to make ourselves comfortable.

A candle was placed in a niche in the wall, and we were left alone for perhaps half an hour. Some scuffling took place at the entrance of the cave, which brought our hearts into our throats, but it was only our escort entering the hiding place. They brought us some food, but I was by then too frightened to eat. The Chinese then settled themselves between us and the entrance and then proceeded calmly to check the loading of their weapons, cock them, and then sat covering the opening. It was all too evident that they were ready to die in our defense. The first foe to stick his head in the doorway would get it blown off. Of course, the second one would toss a hand grenade in, and that would terminate the skirmish. I felt like the proverbial rat in the trap and spent some of the worst moments of my life while we waited for the "Shipu-men" to find us.

We heard the Japanese column arrive outside and break ranks to look for us. Several times we heard the questing footsteps cross the roof of our hiding place, and then we heard them enter the house which hid the entrance to the cave. From there presently arose sounds of struggle and screams and shouts. One of our escorts turned to us and made whipping motions across another's back. The invaders were beating the owner of the house, trying to make him tell where we were. Our friends smoked incessantly but other than this showed no signs of nervousness. The air in the cave, stale to start with, became suffocating. It was all we could do to keep from coughing and thus betraying our position. After nearly two hours of unbearable suspense, someone called out to us. The guerrillas relaxed and started joking among themselves. As we all crawled out into the open, I was never so glad to see the light of day before or since!

The old priest met us outside the farmhouse and told us by signs with great glee how he had fooled the Nipponese. They had evidently entered his temple, defaced his idols, and had even beaten him, but he showed us how he had cried, torn his hair, and wrung his hands and had sworn that he had never seen us. Any of these poor people could have been richly rewarded in cash by betraying us to the Japanese, but the thought apparently never entered their minds. Their mutual sense of responsibility for us and their hatred of the invaders were reasons enough.

Thankfully, this frightening encounter was behind us.

CHAPTER 10

HIDING IN PLAIN SIGHT

THE NEXT TREK STARTED off while it was still quite light, and we walked about 8 miles along narrow trails, back and forth around rice paddies, until we arrived at a house near the water. Here was served a nice hot supper of chicken prepared in various ways, rice, greens, shrimp, and eggs. When it was quite dark, we were taken down to a small quay and boarded a diminutive junk. Goodbye and adieu were said to our friends, as best we could, before setting sail for the mainland. Our first host's number one friend was still with us. The other fishermen had gone back to their home island after turning us over to the guerrillas.

The night was clear for a change. Even while immersed in the exotic Asian otherworldly surroundings, the glimmering stars in the sky and the constellations they formed were familiar because we were still in the Northern Hemisphere. A nice breeze prevailed, providing an excellent opportunity to observe the expertise of the Chinese boatmen. As a boating enthusiast in my spare time, I was fascinated by their technique, boats, sails, and rigging. My personal goal was to master surgery equal to their mastery of sailing.

With that, I pondered and then reaffirmed in the darkness my commitment to survive this ordeal.[1]

There was no moon, fortunately, and aside from the suspense we were relatively comfortable. The trip as uneventful aside from having to duck around a small island to avoid the patrolling Nip gunboat whose lights we could see clearly in the distance, and the fact that we wound up at a totally different place than the one we had started for. Our escort had gotten word at the last moment that the Nips were waiting for us at our original destination!

About 04:00 hours on April 22, we tied up at a little quay, passed a very sleepy outpost, and walked into our first Chinese town. Chen Tao was an amazing and eerie place at night, with only the light of a lantern to guide us. The narrow streets, crooked lanes, strange buildings, and the variety of smells that were then very new and strange to us. After getting used to it, we sarcastically dubbed the odor of human excrement the "national air of China."

These destitute people lived so close to the ragged edge of starvation that nothing could be wasted. Human manure was their chief and most valued fertilizer. In towns and cities, the night soil is collected in wooden tubs and carried thru the streets by workers, either direct to the curing vats on the surrounding farms or it is dumped into the bottom of a small junk and transported wherever needed. Along the trails (there are few roads in China), every farmer sets out from one to several large earthen pots, usually with a small lean-to over them, and there is some competition to get the contributions of the passersby. The smell and the quantity of flies, particularly in hot weather, were colossal.

Upon reaching a certain store, our guides stopped and beat upon the door and shouted until they raised the proprietor, who after the customary bellowed arguments let us in and brewed tea for us. It was evidently some sort of a dry-goods shop, though there were articles of food and some hardware scattered about. After some pointing and other gestures, the shopkeeper understood and proffered socks for us. They were thin and of harsh material, but at least they were clean and dry. We sipped our tea and waited and thawed out while our guides went out and rounded up someone who spoke English. This time it was the local salt-tax collector, a Mr. Yung Yu Yii, his wife, and a Mr. Chu. Mr. Yung was a thin, ascetic-looking man who spoke quite precise English. He had been in England, but not in America. Mr. Chu was a fat and jovial fellow who spoke no English but whose hospitality could not be denied. He was typical of the landed Chinese gentry. Shortly thereafter we all adjourned to his house, a quite ornate two-story residence with a tile roof and a small but pretty garden.

We climbed the typical rickety Chinese stairs to a second-floor sitting room, where we talked until nearly 08:00 hours, had a sumptuous breakfast, and [had] a chance to wash in hot water with soap. This was a real luxury because we were grimy and smelled like the boy's gym. By this time, half the town had collected in the courtyard and were much interested in the strange white men and their antics. The Chinese have practically no hair on their bodies and were much interested and amused by our hairy arms, legs, and chests.

Thus refreshed, we started off on foot for the next town, dodging the Shipu-men along the way. We hired a small boy to carry our few possessions, mostly life vests and spare coats the Chinese had given us. It was good to be traveling by daylight again. All day we trod through fascinating countryside. Once or twice, we hid from passing planes, but aside from that we were in little immediate danger. It was sobering to know that any plane you saw (or heard) was an enemy (and thus a threat), because there were no friendly airplanes in those skies at that time and place.

At a noontime stop in a small village, the local inhabitants provided a rather scanty lunch of rice, eggs, and tea. We were soon on our way again. During that afternoon, I noticed red streaks running up my right arm. I was developing a septic hand from a small scratch I'd gotten on my knuckle climbing up the cliff during our landing. I lanced the abscess that was forming with my knife blade, heated red-hot in a match flame. It drained well and cleared up shortly, though I carried my arm tucked in my shirt for the remainder of that day. The experience gave me a healthy respect for the local bacterial flora. They are flesh eaters. The extreme heat made us thirsty, and our feet became sore and blistered. We were nearly crawling on hands and knees when we finally arrived at a river and boarded two small junks.

It was good to sit and rest while someone else did the work. Griffith Williams, the No. 1 boy, one of the porters,[2] and a couple of other passengers were in my boat. It was run by a geriatric Chinese man who looked as ancient as the hills themselves. He had a wonderful face to paint or photograph, but my cameras had gone down with the old "TNT" though my precious film was safe. Our boat could sail faster than the other, but the boy on the other could scull faster than our skipper. The boats were practically in a dead heat when we reached the destination several miles up the winding stream. Twice during the long trip, we hid from passing planes by lying in the bottoms and covering ourselves with matting.

At the end of the ferry boat ride, we had another stiff walk of 15 Li[3] (5 miles) before reaching Sai Mien, or Hai Yu. Here, however, the chief magistrate, a Mr. Chen Chick, gave us a royal welcome, turning out the guard and everything else. We tried to look as military as possible but were belied by our beards, tattered clothing, and sore feet.

Mr. Chen was a dapper little man, evidently very capable, but speaking no English; however, Chang Sin-jin, a young and well-educated girl, was our translator, with whom we carried on our conversations with the help of the inevitable dictionary. An escort took us to the local army headquarters, where there was a hot bath with soap—the luxury of luxuries. In China you bathe in a small wooden tub, using a towel to wash with and to mop yourself off with afterward. The Chinese see no use in using two towels—one wet and one dry. The thoughtful Mr. Chen also delivered to us clean shirts and shorts. Mine were a bit tight, but they were clean, and it was wonderful to shed my lousy underwear. Everyone in China has lice, from the highest to the lowest; you scratch whenever you're not too busy doing something else. Daily baths and clean undies are the only way to stay ahead of the little beasts, though of course the newer insecticides were effective.

We were next treated to a sumptuous dinner and entertained by several groups of children. One group of very little girls brought us some flowers and then sang and danced about the wonders of flight. After dinner we adjourned to the magistrate's office, where we talked for a while. He gave us each a hundred dollars (Chinese money) from his own pocket and a "Chicken-Blood Precious Stone" signature seal or "chop," from his native province, Chang Hua. Everyone of importance in China has his own individual "chop." They say signatures can be forged but that a "chop" cannot be duplicated. Mr. Chen then told us that Lawson and his crew had been there two days previously. They had been given what first aid was possible and forwarded on to Linhai, the nearest large town, where the local hospital would render care. A single corpsman was the district's total medical staff, aside from the native herbalists, and from his slender stock I drew some iodine and adhesive tape for our blistered feet.

When we turned in to sleep on beds for the first time since the night we landed, we were asked if we required the services of women. We replied that we appreciated the offer but were just too tired. We had mastered the use of the bee (quilt), were used to hard beds, and thus had a wonderful night's sleep—the first solid one for me since leaving the carrier. The next morning (April 23), we awakened much refreshed.

With his usual consideration, Mr. Chen had supplied toothbrushes, and after use my mouth tasted a little less like the bottom of a birdcage. When told we could send telegrams, we wired Chungking announcing our safe arrival. I also filed a cable to Edith, my wife, stating, "safe and well," but this message was never delivered. After breakfast a mass meeting was held in our honor, attended by the local townspeople, soldiers, and schoolchildren.

Everyone gave speeches, and there was much singing and cheering. Two buglers blew some calls. The bugles were old and battered and just a little out of tune, but we took the will for the deed. The magistrate made a well-delivered speech, unfortunately for us in Chinese, and then Miss Chang, the interpreter, made one in Chinese and English. I asked her for her notes and will reproduce them here. The grammar and construction are open to criticism, but not the sincerity.

"Warriors and fliers from America, and my countrymen":

Today our meeting is held to give a farewell of American fliers.

It seems to us that the warriors come from America to our capital containing a special significance. In order to win the power of our nation, the freedom of our people, and justice of the world, we have fought against Japan for six years.

I may assure you that we Chinese pay our deepest respects to the assistance and vigorousness of America.

We are very cheerful and vigorous when America allies herself with China against Japan.

Fliers and warriors, though we welcome your coming to our city, the inconvenience of our communications keeps us from supplying fine things.

Now we summon ourselves to this meeting instead of two million Chinese people [the population of the district] to give our farewell to you.

We wish to drink to your health and to celebrate the Allied victory.

After this, we each got up and stated how much we appreciated the honors they showered upon us. Further, we hoped that our future actions would show how grateful we were to them for saving our lives. Miss Chang translated our words, the meeting was closed, and we were presented with a large silken banner inscribed,

The air heroes of United States of America.
JUSTICE FRIENDS (the "e" in "friends" was penciled in)
Given by the various Public of District of Sai Mein
Chekiang, China.

Everybody adjourned for hot tea following the presentation.

The night before, I requested to purchase a camera since I wanted to have pictures of all that was going on. I was told that there were no cameras of any sort for over 100 Li (at a third of a mile per Li, that would be 33 miles). After tea, a photographer appeared and took our pictures with an ancient 12" × 12" view camera with neither diaphragm nor shutter. They had telegraphed for him, and he had traveled all night by sedan chair to take our pictures.

We said adieu to our new friends, the guerrillas, and the chap from the first island. We wanted to reward them in some way, but they would accept nothing, so we had to be content with giving them our sincere thanks and some small mementos. The one thing which I had which seemed to interest the Chinese the most was a batch of pictures I had taken the preceding Christmas of my two children, then aged two and three, dressed as angels. These pictures are strewn across the breadth of China, and I often wonder what finally became of them. The guerrillas were a tough, hard-bitten crew, as those who fight for freedom without uniforms everywhere must be. I have yet to meet braver, more hospitable, and [more] generous people.

Sedan chairs ("Juh tz") were provided for us so that we could make the next stage of our journey in comfort, but we started out on foot. It was a very triumphant procession with honor guard, firecrackers, confetti, cheers, and songs. We walked about 5 Li before stopping to get into our chairs, and the procession was still winding out of the city gates. Our party consisted of a squad of ten soldiers afoot, their commander, an interpreter, and the five of us in sedan chairs. The chairs were made of wicker and balanced on two long bamboo poles. Each had a bamboo framework over it, with a scrap of cloth draped over it to keep off the sun and part of the rain. They are quite comfortable. You lie back on cushions and hook your feet over the poles. Each chair had four carriers ("Juh Fu"). Two carry the sedan, while the other pair rest as they walk along. They exchange positions without missing a step. The motion is a very pleasant one if you're not inclined to be seasick! The carriers had tremendously developed backs and legs, while their arms appear very skinny. The porters object if you let your legs swing freely. It seems to upset their rhythm somehow.

We went up a broad green valley, and the stone-paved road degenerated into a single muddy track. Rice paddies were everywhere, with the rice coming along in all stages of maturity. The paddies were terraced right up to the tops of the hills, and the irrigation systems were extensive, with all manner of pumps and human-powered bailers to lift the water from level to level. The most interesting type of pump to me was one that looked like a caterpillar tread with small paddles in place of the track. These paddles pushed the water up a long, narrow trough and with two farmhands[4] working the contraption with their feet. It produced an amazingly large stream of water.

Trees were remarkable for their scarcity. A few grew along the more inaccessible ridges, and an occasional one in a farmyard was used for drying rice straw. Apparently, there was a rigid control of the timber, but branches were cut off high up the trunk, which gave all the trees a curious tufted look. We passed two men ripping a short section of tree trunk into boards with a long handsaw, one above and one below the log. We also passed farming settlements everywhere. The age and disrepair of the buildings was the most noticeable feature of the landscape. The Chinese have a saying, "Mean mean-tih," which means "in due course"; they use it much as the Latin Americans do "mañana."

Several Japanese planes flew overhead during the day, apparently on their way to bomb some objective farther ahead. At least they did not molest us, because nothing was evident that would make the enemy think that there was anything unusual about our little procession. In China, every able-bodied person works. On our first night we saw how the old grandmother fed the cooking fire; now we saw young children driving baby water buffalo pulling miniature cultivators and plows, or busy digging clams along the streambeds.

We stopped every 10 Li or so to rest and water the chair carriers, usually at some little wayside building built by some prosperous person to "acquire merit," in the Buddhist tradition. These buildings are usually tended by the people of the locality, who supplied boiled water free (also for merit) and food, sandals, hats, etc. for profit. Occasionally the trail wound under a decorated archway; these we were told were "widow's arches" erected to the memory of some widow who had remained faithful to her first husband and had not remarried.

The local governments, army, and schools are very closely related. The emphasis being placed on education was impressive everywhere. Several types of uniforms were common—gray, yellow, and brown for the army. Black was for the civil guards and officials. Our interpreter, Mr. Tien Sih Chang, had been in the army but was badly burned by mustard gas (he showed us the scars) and was now a civil service worker.

We reached the next town, Ying Yee Chen, about noon and were greeted outside the gates by long lines of schoolchildren and their teachers. All were bearing flags and banners, cheering, and singing. They followed us into town, still cheering and singing songs about airplanes. The boys and girls who were late came running up as we went by. We meandered along the main street, which was about 10 feet wide and lined with shops selling a wonderful variety of objects, but mostly food of some sort—which emitted an astonishing diversification of odors—some good, some not so good. Turning off, we were taken to the local army headquarters and school. The children came in and lined up in front of us and cheered us yet again, and the local governmental officials came in to pay their respects. The local ritual of exchanging calling cards was by now familiar. It is a sincere compliment when a Chinese bestows his card. It means he wishes to be your friend. The card is always given and received with both hands to show it is valued. To use only one hand denotes carelessness.

A fine luncheon of roast pork, more eggs, a kind of sausage, and wine was provided. When both rested and sated, we then set off for the Don Ai Lien Mountains, which must be crossed. Out of town we went over a beautiful arched bridge and up a lovely green valley. The children followed us for several Li, still shouting and singing.

There were many small temples and shrines and of course the inevitable human manure pots and lean-tos along the route. There was also much foot traffic on this trail. The only wheeled vehicle we saw was a bicycle, which was being pushed along. Nearly all loads are carried on some sort of pole supported on the shoulders. The "heavy freight" was carried on a crossed stick to distribute the weight on both shoulders. The "express" was carried on a limber pole with a cane to balance the load on, while resting. The weights carried even by children were amazingly large.

In general, the people were healthy looking, except for skin conditions of all sorts, probably due to the filth and lack of certain vitamins. The people of the islands seemed much cleaner than those of the mainland. The sickly die young in China. Only those who can develop immunity to the local bacteria survive to reach maturity. Consequently, they are by natural selection a very sturdy race.

The weather varied from steamy to cool, depending upon the wind. We came into more and more wooded country with the gain in altitude. The hillside trees were largely pine, and all had been shorn of branches nearly to the top. Once we heard machinery and passed a small mill with an overshot waterwheel (water source from overhead) and wooden gears grinding grain. At the stops we would have water freshly boiled for us. The soldiers would smoke and drink water from the spout of a teapot or from sections of bamboo mounted on handles.

Humans were the only form of draft animal everywhere we went, excepting a few water buffalo used to do heavy plowing. We were amazed to see several girls hobbling along on bound feet.[5] Apparently in the back country, small feet are still a sign of beauty despite the government decree banning the practice. One government decree which was rigidly enforced was against the manufacture of opium. Anyone who was found to have opium poppies on his property was executed immediately.

As the trail steepened to go over a pass, we got out of the chairs. The exercise felt good, though my feet were still plenty sore. We climbed up steps cut out of the rock or built up of bits of stone. The guide said, "Bandits used to lurk in these hills, though of course, there aren't any now." However, I noticed that the soldiers kept a sharp lookout.

We stopped for a breather at the top of the pass. As everywhere we went, the people crowded around to stare, work stopped, and everyone jabbered at once. Everybody was fascinated by our zippers. A small baby crawled under my chair; its mother yanked it out and slapped it and it started to cry. I gave it a penny and it stopped instantly. Chinese children are evidently trained not to cry. On our first night on Tan Do San, a low platform beside our bed collapsed under our weight and onto the foot of a young girl. Her face contorted with pain, but she made no sound.

The other side of the mountain evidently had more rain than the one we had already climbed, because it was covered with lush green and flowering shrubs, a kind of primrose, and many azaleas. The yellowish green of sprouting rice and the deeper green of the more mature plants made pretty patterns in the valley below. As we descended, we passed a hillside village, which was one large rambling communal building.

About 15:15 hours, we arrived at the town of Da Dien (Ta Tien), where "chow water" (hot boiled water) was served. It's surprising how refreshing hot water can be after you get used to it. We waited to be met at the local Chinese dispensary. Hwang Tung, the commanding officer, was a fine-looking man with a distinctive voice and commanding presence. This was a training area for some two thousand conscripts. We were next taken to the headquarters in an abandoned foreign-mission compound. Everything that is not Chinese is called "foreign"; even the missionaries who have lived in China for decades refer to themselves as "foreigners." We met Hwang's wife and their cute ten-month-old boy. Sleep came quickly after the well-prepared dinner.

The next morning was April 24, 1942. I got up early and walked over to the telephone office with Mr. Tien, our guide. The "telegraph" turned out to be an ancient field-type telephone. It looked like Alexander Graham Bell's second model. The next twenty minutes were spent cranking the handle and yelling "Waa, Wae!" into it before we could raise the next town and tell them when to expect us. The telephone office was in an old temple. Peeking behind a partition, I saw several old hand-carved wooden warrior gods, which made my collector's palm itch. Naturally, there was no way I could transport them home even if I could have acquired them.

We went back to the compound for breakfast and a ceremonial send-off. The buglers were in better tune this time as we walked past the ranks of civil guards and their trainees.

It was hazy turning to rainy that morning. The countryside was flat and less interesting than previously. We traveled the 25 Li to Linhai in about two hours, arriving at 10:00 hours. We were taken directly to the public courts for a conference with the chief magistrate or "Jurenjang," past ranks of Boy Scouts and Girl Guides, the cleanest looking of all the people we'd seen. Linhai (Tai Chow Fu, locally called "Too-she-Foo") was a capital city in the old days, the head of a "fu" or group of counties. It had been taken by the Nipponese invaders the year previously and held by them for four days. Thereafter, it had been bombed eight times, although it contained nothing of military utility.

THE
ATLANTIC MONTHLY

VOLUME 171   *NUMBER 6*

JUNE, 1943

86th YEAR OF CONTINUOUS PUBLICATION

THE HORNET STINGS JAPAN

by MAJOR THOMAS ROBERT WHITE

April 1, 1942. — Loaded sixteen B-25's (Mitchell Bombers) onto carrier *Hornet* and pulled Task Force. Lost the 13th crossing the date line. Gassed ships and loaded bombs.

With the sponsorship of his father, noted plant breeder and philanthropist Clarence White, manuscript excerpts were published in *Atlantic Monthly* 171, no. 6 (June 1943). This fast-paced version was greatly condensed and delivered in short (terse) sentences. *White family*

During the idyllic prewar period, Doolittle's copilot, Richard Cole, recalled[1] traveling to Mines Field (now LAX) from Pendleton, Oregon, to accept and fly away a brand-new B-25. Delivery flights were later performed by Ferry Command, where many pilots were women volunteers called WASPs (Women Air Service Pilots). *Boeing*

The standard Doolittle load of four bombs is visible when peering into the bomb bay. Depending on their intended target, they could be any combination of either incendiary or demolition bombs. The inscription reads "I don't want to set the world on fire—just Tokyo." Inert bombs stenciled "drill" were staged as props for a reunion. The photograph is dated April 8, 1958. *Boeing*

Thomas Robert Fisk White
Sunset Drive, Redlands, Calif.
California Institute of Technology,
S.B., 1931
Practice: Los Angeles, Calif.
Orthopedic Surgery
Johns Hopkins Hospital, Baltimore,
Md.
Married in 1934 to Edith K. Eyre

While trained as a top gunner, Thomas Robert White participated as the flight surgeon during Doolittle's raid on Japan. When his plane subsequently ditched (crashed into water), he saved his surgeon's instruments only to lose them when the rubber raft was upended by the surf. *Harvard University yearbook, 1937*

The young aviators are cool, confident, and cocky in their freshly issued attire. A preflight inspection in the sunshine yields an opportunity for a cigarette, time hack, and final check of the navigational charts before takeoff to their next destination. Aviation is an exhilarating experience for those blessed with brand-new airplanes, sexy uniforms, and sanguine blue skies. *Boeing*

Standardizing aviation gasoline (avgas) at 100 octane was probably Jimmy Doolittle's greatest lifetime accomplishment. Consistent avgas was a godsend during World War II because it simplified the logistics of refining, transportation, and storage. *Boeing*

NAA president James Howard "Dutch" Kindelberger meets with Doolittle at the Los Angeles plant. NAA took pride in three primary wartime products: AT-6 Texan, a trainer; B-25 Mitchell, a medium fast-attack bomber; and the P-51 Mustang, arguably the best escort fighter aircraft of World War II. *Boeing*

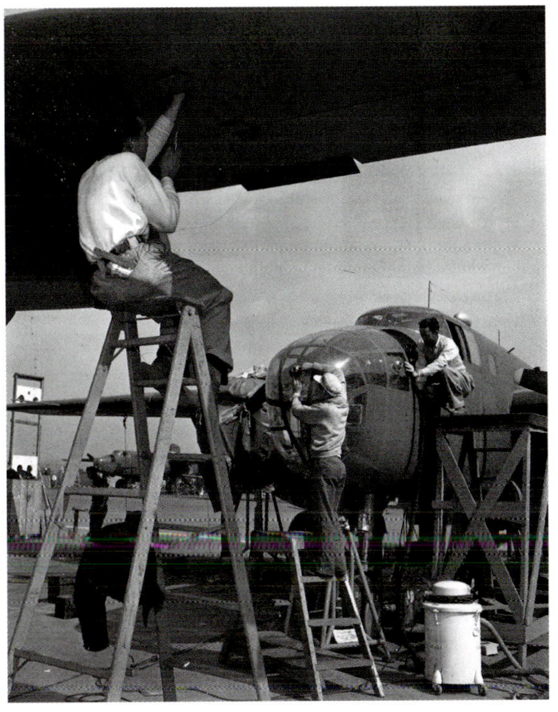

In the wake of the Pearl Harbor debacle, workers at factories, rework facilities, and repair depots scrambled to prepare these and other B-25s for their combat assignments. Simplicity of design and rugged construction facilitated operational reliability while minimizing downtime for maintenance. *Boeing*

Consistent with a highly educated person of proper upbringing and raised in an established family, White maintained an even temperament when confronted by adversity. Frustrations with either people or events were written down using measured terms. *White family*

The NAA main Los Angeles plant was located at Inglewood within sight of the Pacific beach. For reasons undocumented and not fully understood, members of the employee marksmanship club gathered and assumed a menacing stance for the photographer. *Boeing*

A militia quickly formed after the Pearl Harbor attack. Men bearing World War I-era bolt-action rifles gathered the guard the newly constructed Kansas City B-25 factory during the cold winter of 1941–42. *Boeing*

Despite the Great Depression of the 1930s, Americans then enjoyed a lifestyle a world apart from the typical Asian because of Western technical advances including indoor plumbing, radio, movies, various appliances, and electricity. Even a defense plant carpool was far more exciting as compared to cultivating an Asian rice paddy. *Boeing*

For eighty of the Raiders, their sole Navy cruise was a one-way trip with no opportunities for exotic ports of call. Boarding a Navy ship comes with ancient rituals alien to most Army fliers but deeply ingrained into every sailor or marine. USS *Missouri* (BB-63) circa 1991.

A Fletcher-class destroyer is underway at sea. Dr. White loved to watch the nimble destroyers move about Task Force 16. Designed in 1939, a total of 175 of the type joined the US Navy's worldwide wartime fleet. *Boeing*

War planner Admiral Isoroku Yamamoto (1884–1943) was exalted by the Nipponese hierarchy but despised by the US military for the Pearl Harbor treachery. When an encrypted enemy message was intercepted and decoded, Yamamoto was then ambushed on a flight out of Bougainville (Solomon Islands) and assassinated by the pilot of a USAAF Lockheed P-38. The date was April 18, 1943, or exactly one year after the Doolittle Raid. *NARA*

Xenophobia was rife on both sides of the Pacific. Hateful racial stereotypes were pervasive, as is evident in this sketch from an industrial artist. Similar artwork was found everywhere from factory walls, post office bulletin boards, and military recruiting stations. *Boeing*

Even when interviewed at age ninety-six, Abraham M. S. Goo (b. 1925) had sharp recall of the Pearl Harbor attack, the consequences, and his own World War II military service, which started in 1943.

A dozen unarmed Boeing B-17s arrived over the island of Oahu in the middle of the Pearl Harbor attack. Normally armed with .50-caliber machine guns (like the one seen here), could they have made a difference by making their arrival with guns blazing? *Boeing*

The metal parts in a radial engine shrink as they cool. Loose fitting pistons allow oil to leak past the rings and puddle in the lower cylinders. Therefore, ground crews manually push the big Hamilton-Standard blades a dozen times to smear that lubricant onto the cylinder walls before attempting engine startup. *Boeing*

This Navy medical officer was photographed sitting contentedly at his desk. The medical officers aboard *Hornet* were kinder, more helpful, and generous with their supplies as compared to their Army counterparts. They provided several needed items that I had previously been unable to acquire. *Boeing*

The cold, damp air of the northern Pacific demanded a stylish aviator's leather jacket to stay warm; however, sunglasses were not needed in the heavy overcast. *White family*

One of the greatest feats of seamanship I have ever witnessed was the refueling of the convoy at sea. The sheer ability and coordination of the maneuver was breathtaking. Destroyers are speedy but thirsty and need refueling every three or four days when underway. *Navy*

The crew of "TNT", *left to right*: Lt. Howard "Ses" Sessler was the combined bombardier-navigator, who also operated the .30-caliber nose gun. Lt. Donald G. Smith ("Smitty"), pilot. Dr. Thomas Robert White. Lt. Griffith P. "Grif" Williams, copilot. Sgt. Edward Saylor, engineer and top gunner. The engineer handles mechanical chores when on the ground. *USAF*

An unknown NAA artist captured the image of a Doolittle Raider penetrating Asian waters at low altitude on April 18, 1942. The mission was celebrated by most every US citizen, while remorse, shame, and discredit descended upon the military elite of Tokyo. The Pearl Harbor attack had seared American emotional resolve in a manner not anticipated by the cold calculations of the Nipponese militants. *Boeing*

"Yes sir, setting course for China." Pilot and copilot shared flying duties on a flight of thirteen-hour duration. The exterior of the B-25 was small, and the interior cramped. The photograph reveals a claustrophobic cockpit as visible only when the overhead emergency escape hatch is removed. *Boeing*

Rather than the pastoral midwestern scene depicted by this NAA sketch, many Raiders jumped into total darkness, dangled amid rain squalls beneath parachutes, and landed on a broad swath of sometimes rugged Chinese countryside. Three died, others were injured, and some were captured. *Boeing*

Aboard number 7, "Ruptured Duck," *left to right*: It was navigator Charles McClure who endured the pain of dislocated shoulders. Pilot Lt. Ted Lawson was the most seriously injured and sometimes was not expected to live. His injuries included smashed teeth, torn lips, and a serious gash to the left lower leg, which became infected. Cpl. David Thatcher, flight mechanic and top gunner, was not seriously injured. Lt. Dean Davenport, copilot, suffered a fractured leg and concussion. Lt. Robert Clever, nose gunner and bombardier, encountered serious facial injuries and blood loss caused by crashing through the Plexiglas nose cone. *USAF*

A staged maintenance manual photograph in a parking lot has nothing in common with a squishy life raft adrift in the ocean on a stormy night. Accessories including oars, air pump, and a flare gun (properly named a "very pistol") are being demonstrated. *Boeing*

Historians believe that the crew of "TNT" (plane 15), shivering from cold and gasping for breath, crawled ashore on Tantou Mountain Island (also written "Tan To San"). Today the island has become a pleasant seaside tourist destination for Chinese vacationers.

This sketch of the Japanese soldier is more menacing than a photograph. The encounter in the underground "hideout" was probably the most fearsome because the cadre of Raiders were confined to a small claustrophobic space with no options for escape. *NARA sketch*

Even in 1942, the standard form of overland transportation in some rural areas of China was human-powered sedan chairs. The procession never moved faster than a walk on ancient trails too narrow for vehicles. Trains, planes, and automobiles were encountered only later in the western provinces. *Alamy*

Like young men of the Mormon faith, many monks make the transition from their teen years to adulthood by serving a year of devotion to Lord Buddha's service before returning to their normal lives. A few opt for a lifetime of chastity, introspection, and poverty by forever remaining as monks.

I tried to buy the soldiers more cigarettes, but the interpreter said, "Oh, the nation furnishes them," and forbade it. The most popular brand of cigarette was "Victory," which were on sale everywhere. They had fancy gold and blue packages (the colors of China) and were manufactured in Shanghai by Japanese merchants.

Electric energy, while widely utilized for many purposes in America, was in its infancy and a godsend when available at a hospital in wartime China. Here, a jeweler relies upon a lightbulb to perform his delicate artistry.

Seaplanes were losing favor within the War Department as World War II began. The Navy canceled its order for Boeing PBB-1 flying boats in 1942. Only this single prototype was ever built. Instead, the Navy relied upon land-based PBJs (same as an Army B-25) for maritime surveillance. *Boeing*

The abacus was the universal merchant's tabulating and accounting tool in pre-electronic Asia; however, the Chinese version was distinct and separate from the Japanese abacus. *Stock photo*

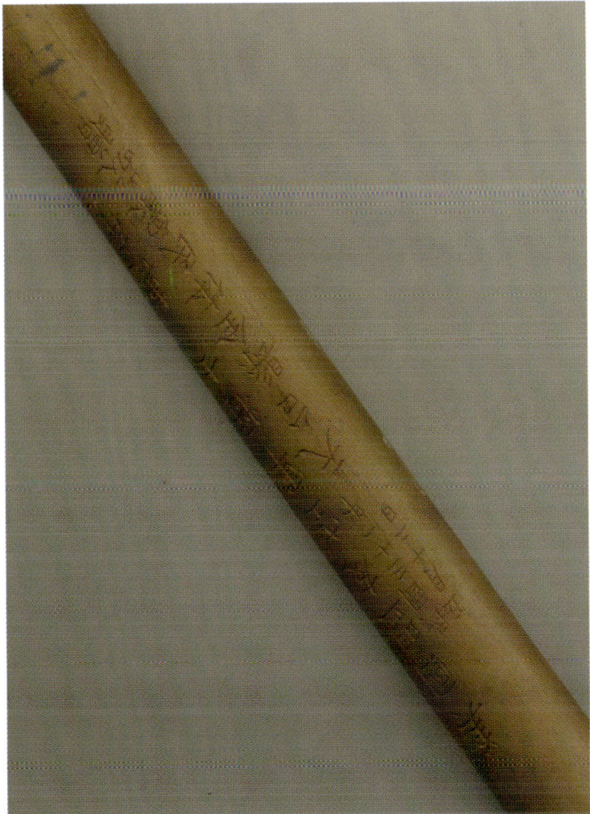

The walking sticks were inscribed in Chinese: "A keepsake to the officers of our friends and allies of the American Air Force. The 31st year of the Chinese Republic, the fifth month, the 12th day of May 1942. Presented by the people of the district of Tien Ta." *White family*

The knife, fork, and spoon were crafted of coin-quality silver. The international standard was then 75 to 90 percent silver mixed with copper. In a country founded on chopsticks, a set of eating utensils might be a godsend when a Westerner eats items such as rice, soup, or fried egg. *White family*

One of the memorable things obvious in traversing China was that each district seemed to have a different style of straw hat. All are large, but some are wide and flat. Others are conical and have very high peaks.

In China, everybody works. Children tend to their younger siblings so adults can do the serious work of securing survival for the family. Our presence always created curious looks, but a wink, smile, or other friendly gesture fended off hostility.

Dr. White was less enamored with airplanes after the war than before. In any case, he poses with the ubiquitous Douglas transport during more-sanguine times. *White family*

Dr. White knew he was on the trip of a lifetime. As soon as survival became likely, the consummate shopper eagerly sought those souvenirs that either captured his fancy or helped him recount the adventure. This superbly crafted pocket watch is an enduring example. *White family*

One of my purchases was a very interesting pair of elephant hair earrings. They were made of three concentric rings of elephant-tail hairs, each about 2 millimeters thick, wound with strips of thin gold. We haggled and I bought them for nearly a quarter of the original price. *White family*

A Model 307 Stratoliner in flight. Production was halted on this advanced airliner at only ten units so Boeing could instead focus on B-17 wartime production. The TWA fleet was pressed into military service. One of them airlifted Doc (and entourage) all the way from Karachi, Pakistan, to Washington, DC. *Boeing*

This small stone head measures about 2 inches in height and came with a "certificate of authenticity." Imhotep was the Egyptian god of medicine. Since it's a handsome piece, I plan to someday have it mounted as a companion to the small plaster head of Nefertiti, which was my next purchase. Nefertiti was the mother of the famous King Tut and one of the most attractive women in all of history. *White family*

This time I found the place where they made the beautifully inlaid jewelry boxes that we had previously seen in some of the stores. I bought some mother-of-pearl inlay work and a cute little box made of tiny turnings of ivory, ebony, and teak. It was surprising to me how fine and accurate work the native craftsmen could do with their crude tools. *White family*

Only fourteen examples of the Boeing Model 314 Clipper were built. All were pressed into worldwide military service and flew over four thousand high-priority missions. None were preserved. Two sank to the bottom of the ocean (one in the Pacific, one in the Atlantic). All others went to scrap. *Boeing*

Silver Star

AWARDED FOR ACTIONS
DURING World War II

Service: Army Air Forces

Rank: First Lieutenant

Division: Doolittle Tokyo Raider Force

GENERAL ORDERS:

War Department, General Orders No. 33
(July 18, 1942)

CITATION:

The President of the United States of America, authorized by Act of Congress July 9, 1918, takes pleasure in presenting the Silver Star to First Lieutenant (Medical Corps) Thomas Robert White (ASN: 0-420191), United States Army Air Forces, for conspicuous gallantry in action against the enemy while serving as Flight Surgeon in the 1st Special Aviation Project (Doolittle Raider Force), subsequent to the raid on Japan, 18 April 1942.

Richard Cole and David Thatcher were the final Doolittle survivors but relished each annual event even as their ranks thinned.

Like George Washington to Americans, Emperor Hirohito was highly revered by his countrymen while also celebrated as an equestrian. In fact, he was a shy, reticent, and introverted person who escaped war criminal status by becoming MacArthur's collaborator in exchange for retaining the castle, the throne, his family, and an oversized white horse. *Alamy*

It was early on another Sunday morning when the Pacific war ended aboard USS *Missouri* on September 2, 1945. War crime investigations were already underway. Only those cases considered most egregious went to trial. Allied enthusiasm for further individual retribution eroded in the wake of the ongoing Nuremberg prosecutions. Thus, many culpable Japanese troops sidestepped justice for their sadistic actions. *US Army*

At age eighty-three, Dr. White contracted a lethal combination of pneumonia and heart disease. After adroitly sidestepping the Grim Reaper fifty years earlier, the end came at the Eisenhower Medical Center in Rancho Mirage, California, on Sunday, November 29, 1992. *White family*

Plant Sites: North American Aviation, Inc.

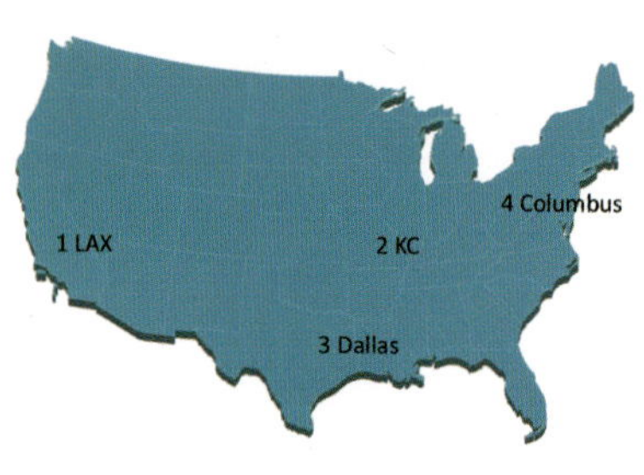

Location:	Years Active:	Aircraft Built:
1 Los Angeles	1936-1986	P-51, B-25, AT-6
2 Kansas City	1941-1945	B-25
3 Dallas	1941-1945	AT-6, P-51, B-24
4 Columbus	1950-1988	FJ-Fury, etc.

Aviation Manufacturing: Wartime Workforce

Workforce Demographic: Male & Female 45%, People of Color 10%

Typical Headcount Trend – Boeing & NAA

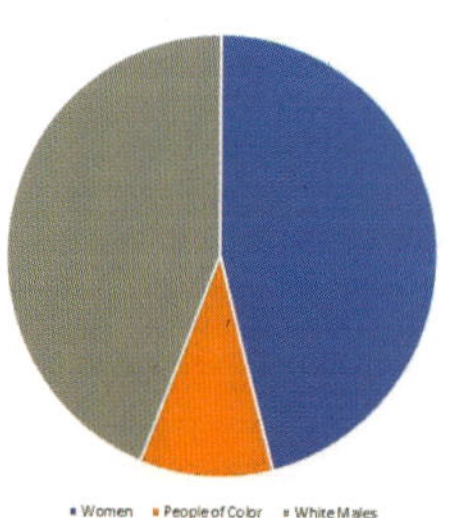

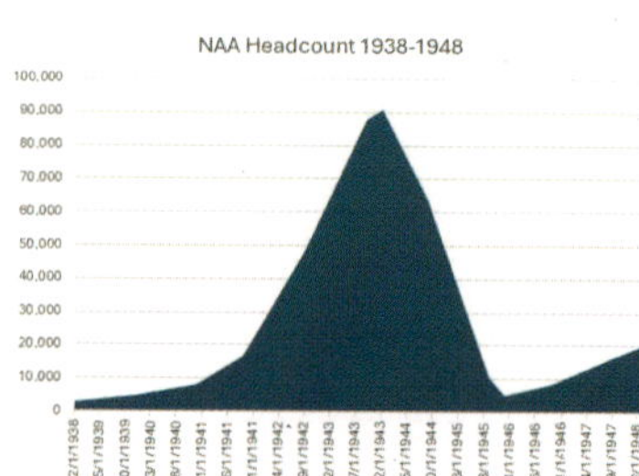

The NAA wartime workforce peaked in the autumn of 1943 at 91,000, with about 46 percent female and 10 percent people of color. The Los Angeles headquarters was augmented by huge government-built plants at Kansas City (B-25 production) and Dallas (AT-6 trainers and P-51 Mustangs). NAA ceased at Dallas and Kansas City soon after Japan capitulated (V-J Day). Columbus, Ohio, was a Navy war plant reassigned from Curtiss-Wright to NAA in 1950.

The bottom turret is visible on the lower right. The turret was problematic, so Doolittle discarded it from each of his aircraft. The resulting hole was plugged with sheet metal. The weight saved was traded for additional fuel. Soon thereafter, the lower turret was also deleted from the factory bill of material. Note the various insignias. B-25s were supplied to many Allied nations. *Boeing*

Army Air Forces units took great pride in their military heraldry. Forged in combat, this was the patch of the 75th Bombardment Squadron, a medium-bomber unit that arrived in the Southwest Pacific during the time of the Royce Raid. *Boeing*

Jack Fox plied his trade in the backwaters of the South Pacific. He knew both the B-25 and their crews like the back of his hand. A master mechanic, Fox was the first to install additional forward-firing guns at an overhaul depot in Australia. The stateside factories followed his lead, and the B-25 "Strafer" version was born. *Boeing*

Paul "Pappy" Gunn (*right*) with an unknown officer, was of a rare breed: a retired Navy enlisted pilot, a former Philippine Airlines expatriate pilot, and now a freshly minted US Army aviator with a hatred of the Japanese because they were holding his wife, Polly, and their four children as prisoners in the Philippines. *Boeing*

Housing at Charters Towers for "Pappy" Gunn, Fox, and the others consisted of small tents. Fortunately, the climate there was generally warm and dry. Local ranchers contributed one beef steer per week, and when butchered it became the main course at the weekly barbecue and beer bash. *Boeing*

The optional B-25 bomb bay fuel tank yields a reliable ferry range exceeding 2,400 miles—or the distance from San Francisco to Honolulu. "Pappy" Gunn used them to get from Darwin, Australia, to Del Monte Air Base and back during the Royce Raid. *Boeing*

"Pappy" Gunn led a dozen B-25s on a brazen attack on Japanese targets in the Philippines during April 1942. The lieutenant colonel is seen here with his spouse, Polly, and NAA president "Dutch" Kindelberger at the main Los Angeles plant in 1945. Gunn's finger was crushed between bombs, and the painful injury was slow to heal. *Boeing*

CHAPTER 11

AMPUTATION

I IMMEDIATELY WENT to the hospital where Ted Lawson (pilot of number 7) and his three injured comrades were admitted. The hospital was on a hill behind the town, which rejoiced in the name of "Hill to View the Heavens," though those who climbed it regularly came to call it the "Hill of Difficulty" (from the *Pilgrim's Progress*, John Bunyan, 1678). The hospital was established by Dr. Bevington, who left behind such a reputation for cures that even two decades after his departure, the hospital still reflected his glory.

The Church Mission Society had operated it for several years, and then it was purchased by two Chinese doctors, a father-and-son team, the doctors Chen (pronounced "Jing" locally). The son, Dr. Chen Sen-nyi, had trained in an American Mission Hospital and so knew considerably more than the rudiments of modern first aid. No doubt, Lawson's and Davenport's eventual recoveries were largely due to the excellent care they received there. Through the kindness of the State Department, Dr. Chen achieved his lifelong ambition by the study of medicine in the United States. The fact that Ted and Dean were still alive is just one of the miracles which occurred on and after April 18.

Both pilots assigned to Ruptured Duck, Ted Lawson and Dean Davenport, were in very bad shape when I arrived, some six days after the accident. Both had lost a lot of weight and appeared to be on a downhill grade. Ted was much sicker. He lost all eight of his front teeth and had minor cuts all about the face and chin and a bad cut in his left upper arm. His worst injury was a deep laceration extending from 2 two inches above his left knee diagonally downward and inward through the lower end of his femur, patella, [and] knee joint and into the upper end of his tibia. There were several minor cuts and abrasions on his lower leg, but all the wounds were hideously infected with a very virulent organism, apparently one of the fecal-contamination types of symbiotic, anaerobic bacteria. The whole leg was swollen, crepitant, and fluctuant, with a foul watery discharge seeping from every opening. There was an area of dry gangrene over the inner aspect of the ankle. Motion at the knee joint was of course extremely painful, and Ted was delirious most of the time from weakness and toxic absorption.

Davenport's primary injuries consisted of several deep cuts on his right leg, which were badly infected with the same foul organisms. McClure had dislocated both shoulders, but at the time, with no x-ray available, I did not make the diagnosis. Both shoulders were hugely swollen and ecchymotic (bruised). The deformity was not apparent. I thought he had sustained a possible fracture of the right shoulder and a nerve injury on the left, with an almost complete left wrist drop. Mac also had several minor cuts, all badly infected. Robert Clever (bombardier) manifested a basilar skull fracture with bleeding from the nose and ears but was well on the road to recovery when I arrived. He also had a sprained right ankle and infected cuts on the right hand, leg, and scalp. Thatcher had the small scalp wound I mentioned before, and this was nearly healed when I first saw it.

I immediately went to work on the injured, inspecting and dressing their wounds and making some changes in their nursing care. I wore some old and much-patched rubber gloves to avoid any mixing of the infections of my several patients and to prevent contaminating their wounds with my own still-draining hand. I was determined to save Ted's leg if possible and so ransacked the hospital and finally found some Japanese-brand sulfanilamide. I started both Ted and Dean on this by mouth, doubtful as I was of its potency, and then tried to improve the drainage of Ted's wounds. The area of gangrene over his left ankle was insensitive, and I was able to excise (cut out entirely) with scissors with a minimum of discomfort. My labors were rewarded when over a cupful of stinking pus gushed forth.

For McClure's shoulders, I rigged a small table over his bed for him to rest his arms on, in lieu of an airplane splint. A cock-up[1] splint was also contrived for his left wrist to prevent any contractures. The two Chinese doctors and their staff of nurses and orderlies were of great assistance to me, as were local foreign Christian missionaries. There were two missions in town, the China Inland Mission, represented by Mr. and Mrs. Frank England, and the Church Mission Society, represented by Misses Andrews and Marrian. From the nearby town of Sienku (or Sienju) came Mr. and Mrs. Smyth and their two children, Francis (aged two and a half, and looking just like the pictures of Christopher Robin in A. A. Milne's books) and Morris (aged ten months). Mr. Smyth represented the China Inland Mission too, and Mrs. Smyth was an American-trained nurse. A qualified nurse was a godsend to me because she took much of the responsibility for the care of the injured men onto her capable shoulders.

Medical supplies of all sorts were very short. Their scarcity can best be illustrated by quoting the local prices of some representative items. Of course, much that I would have liked was simply unobtainable at any price. Quinine was a dollar a grain, and we were all taking 10 grains a day to prevent malaria; sulfanilamide of doubtful potency was five dollars a tablet; emetine, for the treatment of amoebic dysentery, $100 to $120 an ampoule; cod liver oil, $85 a bottle; and so on. I wired Chungking to fly in some supplies to me. I especially wanted a transfusion outfit and some citrate (to keep blood from clotting while it is transferred from one individual to another) and more sulfa drugs.

I was still unaware that none of Doolittle's planes survived. We were well within the sphere of action of enemy airplanes, so it was out of the question to send other than combat-type aircraft. That afternoon the Chinese newspapers were headlined with news of the raid and even printed photographs of our planes flying low over Tokyo, along with some of the bomb damage. These pictures had been purloined from smuggled Tokyo papers. The news caused great excitement among the Chinese. After being at war with Japan for nearly eight years, it was the first sign of any real help. They must have been very much disappointed when the raids were not continued, because I know we were.

Many deputations from the city, schools, and various civic and military organizations appeared. They brought abundant gifts and scarce supplies of many kinds, including oranges (quite rare), eggs (four for a dollar), cookies, decorative banners, and so forth. The local city government, headed by the chief magistrate, a Mr. Tsong (pronounced Chuwang in Mandarin), was very helpful by furnishing all our other food, many supplies, clothing, and a cook. Wong (the cook) had worked in the YMCA at Shanghai and thus knew how to prepare "foreign" dishes, which was a great help for the patients, some of whom did not care for Chinese food; however, Wong was a rascal who absconded with a large part of the food furnished to us by selling it on the black market.

Those of us who could still navigate went to Mr. England's home and deloused. I had a lovely hot bath, and Mr. England loaned me some attire. Fortunately, he was also a big man, and his clothes fit me. The Englands' home was in a little compound on the other side of the town. They had a nice frame house, a garden, and, wonder of wonders—a lawn. Stepping through their gate was like stepping out of China [and] into England. We all enjoyed many pleasant afternoons and evenings there.

That same day I had a telegram from Maj. Hilger, asking me to retrieve the bodies of two of our compatriots at a nearby town for identification and burial. I checked with the authorities. No bodies were there, but they stated [that] several of our group had been captured by the Japanese, and some had been killed. This news naturally upset us. We also heard that Chushien and Lishui had been badly bombed.

Saturday, April 25, 1942, marked the beginning of our second week in China. Lawson had a bad night. It was apparent that he needed some more-effective supportive treatment. He wasn't eating well and was very toxic from his wounds and the sulfanilamide. He was blood type "A," and since Griffith Williams (my copilot) was also type "A," I decided to try a direct transfusion. I had no means of doing a proper crossmatching so had to take the chance of subgroups and a reaction. The only apparatus available was a couple of ancient syringes, a 10 cc and a 20 cc, and so young Dr. Chen and I commenced the procedure. Of course, we had the expected trouble with clogging needles and syringes but managed to get in 150 cc the first try, and later, after cleaning and boiling the outfit, 200 cc on the second try. Ted seemed stronger afterward.

We were all given Chinese names by a scholar friend of Frank England's. I was "Way Beh Tih," which means "Great and powerful one who walks in the path of virtue." Heh, if they only knew. "Esang" means doctor, so I was also called "Way Esang." The Chinese were also having cards printed for us and getting our Chinese names carved on our "chops."

It rained all day, and there were several air-raid alarms. Enemy planes flew overhead but were apparently on their way to bomb other towns, because they did not bother us. The alarm was sounded on an old temple bell, which was mounted on a hill opposite us. Sounded slowly, it meant that an enemy plane was coming. Faster cadence meant it was near, and very rapidly meant it was nearly overhead. When sounded slowly in couples, it signaled "all clear."

The next day, Mr. England conducted Sunday services at the hospital. Afterward I went to his house and built a modified Roger Anderson splint[2] for Lawson's leg. Installing the splint was a painful process, but immobilizing the knee joint and elevating the leg made him more comfortable and I hoped would improve drainage.

The "Jurenjang"[3] visited and brought us a big basket of oranges, which were very welcome. Later, other government and military officials called and brought a variety of presents. Many were nearly priceless at the time. Raisins were 2 ounces for a dollar; [also there were] preserves (six to ten dollars a jar), wine, grapefruit, eggs, thermos bottles ($120 to $150 each), clothing, and, a great treat—canned butter ($15, when you could get it). The missionaries were google-eyed. They said they hadn't seen any butter for over two years. Naturally we shared it with them.

The electric-generation plant finally failed. The lights had been weak and flickering, but now the lack of nighttime illumination was a curse. The power had been supplied by a diesel motor running on charcoal gas, but it had finally broken down beyond the skills of local mechanics to fix. The faulty part was sent away for repair. We were now reduced to candles and occasionally a kerosene lamp (kerosene was scarcer than rubies). Imported candles cost $2.50 each. Local ones were cheaper but burned much more quickly, while yielding a rancid odor.

On Monday, I gave Lawson our only ampoule of glucose in saline. He had a very sharp reaction. We were running out of sulfanilamide, and I was feeling rather unwell myself, so things looked grim. I didn't see the necessity for keeping healthy fighting men hanging around the hospital, especially since I knew we'd be there some time. So, I sent Smith, Williams, Sessler, Saylor, and Thatcher on to Chushien, our original destination. They went by sedan chair, and we all dispatched letters with them. I felt lonesome after they were gone.

Tuesday, April 28, dawned cold, and I had fires lit in the sickroom and Frank England loaned me a sweater and a coat. Lawson was no better, so I gave him some chloroform and enlarged his wounds and opened several other pockets of pus to try to improve drainage. Ted stopped breathing, and I had some anxious moments before we could get him going properly again.

The missionaries told us that when Chefoo was occupied by the Army of Nippon, some 375 missionary children were captured at a school there—while their parents were proselytizing in Free China. The malevolent enemy forbade any communication between the parents and their children.

Lawson's wounds looked better by Wednesday, and for the first time I began to hope we could save his leg. I went downtown for shopping and had an interesting morning looking the town over. The streets were small, twisting, and lined with all manner of shops. I bought a thermos, $120, and a suitcase (paper), $85, a hat, umbrella, and $40 worth of sulfanilamide. When I got back up the hill, I wasn't feeling too well [*sic*] and then had a hard chill. I thought I was probably coming down with malaria and so went to bed with 30 grains of quinine. I spent Thursday in bed with my ears making like bells,[4] but the fever broke later in the afternoon, and I felt much better. I had a telegram message from Davy Jones saying that Smitty (my pilot) and the others had arrived intact, which gave us considerable relief, and that they would somehow get supplies to us.

Friday was May Day (May 1, 1942), and I was able to get myself moving. I was feeling much better, although I had a swell drug rash from the quinine. Ted's wounds looked worse again, so I ground up our entire supply of sulfanilamide tablets into powder and put this in the wounds. This seemed to help a little; with the other boys, the sulfanilamide powder seemed to be the only treatment that was of any value in clearing up their infections. Fortunately, the elder Dr. Chen was able to find some more sulfa for us.

Saturday a Dr. Ding, from the "Plague Prevention Unit" of the Public Health Hospital at Kinwah, arrived. He brought a little morphine, some sulfanilamide, and, best of all, a transfusion kit with some citrate. The kit was Japanese in manufacture and a cleverly designed outfit. The carrying case did double duty as the sterilizer. You just poured a little water in it and set it on a stove. I put this to immediate use and gave Lawson 500 cc of blood, using Clever and McClure as donors; both were type "A," but I didn't want to take a full pint from either. I had also hoped they might have some specific antibodies in their blood—since they were recovering from the same type of infection.

Sunday, Dr. Seng from the Provincial Medical School arrived with a few more supplies. Both Dr. Ding and Dr. Seng were a big help. Their supplies were a godsend. Church services were conducted in the hospital, with Mr. England (again) officiating. Following the services, another group of deputations arrived from the Chinese air force and various nearby communities and organizations. All brought gifts and eggs—most of which I think Wong sold on the black market.

In the late afternoon I went for a walk on the city wall. It was very interesting and in a remarkable state of preservation. Many of China's cities are still walled, and some are still put to good use. We heard of one small town that held off one of the Communist armies for several weeks until help arrived. I was also interested in surveying the river and decided that it would be possible for an amphibian or seaplane to land there. No other kind of plane could land except a blimp or a helicopter.[5] All the level (or nearly level) land was taken up with rice paddies.

I telegraphed a message to Chungking and asked them to send a seaplane so Lawson could be flown to more-adequate medical facilities. I received no reply but later found out that the authorities had made a serious effort to comply; however, they were stymied by the fact there wasn't a seaplane nearer than Australia that could make the trip.[6] In my opinion, small seaplanes or amphibians would be very useful in China. There are small rivers everywhere, most of which could be used for landings and takeoffs. Most of the level ground is intensively farmed. The construction of even a small landing strip is a formidable undertaking.

By Monday, Lawson was in such poor shape that it was evident that both his leg and his life could not be saved—so it was decided to amputate the leg. The Chinese had smuggled an ampoule of novocaine out of Shanghai at my request, so we were able to give Ted a spinal anesthetic. After our first experience, I didn't want to repeat the inhalation anesthetic. I gave the spinal in his room so he could be moved to the operating room in relative comfort. Mrs. Smyth had sterilized the packs and instruments, and then she and Dr. Chen (the younger) scrubbed with me. The instruments were of the 1890 vintage but were adequate for the task.

We blocked off the infected part of Ted's left leg with drapes and prepared the operative field, applying a tourniquet up as high as we could. We had to make our skin incision about the middle of the thigh in order to get a decent margin of healthy tissue above the infected area. I made fairly large skin flaps and undercut each layer of muscle as I came to it. The large vessels were clamped and tied as we came to them, though because of the tourniquet they naturally didn't bleed. The large nerves were dissected up a short distance and cut. The bone was sawed through at a still-higher level, and the edges beveled. Then the wound was closed in layers and the skin approximated without tension, with drains in the angles of the incision. We used raw-silk sutures ties. Incidentally, it is one of the sweetest suture materials I have ever used. We came out about even on the anesthetic. Ted said he felt the last few stitches.

Following the operation, I gave Ted another 500 cc of blood. I had no other type "A" donors so gave the blood myself, since I was type "O" or the "universal donor." There were no facilities for doing serology tests or crossmatching, so I couldn't consider any Chinese donors.

It may be that I will be criticized for not doing a guillotine type of amputation, such as is done routinely where medical facilities are more adequate, but in my own mind at least I was convinced that I did the right thing.[7] We were over 1,000 trackless miles from the nearest medical installation of any adequacy, and, conditions being what they were in China, the contamination of any open wound would have been a certainty. We were faced with the imminent prospect of having to move out suddenly to avoid capture should the Japanese discover our presence and send a column after us. With inadequate supplies and what crude shelter might be available, I just couldn't see trying to care for a large gaping wound.

The next day, Tuesday, May 5, Ted was better. He was comfortable for the first time since the accident and was lucid for the first time in weeks. The wound was draining only a very little serum. Dean Davenport and Robert Clever were able to be up and about by now, though on crutches or canes, and Charles McClure could get about, though his shoulders still bothered him.

Madame Chiang Kai-shek Hosts the Raiders

Dr. White is silent about this event because he was absent. As previously stated, White sent the balance of crew 15 (pilot Smith, copilot Williams, navigator Sessler, gunner Saylor) plus Ted Lawson's top gunner (David Thatcher, crew 7) on to Chusien, where they met up with the others on their way to the Nationalist Chinese capital of Chungking. The doctor opted to remain with his patients at the Linhai hospital.

Chungking was then described as a rat-infested slum city that suffered too-frequent aerial bombardment. The Raiders were hosted at the official presidential residence for a wonderful lunch by Madame Chiang Kai-shek. Doolittle's men were awed by the beauty and grace of Madame Chiang. General Joseph Stilwell found the slender, American-educated, forty-four-year-old much more impressive than her inept husband. Stilwell wrote in his diary, "a clever brainy woman." "Direct, forceful, energetic, loves power, eats up publicity and flattery, pretty weak on her history," he wrote. "Can turn on the charm in an instant and knows it."[8]

The main gathering was in the afternoon, but the Raiders were called back around 9:30 p.m. to the drawing room. They received instructions on how to behave before Madame Chiang arrived with an entourage of local officials and press people. Medals and letters of appreciation were awarded to each. She then posed with the airmen as flashbulbs popped and motion picture cameras rolled.

Meanwhile, back in Tacoma, Washington, with Ed Saylor away on military duty at some unknown location, his young wife moved in with her mother-in-law. The duo shared a brownstone apartment in the downtown district. The feature movies were always preceded by a Universal Studios newsreel narrated by Ed Herlihy. Some weeks later, the pair attended the nearby movie theater for a double feature (two first-run motion pictures for the price of one) and were dumbstruck when Ed Saylor appeared on the newsreel feature proximate to the sultry-clad Madame Chiang Kai-shek. Was Ed's wife jealous? Not a bit, according to Ed's stated recollection.[9]

Dr. White at the Hospital

On May 6, we heard the depressing news of Corregidor's surrender on Mr. England's radio. Drs. Seng and Ding left, since their services were no longer required and they didn't relish an exposed position with enemy planes passing frequently overhead.

Ted Lawson was showing definite improvements, so I took Dean Davenport, Charles McClure, and Robert Clever on a shopping trip in sedan chairs to see how they would withstand that means of travel. Mr. England and I joined on foot. We went for a tour of the city and wound up at the England residence for tea and a fine dinner. I had a close shave by nearly stepping on a cobra. Fortunately, the snake was nearly as frightened as I, and we both went our separate ways. We returned to the hospital after dark—which was an interesting experience. Walking down the eerie echoing streets in the black night, relieved only by the flickering light of two paper lanterns, the silence was broken only by the sound of our footfalls and the slither of the chair bearers' slippers. The patients withstood the trip well. I was much encouraged.

The next day, Lawson was still running a low fever—but improved. I gave him a second pint of my blood and felt briefly faint. It was a nice cool day, and my other patients were all doing nicely. Wealthy and influential people from the entire surrounding countryside sought appointments for treatment by the "foreign" doctor. I had quite a problem in keeping my schedule clear while taking care of the whole district.

I was glad to do what I could for the Christian missionaries but maintained that as a military surgeon, I could not treat civilians except in consultation with the Drs. Chen. In this way I was able to repay in some small measure the many kindnesses and great generosity of these two men. In this manner I saw several very interesting cases. One was the son of General Du, the "wu juren" or military head of the six local districts. This patient had an extensive tuberculous ischeo-rectal abscess, which we later incised and drained with considerable success.

We were all very proud of the excellent work that the American Red Cross was doing to relieve the suffering of many of the near-starving people. All money and supplies are administered by Christian missionaries, and each case was thoroughly investigated by someone familiar with the district and its people, thus ensuring [that] very little of the benefits fell into the wrong hands. The people everywhere showed great respect and gratitude for the equitable manner the relief was administered.

An amusing incident was observed on this day. There were a great number of small hawks about, and the Chinese have a habit of carrying parcels dangling from a long cord or string rather than holding them in their hands. One old gentleman was carrying home a piece of meat in this manner when a hawk swooped down, seized the meat, and flew off, triggering the finest accompaniment of Chinese profanity I've ever heard!

Mr. Jack Sharman, a Welshman, arrived in town to do what he could to help. He had a bicycle on which he could travel much faster than the sedan chairs; however, I never could fathom how he could navigate those rutted rocky trails with it.

Friday, May 8, found Ted worse again. The stump was draining a purulent material from the angles; he was "off the beam" (irrational) and not eating. Dr. Chen said he knew of a source with sulfathiazole, so I encouraged him to do his utmost to get some.

That afternoon, I went downtown again, looking for some dental instruments. Dentistry, watchmaking, and photography are combined in China into one specialty. As usual whenever any of us appeared in public, a big crowd congregated. The Chinese were much amused by some pheasant feathers I had stuck into my straw hat. The shop I visited had the watchmaking and dentistry downstairs and the photography upstairs. The studio backdrop was the antithesis of Chinese—a much-cracked and worn mural portraying a Victorian interior. It turned out that this was the man who had made the trip to Sai Mien to take our pictures, and so I was able to get copies of the photographs. I collected a few dental instruments and returned up the hill. I had been doing a little impromptu dentistry on the missionaries, who had not been able to see a "foreign" dentist for several years. I had neither drill nor training in dentistry—but scooped out the cavities as best I could with chisels and curettes. I did my best to sterilize the cavities with iodine and made up an amalgam of powdered silver and mercury from a broken thermometer. I did not expect to do a first-rate job but hoped it would suffice until they could see a proper dentist.

That night, Dr. Chen invited us all to a "feast" at his home. It was a marvelous dinner and the best food I've ever eaten. Sixteen courses plus six "extra" courses were served! I made the common mistake of eating too much of the first courses and had to go rather light thereafter. Everyone attended except Ted Lawson, Charles McClure (who didn't like Chinese food), and Mrs. Smyth. It is considered very polite to ask the ingredients of a given dish and how much they cost. After dinner, when we were all sitting glassy-eyed and gorged up to the gills, Dr. Chen apologized for not having served anything worth eating. I also imbibed a little too much of the deceptively smooth "water wine" and got mildly lit; however, it was Dean Davenport who was carried home on a stretcher.

On May 9, news of a victory at the Battle of Coral Sea was received and our morale improved. I had four dentistry patients, examined three eye cases, and did ophthalmoscopy and retinoscopy by candlelight with instruments which should have been in a museum. It was an interesting experience, although the fundi (the part of the inner eye opposite the pupil) were hard to see in the poor light and increased retinal pigment of the Chinese people.

May 10 was Sunday, and after services, $410 worth of sulfathiazole arrived, which was certainly an answer to my prayers. I put Ted Lawson on it immediately and took the stitches out of his stump. The stump had healed nicely except for the angles of folded skin, which had developed a low-grade infection. This was annoying, but not serious, but gave an indication of what could have happened to a large gaping wound.

Again, we had dinner at the Englands' and had a delicious pheasant (out of season!). The bird was supplied by the Chinese pastor of Mr. England's church, a Mr. Wong, who shot it with an old muzzle-loading, percussion-lock fowling piece. The powder was made locally, and the shot was cut out of sheet lead (lead metal in sheet form) by hand and then rolled between two stones until it was relatively round! No percussion caps were available, but the ingenious Chinese got around this by putting a couple of safety-match heads and a bit of the friction paper into an old cap. This device worked nearly every time, though there was nearly two-tenths-of-a-second hang fire that you had to get used to.

I spilled the soup on my only pair of pants and had to have them washed. I lived in my summer flight suit for several days.

Mr. Liu, who guided my pilot, Donald Smith, and his gang to Chushien, returned with letters from Davy Jones and the others. Thirteen of our planes were accounted for by that time. We further heard that York and Farrow were in enemy hands and that Hallmark had gone to Siberia. [This information was incorrect. York and crew were under house arrest in Russia. Farrow was captured by the Japanese and one of the three later executed.] Jimmy Doolittle was safe and already in transit to the United States—which made us all very happy.

The next day, Ted Lawson's temperature was normal for the first time. It was evidence of recovery and certainly was a big relief. We got him out of bed twice during the day and let him sit up in a chair.

CHAPTER 12

DODGING A PERSISTENT ENEMY

INVITATIONS TO A FEAST ARRIVED that afternoon. They were on red paper, and red is very complimentary. A celebration was being given in our honor by twenty local organizations. Later, the "Yuentsaing" (pronounced "yuren-jaing"), the chief magistrate, arrived to escort us to the feast, a further signal of honor. The regal event was held in the new Chamber of Commerce building, and we had our pictures taken. We were presented with another banner and a solid coin-silver knife, fork and spoon, and napkin ring. The latter were engraved in Chinese: "Presented to Dr. White in remembrance of the event of the first bombing of the Country of the Dwarfs (Japan), by the Linhai Chamber of Commerce." I had borrowed a shirt and some pants from Mr. England and wore Charles McClure's blouse and so was almost in uniform. We had nine courses and five "extras" in addition to pieces of sugar cane, watermelon seed, water chestnuts, and some candy, which tasted like mothballs. We consumed some very rare delicacies, including shark fins. Remembering my last experience, I ate only small helpings and went easy on the wine.

Tuesday, May 12, Ted Lawson was much better. Dean Davenport, Robert Clever, and I went to the Englands' for tiffin (light teatime meal) and dinner. Bessy England, a refined Scotch lassie, made us some Scotch pancakes, which were delicious. I fixed Frank's camera and tinkered with his electrical system. He had a wind charger attached to his house, which powered electric lights while the rest of the town was in darkness until the diesel generator was fixed.

Wednesday was routine except for a visit to the post office in search of stamps to purchase for my collection. The postmaster, a Mr. Tsiang, gave me some rare issues from his own collection, and his assistant, Miss Hong, gave me an interesting miniature sheet. There seemed to be no limit to the generosity of these people.

Every day the "Tsingfu" (pronounced "jing-fu") man would stop by to see if there was anything that we wanted or needed. As representative of the city government, he was able to do a lot for us. Any clothing, articles of diet, or curios we wanted he would either dig up or produce a reasonable substitute. The next day, five canes arrived for us.

Mr. and Mrs. Thompson (missionaries[1] from Hwan-yen) arrived, and I performed a medical examination on Mrs. Thompson and did some dentistry on Mr. Thompson. Ted Lawson and Charles McClure both had temperatures, so I put each of them on sulfanilamide.

Robert Clever, Dean Davenport, and I walked over to Yuentsaing's office, which was in an old temple. The place had a magnificent view, and the temple was filled with interesting scrolls and idols. One of the latter was of a physician. Young Dr. Chen came with us to Chungking because he wanted to join the Chinese air force as a surgeon and eventually complete his medical studies in the United States. With Ted Lawson's persistent advocacy, Dr. Chen finally received a scholarship and was (by 1949) a medical school student in America.

It was silkworm season, and I spent nearly an hour watching an old woman wind silk from the cocoon onto a reel. We think the worm-driven gadget on a bait-casting fishing reel (moves the line back and forth) is a new development; however, this old woman had one on her reel. It was crude but it worked. She put the cocoons into hot water, teased a free end loose, passed this on to her reel, and unraveled the single thread from the entire cocoon. Everywhere big hanks of raw silk in their natural colors were drying in the sun. Some silk was pure white, some reddish, and the remainder a brilliant orange.

Friday, May 15. I did some more dentistry and saw a high-ranking fish commissioner in consultation with the two doctors named Chen. It was an interesting problem to tackle with none of the usual diagnostic aids, but I finally decided he probably had a gastric ulcer. I developed a great deal of respect for the elder Dr. Chen. He had had none of the advantages of a Western education and indeed spoke no English, but his commonsense judgment and (above all) his ability to get along with what limited available supplies and equipment [were what] marked him as a true healer.

I had tiffin and dinner at the Englands' residence and took a couple of shots at a squirrel with the old muzzleloader. The critter had been eating the plants in Frank's vegetable garden. I winged him on the second shot, and Frank poked his nest down in case there might be some small ones in it. We heard some news which reminded us that the Japanese weren't far away. They had bombed nearby Tien Ta and were reported to have massed some 30,000 troops in

Hangchow. We also heard of attacks along the Burma Road in Yunnan Province. One plane flew over during the afternoon without pause. Plans were made for a quick exit should the Japanese army advance in our direction.

Jack Sharmon telephoned the next day. The enemy was closing in on his town, and he was leaving. This alarmed us because his district was only two days' travel from us. To further condition our team, I planned to take them all down to the Englands' residence for dinner.

Sunday, May 17, was a wonderful day. After services, the elder Dr. Chen presented all of us with some very valuable and beautiful presents of Han-dynasty jade. He was a collector of jade and was interested only in pieces that were at least 1,500 years old. The Han dynasty was one of the most prosperous periods of China's long history, and the people had the time and resources to turn out some of the best examples of Chinese art in existence. He gave me a lovely belt buckle of white and green jade, which had once belonged to a Mandarin, and a beautifully carved jade snuff bottle, both of which are museum pieces.

I calculated that we had used over $10,000 worth of medical supplies alone, plus use of the hospital, operating room, [and] nursing staff and the services of both Drs. Chen, and yet, when I mentioned repaying the old doctor, he was genuinely insulted and said, "In times like these, everyone must do his part; this is just my small contribution!" If you ask me, a fine sentiment.

Letters of thanks were written to Dr. Chen and the Juenjang before departing with the men to the Englands' for the afternoon and dinner. Mrs. England presented me with a collection of fancy embroidered doilies for my wife and some cute Chinese doll shoes for my daughter, Roberta. Mr. Thompson gave me a rare old stamp. Some more deputations arrived as we rested after dinner. We were next presented with a silken banner and many other gifts.

The news of the enemy advancing quickly was frightening. The Chinese tanks and army headquarters had departed town already. There were not enough troops or supplies to defend the city, nor [to] do much more than irritate the advancing Nips. We planned to leave the next morning as early as possible. Lawson had stood the short trip very well, so we spent the rest of the evening packing our few belongings before turning in for one last good sleep on mattresses teamed with innersprings.

Whatever else people may say about the unsanitary conditions in China, the poverty and disease, nobody can disparage their courage, hospitality, or generosity of the Indigenous Chinese people.

Monday, May 18, marked one full month after the Raid. It dawned cold and rainy as we scurried about in the inevitable last-minute preparations. After a substantial breakfast, we bid our many good friends farewell. The Englands, Miss Marian, and Miss Andres were going to stay put to carry out their self-appointed labors until the last possible moment. We worried about them constantly, but they said that they would take to the hills if worst came to worst. There they would be hidden and cared for by their Chinese friends. These brave people stayed on for nearly three years before the repeated calls for them to come to safety were heeded. Only then did they make nearly the same trek as we did through dangerous enemy territory. I am very happy to report they all reached India unharmed.

We bundled into our chairs and were covered with oilcloth (a kind of semiwaterproof paper) and were reasonably comfortable, if a little damp around the edges. The entourage finally got underway. It consisted of my colleagues in arms, Mr. and Mrs. Smyth, and their two children, Dr. Chen (the younger), an interpreter, guide, and general factotum (jack-of-all-trades). Along with armed escort and porters carrying our luggage, we made quite an imposing procession as we descended the "hill to view the heavens" for the last time, passed through the city, and out the Water Gate. The pontoon bridge over the river was crossed, and then we headed up the valley. The route followed the river, crossing and recrossing its stream many times, sometimes on bridges but more often by ferries—small boats poled by crewmen or towed across by ropes. The countryside was lovely and green. The weather shifted from rainy to sunny as the day progressed and we dried out.

We passed several rapids and watched with interest the boats going and coming. Going downstream, they would shoot through the swiftest part of the stream. Coming upstream, they were poled or laboriously hauled upstream where the current was weakest. We also passed several old mills busily and noisily at work. Their wooden wheels and gears were evidence that many of these people were not yet arrived at the Iron Age.

Pah Shu Yiang was reached at about 14:00 hours. It took a leisurely lunch to satisfy our ravenous appetites, and then our slow trek resumed. Many of the hills along the way had beautiful old pagodas on them. New patches of rice seedlings looked like rich lawns. Occasionally we would pass through a small grove of young pine trees. It was a very interesting and beautiful country.

The Chinese calendar is composed of lunar months, each twenty-eight to twenty-nine days long and ending with the full moon. The "seasons" are a fortnight long (two weeks). We had just finished the "excited insect season" and were entering upon the "mildew season." Once during the day, Robert Clever's porters slipped and spilled him out. Fortunately, he was unhurt. It was equally fortunate that none of the other porters slipped, because the steep cliffside immediately adjacent to the trail would have been unforgiving.

I walked the last 17 Li to Sain Ku (meaning home of the "mountain men" or fairies), another old walled city with beautiful pagodas nearby. We arrived late due to the wet[ness] and were met outside the gates by local officials. The chief magistrate was in bed with an attack of malaria, but his representative and the maritime customs officials entertained us with a nice dinner and put us up for the night. Mac and Ted continued to the Smyths' house for dinner and bed, since this was the Smyths' district. I walked over after dinner to change the dressing on Ted's leg and to see how they withstood the trip. I was very pleased with the way the patients were taking it. They were a plucky lot.

During dinner, some of the officials were called away. They left saying they had just received an emergency telegram from Tien Tai. It appeared the Japanese ground forces were close on our heels. I sent a wire to Chungking saying: "En route Chushien with four injured officers. ETA (estimated time of arrival) 22 May. Stop. Request an airplane meet us." I still didn't know that all our planes crashed. We heard later that the boatmen refused to take our escort back to Linhai because of enemy proximity.

Robert Clever was dubbed "General Kuh" because Kuh was his Chinese name. He further joshed that he was going to join the guerrillas and become a general. Our trip would have been much harder if it had not been for General Kuh's continued good humor and cheerfulness. Many times, when the rest of us were discouraged or blue, he would come forth with some wise remark or an apropos joke and get us laughing. The poor chap was killed[2] shortly after reaching the US in one of a series of accidents which earned the Martin B-26 Marauder the title of "pilot killer."

We were up early the following morning and after breakfast heard the news that the Japanese had captured Tien Tai and one other town. Shortly thereafter, a wire (telegraph message) arrived from the provincial governor, advising a detour around Kinwah because the enemy forces were very near that city. This meant two more days on the road and that we might finally have to go to Lishui instead of Chushien. We bid the Smyths goodbye, as they too had decided to stay on in their district and continue their work for as long as possible. We urged Smyth to send his wife and children out with us, but after some discussion they all decided to stay. The menace of the Japanese was getting progressively more ominous, but the spirit and pluck of these people never ceased to amaze me.

We finally got underway about 07:55 hours and continued up the river valley. At the first stop, Lawson's chair was over fifteen minutes late. One of his bearers, an older fellow beset with nausea, was either sick or drunk. We made some readjustments and continued onward. We crossed a ferry and passed through occasional thickets of pine and groves of bamboo. The mountains on either side were becoming higher and more rugged, and we passed through some lovely scenery. The riverbed was wide and gravelly. I remember thinking that they must have occasional severe floods. There were many long rafts of bamboo drifting downstream to the markets of Sian Ku and Lishui. As before, we crossed and recrossed the stream repeatedly, sometimes by bridge, more often by ferry. We passed many busy mills. The wheat harvest was already in, and the next crop of rice was being planted. As on the first day, the age and disrepair of everything in general was startling.

I walked the last 15 Li to Wonchi, reaching that city about 16:45 hours. Again, we were greeted by the local officials and taken to the local army headquarters, where a very nice dinner was prepared for us. Wonchi was the first town in China, aside from the fishing village at which we first landed, where no one was found who could speak English, so we were forced to fall back on Dr. Chen's rather halting translations. I did the routine dressings on my patients, and we all turned in early.

Ted and I were bunked in the headquarters building while the rest were guests in a local hotel. I remember that night mostly by the size and pugnacity of the mosquitoes. We burned punk all night long in a vain effort to make them keep their distance. All we accomplished was to scorch a hole in my only pair of pants! Those who went to the hotel had some very amusing experiences. It was hardly the Ritz!

On Wednesday, May 20, sleep ended at 05:00 hours and a sumptuous breakfast of five courses was served. Eating fried eggs with chopsticks is quite a feat. Dr. Chen telephoned around and found that we would have to go by way of Lishui after all. This was to be our most difficult day, since crossing a rather high mountain was required to reach Hwotsing, our next stop. However, the possibility of a car meeting us there energized us to meet the ordeal.

The valley was now getting narrower and steeper with our ascent. The scenery was becoming more rugged and wild. There were veritable cliff dwellings, which reminded me of some in our own Southwest. Whole villages were built into a crevice in the rocky face of the mountain. Ted had faster porters this time, and we all made better time. The weather was lovely. There were many small towns along the trail—each with a temple converted into a local party or army headquarters. The route paralleled the telephone or telegraph wires. Several times we heard shots and saw puffs of smoke on the hillsides. Evidently hunters were using ancient guns consistent with the weapon I had used to shoot the squirrel. We passed numerous graves and tombs scattered all over the countryside. Some were plain stones without inscription, while others were elaborately carved and decorated sarcophagi.

The farmers along the way were threshing their wheat into large wooden tubs. Each had a matting screen behind to catch any "spray." The threshing was accomplished by hitting the wheat on a grillwork of bamboo in the tub.

Later the wheat was separated from the chaff by winnowing or in a very ingenious gadget made of wood, whereupon a hand-turned blower separated the grain from the useless portion.

We reached the foot of the mountain about 09:20 hours. I decided to proceed by foot because I was a heavy load, and my porters didn't look too strong. The path followed a cascading mountain stream through some very beautiful scenery. In one place, three arched bridges and a small hamlet made for a lovely picture. The traffic over this trail was very heavy, and the loads carried by the porters were amazing. Nearly all the traffic between Free China and the provinces just departed went up and over this mountain on this single narrow trail. The only other trail passed within a half Li of the Japanese lines.

I reached the 3,000-foot summit well winded and panting at about 11:20 hours and paused in the little town of Nurtia. Lawson arrived first, I was second, and the rest were far behind and arrived about noon. Lunch consisted of sandwiches, hot condensed milk, and cookies. "General" Tung was encountered going the other way. He said he had "just" (in January) seen General Stilwell in India. He gave us some good cigarettes and chocolate.

I also opted to walk down. The descent started at 13:05, and the bottom was reached about 15:10 hours—after negotiating 2,454 steps (I counted them). The scenery was just as lovely on this side of the mountain, though not so rugged: rice paddies terraced nearly to the top, many quaint little villages. The path was wider and paved with stone worn smooth by the passage of generations of bare or sandaled feet. The trail wound up and down. The Chinese roadmakers have a fine disregard for the comfort of the wayfarer, and the trails generally go over a hill rather than around it.

We arrived at Hwotsing about 16:00 hours and were met by officials and ranks of Boy Scouts and Girl Guides carrying banners inscribed "Welcome to American Air Heroes" and the like. We were taken to the local party headquarters, where we freshened up a bit and then were treated to another feast. I put on the long blue Chinese robe which had been given me in Linhai. Blue is the color worn by professional men and scholars. It always makes a hit with the Chinese when you adopt some of their dress or customs. Hwotsing is a pretty little town built around a central lake. It was quite clean too, even by Western standards. The beds were particularly hard for some reason, so I borrowed some extra bees (quilts) for padding.

On Thursday, May 21, wake-up came at 04:00 hours, followed by breakfast. Our departure was delayed until 06:30 because of trouble with the rickshaw drivers. They were apparently demanding pay in advance. Finally, we got started. Clever, Davenport, McClure, and I were in rickshaws. Dr. Chen and Ted were in sedan chairs. The latter seemed much more comfortable and turned out to be a good idea because of troubles encountered later. Our porters were a lazy bunch and were always wanting to stop for a "wee bite"—usually about three great heaping bowls of rice. Fortunately, we had a couple of soldiers along as guards, so with a certain amount of prodding and much shouting of "Quaddy, quaddy!" (Hurry, hurry!), we managed to keep going. It soon developed that my porter was either too weak or too lazy to pull me, so I traded conveyances with Robert Clever. Even then, I had to walk up most of the hills. Whenever we'd bog down, I'd get a chorus of bravado airplane lingo (slang) from the others: "Put him in low pitch, Doc!" or "Shift him into high blower!" or "Doc, raise his manifold pressure!" To which I'd usually reply: "It's no use; he's conked out—I've got to hit the silk."[3]

About 40 Li from Hwotsing, we stopped for some tea at a wayside house. Ted found firecrackers for sale, and he purchased some. Shooting them off provided fun and a diversion. There were three breakdowns out of the four rickshaws. About 20 Li from Tsing Yung, our destination, Mac's rickshaw broke a rim, so I put him in my buggy, and I walked. About 10 Li later, that one broke a spring and Davenport's had a flat tire. We were stuck until I spotted an empty rickshaw going by, which I commandeered with the aid of the soldiers and put Mac in it. The luggage rode in the one with the broken rim. Davenport rode in Clever's, and "General Kuh" and I walked until we caught up with the chairs, then Dr. Chen gave Clever his chair and the medical doctors walked the rest of the way to Tsing Yung.

During that day, it was down one valley, up another. Over a low pass and down a third. We passed many refugees plodding along with their few belongings on their backs or on small carts. The scenery here was very lovely, quite rugged, and with many sharp pinnacles. An airplane passed harmlessly overhead without attacking.

We reached Tsing Yung at 13:50 hours and were met outside the city by officials who accompanied us through the city, across a bridge, and onto a large house hidden in trees on the far side. They didn't want us to stay in town because they were expecting a bombing raid. The house was at the end of the motor road, the first road we'd seen in China wide enough to accommodate automobiles. A station wagon and three trucks were hidden under the trees. One of the trucks was a charcoal burner—the first I'd seen of that type. Later, I saw many of them in China, India, Egypt, North Africa, and England, or wherever else gasoline is scarce. The generator looked like a hot-water tank with pipes of various sizes coming off at different levels. These generators work (after a fashion) by getting a good fire going and then cutting down on the draft and adding small amounts of water to generate producer gas—largely carbon monoxide. The Chinese seem to have the theory that the louder they beat upon the sides of these tanks, the better they work. The trucks and buses thus fueled ran okay on the level but didn't produce full power and always bogged down on the hills.

I was extremely thirsty when we arrived. The day had been warm and muggy, and I drank about a quart of tea, hot condensed milk, and chow water. Ted Lawson and Charles McClure were put to bed while Bob Clever, Dean Davenport, and I sat around dabbing mosquito and flea bites with iodine. After a nice dinner, our pictures were taken again. We then loafed around all afternoon waiting for our car to arrive. In this area, nearly all road traffic was at night because of lurking Japanese aircraft. A company of Chinese troops marched by during the afternoon, heading for the battle that was developing around Kinwah. They were the best-equipped troops I had seen in China, a young, tough, and apparently well-trained outfit. They had rifles of Chinese manufacture, Bren-guns (light machine guns from Britain), potato-masher grenades, and rifle grenades, but no heavy equipment. Against these troops the Nipponese were using airplanes, tanks, artillery, flamethrowers, and poison gas.

At about 17:30 hours, our car arrived, and to our great surprise it was a 1941 Ford station wagon. It must have been strafed at one time because it sported several bullet holes. One had evidently passed through the windshield and penetrated the driver's seat. It had been neatly patched but it gave us something to ponder.

Loading and departure for Lishui came at about 19:00 hours. Ted and Dr. Chen were put aboard the truck. I thought Ted would ride better lying down in a stretcher. This turned out to be a mistake, and thereafter he always rode with us. It was a real luxury to lean back on the leather cushions and whiz down the road at ten to twenty times the speed at which we had traveled for the previous five days.

Two peculiar things became evident along the roadway. First, many of the pedestrians walking on the road would wait until the last possible moment and then duck across the road in front of the car. The driver seemed to think nothing of this strange behavior, since he neither slowed down nor swerved for them. How he missed some of them I'll never know. Later it turned out that the reason for this dangerous maneuver was that the natives thought that by cutting across in front of the car, any devils which might be following them would be run down and thus disposed of!

Second, work crews were waiting at every bridge and at every straight stretch of road. As soon as we passed over a bridge and often before we were out of sight, there would be a boom as the bridge was detonated. As soon as we cleared a straight stretch of road, workers would swarm out and demolish it. It gave us an ominous feeling to know that the Japs were close enough for the Chinese to be carrying out demolitions as soon as we were safely by.

We reached Lishui about 21:10 hours and found another feast awaiting us. This was the location of one of the secondary airdromes we had been heading for that memorable April 18, and now we were finally arriving with hopes that a plane would be able to pick us up there. Instead, we were told that the enemy had been over every day bombing the airdrome, so there was no chance of a plane landing there. We finally got to bed about 22:10, plenty tired out. I dressed Ted's stump and got quite a bit of drainage out, which made him feel better. All things considered, he was standing the trip much better than I had dared hope.

Friday morning, we were up at 03:00 hours, had breakfast, and learned that we could no longer go to Chushien because the Japanese had captured Yung Kong and were fighting close to Kinwah. Therefore, we planned to go southwest to Puchong and on from there. We were loaded into a small bus, which smelled strongly of camphor, and got started at 04:15 hours—just as the first air-raid warning began sounding. The Chinese have long been noted for their ability to get along with what they have available. The strong smell of camphor in our conveyance was due to the fuel, which was largely derived from the cracking of camphor and other vegetable oils. They had lots of camphor but very little petroleum.

Our driver, whom we named "Johnny Beep-Beep," must have gotten his training on the Burma Road, because he was a terror. Johnny didn't know the car had brakes. He used only the horn and gas pedal. He drove like the wind around blind corners, through towns and villages—without slowing down in the slightest. We found that all Chinese cars carry a mechanic in addition to the driver. The reason being that the fuel is so poor that the carburetor jets needed cleaning every few miles, and other repairs were constantly required. The only time we were very worried was when the horn quit working. Even Johnny seemed upset at that!

Several rivers were ferried on the ascent of a river valley. The scenery was rugged and beautiful, a bit too rugged in spots, especially when the scenery coincided with a sharp blind turn! About midmorning, Johnny pulled up under a large tree and turned around and grinned at us. He said something to our guide/interpreter and climbed out of the bus to light a cigarette. Our guide, named Mr. Fong, said an air-raid alert was in effect. Johnny had sense enough to know that a moving car makes a much more obvious target than a stationary one.

We professed ignorance, but Johnny said he'd seen a warning sign hoisted in the last village as we sped through. We all got out and lolled around in the grass and admired the view until word arrived that it was safe to proceed. Later it was stated that the Japanese bombed the daylights out of a village we'd just been through. Apparently, they were still on our trail.

The next brief stop was at Lung Twang, meaning "Long Bow." The countryside in that very mountainous region was lovely. The road wound up and down deep gorges pierced by gushing mountain streams. Every possible piece of land was cultivated, but apparently some was so rough and precipitous that even the energetic Chinese farmers were stymied. One river was ferried aboard a rickety bamboo raft, a very shaky-looking contraption which nearly sank under the weight of our bus; however, the ferrymen and our guides appeared unconcerned—so we took heart and arrived safely at the other shore.

The Chinese have a unique system worked out for ferrying swift streams. There are two ramps on each side, one quite a bit upstream from the other. You start off from the upstream ramp and paddle and pole like crazy and hope you make it across before you are swept past the downstream ramp on the other side! The ferry is then hauled upstream light and is ready for the trip back.

It was a long day and nearly 300 kilometers[4] to Puchong, where we arrived about 15:30 hours. A single day aboard the bus had taken us as far as the five previous days in chairs. This was another old walled city. The fortifications and battlements were still in remarkably good repair. To enter the city, we had to cross a very rickety bridge and squeeze through a very narrow gate. To lighten the bus, everybody dismounted except Ted Lawson and Johnny. Johnny looked the situation over and then backed off to take a running start. He roared over the bridge and slammed through the gate, taking paint off both sides of the bus in the process—but he made it.

While [we were] driving through the narrow streets, there was a band of strolling entertainers, complete with musical instruments and costumes—a very interesting spectacle. We would have liked to have seen the show but were too tired and hungry. We stopped at a Chinese hotel, but after looking it over I decided it was entirely too verminous and opted for the Bank of Commerce—which seemed to do double duty as a hotel and banquet hall.

The reception by the chief magistrate, Mr. Chow, and Mr. Tsung of the Maritime Customs office was warm and hospitable. Both spoke English, though the magistrate's was a little rusty since he hadn't used it for nearly twenty years. Two English women visited: Misses Armstrong and Wade. They represented the Church Mission Society in that district and brought us some very welcome delicacies, some ham, peanut butter, and bread. The feast that night was a very well-prepared one, but we were all so tired that we excused ourselves early and turned in. I wired Chungking of our change in plans.

The sandals seem to vary in design—perhaps in conformance with the local terrain. Another thing I noticed was that the boats on the streams appeared to be lighter and better built than those along the seacoast. They had high narrow sails and were pulled up the rapids by long ropes.

Saturday, May 23, we were up, ate breakfast, and fully loaded by 05:15 and on our way. Our goal was getting to Nan Chang that night to receive further orders. This time we roared through the narrow gate and over the bridge without stopping. Three large planks fell out of the bridge just as we got across, and [we] next stopped at a large motor park just outside the city to get some gasoline. The park resembled a junkyard more than anything else. It was a mass of broken-down and cannibalized buses, trucks, and cars.

After considerable delay, we got started again and, after several stops to clean the carburetor, covered nearly 120 kilometers to Chung Yanks, arriving at 11:15 hours. Two streams were ferried. The second one was very full and swift because it had been raining hard all day. It was a wild boat ride. We missed the downstream docking ramp on the other side by a wide margin. Finally, one of the ferrymen threw a line to one of the men onshore, and it was secured around a large rock just in time to prevent our being carried into sizable rapids. After a struggle, they were able to tow us back upstream to the ramp and send us on our way again. One bridge we crossed was partially hidden under floodwater. Johnny had to guess where the roadway was, since there were no handrails, but fortunately he guessed right.

It was a long day's ride, rather dreary with the rain. We had lunch in the car on ham sandwiches manufactured from the fixings the two ladies had given us the night before. They tasted very good for a change.

About 18:30 we arrived at Quong Sah, a small though quite modern town, where we stopped for supper. I had noticed a large sign outside the town illustrating a bunch of dead rats and wondered if that meant that there was plague about; we were told later that it was just an advertisement for "rat-killing week." There we met some German missionaries who were awaiting transportation to a concentration camp, and a Chinese lady, a graduate of the University of Southern California (USC), who was a widow trying to get along on $80 a month (Chinese money). We continued forward and finally arrived at Nan Chang at 01:30 hours Sunday morning. A paper chase of nearly an hour and a half ensued trying to get our orders straightened out. The phone lines were down because of the rain, and our party was unexpected. We were finally put up at the army headquarters outside the city. Everybody was exhausted by then.

Sleeping until 09:30 on that morning was a real treat after getting up at the crack of dawn or earlier for so long. I had a bath, shaved, ate breakfast, and felt considerably refreshed. It was raining hard, and the countryside was a sea of mud. We finally got word that a station wagon was coming from Kian to pick us up and that we would stay there until it arrived. After traveling for a week without letup, a day of rest was much welcomed by all. I wrote letters while Clever shaved with my razor. It was his first crack at a straightedge razor, but he made out all right. At least he didn't cut his throat. The bedbugs were ravenous, so we spent a good part of our time doctoring bites. The Chinese had salvaged the machine guns out of "Doc" Watson's airplane. I had some fun trying to get them in working order. By swapping parts around, I was able to get one .50- and the .30-caliber nose gun operational.[5] This pleased the Chinese to no end.

The rain let up in the afternoon, so we went into the city in rickshaws to view the sights. There were some fair-sized retail stores, and I bought some much-needed handkerchiefs and a solar toupee (pith helmet). The town was an interesting one, with very extensive walls and some more-modern fortifications, pillboxes,[6] blockhouses, and like structures. Davenport met some Catholic missionaries and got the latest news. For the first time we heard [that] Jimmy Doolittle was now a brigadier general (one star) and recipient of the Congressional Medal of Honor. Furthermore, each of us was awarded our own Distinguished Flying Cross (or DFC). This was indeed exciting!

The weather turned hot and muggy, so after puttering around we went back to our quarters, where a feast of eleven courses awaited us. It was well prepared, and we met some Chinese air force officers. Their insignia was much like ours except that their wings had a three-bladed prop where ours was two-bladed. Mr. Ye arrived from Kian with a beautiful, brand-new Ford station wagon for our use. The priests came to call and told us that they had cared for Lt. Harold "Doc" Watson (pilot on airplane number 9) when he came through there, and had attempted to set his arm. ("Doc" got his nickname from rooming with a chap named Holmes; you know, "Marvelous, my dear Holmes!") Later we learned that "Doc" had unfortunately sustained a fracture dislocation of his right shoulder when he bailed out of his plane over China the night of April 18.

His arm became entangled in the shrouds, and the shock of the opening of the parachute had snapped his humerus. He landed in a mountain stream and was unable to get out of his harness in the dark, using only his left hand. In considerable pain, he gave himself an injection of morphine from the kit I'd provided and went to sleep right there in the brook. Why he didn't get pneumonia, I'll never know—unless the vaccine helped. Anyhow, he was able to get untangled the next morning and made his way to a Chinese village, where they put him to bed with charcoal braziers fore and aft and finally got him thawed out. I didn't see him until much later—at Walter Reed Hospital in Washington, DC.

Monday morning, May 25, we were up at 04:30 hours, had breakfast, and said so long to Fong, driver Johnny Beep-Beep, and set off for Kian. Our long trek resumed after some much-needed rest. With a new car, smoother roads, and a fresh driver we soon named Beep-Beep II, we averaged 60 kilometers an hour. The new driver was reckless and took too many chances. Despite this, we were all much more comfortable than we had been in the smelly bus, even though Ted had to sit up since there was no room for him to lie down. It was 09:00 hours when we stopped in a little town called Ling Tu for food. There was a little shop selling delicate Chen Su pottery. I bought some pottery along with a Ling Tu porcelain painting. They are lovely pieces.

The weather was clearing up as we traveled through a very scenic rural area. [As we were] going down one twisting canyon, a tire blew out while going around a corner, and it nearly landed us in the creek! Robert Clever took a swim while we changed tires. Shortly, we were on our way again. We passed a British military detachment on their way to observe the battle that was developing around Kinwah ("Gin wah"). The colonel in charge could double for Colonel Blimp.[7] "Cheerio," he told us in parting. "I must be off to the battle!"

About 15:00 hours we arrived at the Kan Kiang (Kan River), a sizable stream. The ferry this time was a barge carrying several automobiles and towed by a small launch powered by an old auto engine running on charcoal gas created by two large generators on the stern. My doubts as to its reliability were borne out when the engine quit about halfway across the river. No amount of banging on the generators seemed to have any effect. We drifted rapidly downstream until someone had presence of mind to throw out an anchor—which slowed but did not halt the drift. A second towboat arrived shortly but lacked sufficient power to tow both us and our failed tug. Finally, after a rendition that would put the "Anvil Chorus"[8] to shame, they got both tugs running and delivered us safely to the far shore. There were some lovely cloud formations and a gorgeous rainbow while all this was going on. I wished more than ever for a movie camera and some color film.

We arrived at Kian about 18:00 hours without further adventure and were taken to the AVG Hostel, where we met an American radioman named Miller. The hostel was quite a modern structure and boasted showers. We all bathed, and I dressed for dinner in my blue robe—which always pleased the Chinese. We had a nice "foreign" dinner and met the station master—the local Chinese commander. The hostel manager, Mr. Wang, and several others also spoke good English, so we got along fine. It was hot and muggy, but we turned in early and I (for one) slept like a rock.

Tuesday morning, we all slept late and finally awoke about 09:30 hours—but still in time for breakfast. An air-raid alert followed that morning. The station master, Field Marshal Chan, strolled in while we were eating breakfast and said: "Oh yes, there'll be a Japanese plane overhead in about twenty-minutes, but don't be alarmed; it isn't carrying any bombs!" Sure enough, in about half an hour, an old Japanese attack bomber showed up and, after circling over the city for a while, flew away without molesting anyone. China, at every level, was rife with leaks and leakers. This was just another example of what the Chinese "grapevine telegraph" was capable.

I played Chinese table tennis (ping-pong) with Davenport and lost 17 to 20 before taking a walk. It was very hot and muggy, so I spent most of my time ducking from one store to the next. I bought a lovely little vase in the "Thousand Flowers" pattern, a bottle of ink, and a fancy Chinese flashlight. After lunch at the hostel, we were measured for shirts and shorts to be presented to us by the Kian Chamber of Commerce. We went shopping again in the afternoon with Mr. Koo as a guide. He was a young ex-soldier who, like another of our guides, was poison-gassed by the Japanese. I was looking for one of those long Chinese knives, the "Dah Tao," which are used effectively to exterminate the invaders. The enemy soldier fears beheading like no other form of death because he believes that he cannot enter heaven without his head. I saw a white man riding along on a bicycle and hailed him. He was surprised to see us and turned out to be one of the China Inland missionaries of the district. He invited us over to the mission to hear the news on their radio (or "wireless" as the British call them).

As members of the wartime United States Army in a hostile land, we needed to be armed. Everywhere we went, I'd ask for pistols because I badly wanted one for defense, but they were very scarce. Our total weaponry consisted of a vest-pocket .25-caliber automatic that Ted's wife had given him. It was in very bad shape from its dunking in the sea. At my suggestion, Ted gave it to Mr. Koo, who needed one badly, and he was very grateful. A Dr. Shen, an old friend of Dr. Chen's, showed up and was very much interested in our group.

Wednesday morning wake-up came at 05:00 hours, and breakfast followed. The Chamber of Commerce members arrived with our shirts and shorts, which we put on and had our pictures taken. The clothes suited the climate much better than our woolens, so we were very appreciative. The shirts had pictures of airplanes printed on the pockets and Chinese characters saying that we were "Heroes of the Chinese Republic." Mr. Koo gave us some nice souvenirs, Chinese coins, and good-luck charms. Silver money was nearly unheard of in those days; everything was paper money, even the smallest denominations.

A flat tire was suffered almost immediately after getting started at about 07:05 hours. After changing it, we proceeded onward by crossing the Mi Kiang River on a pontoon bridge but then had another flat tire. Having only a single spare tire, we limped into the village of Cha Ling, where nearly four hours was squandered while getting the two tires repaired. Passing time included drinking tea and noisemaking with more firecrackers. While getting ready to proceed, a warning was received regarding bandits on the road ahead, so we picked up a tough-looking soldier with two big Mauser automatic rifles. Lt. Davenport and I immediately appropriated those weapons and were fully prepared to use them; however, no need arose. After crossing another pontoon bridge and ferrying across the Siang Kiang, and Hong Yang Rivers, the hostel was reached at about 21:00 hours. After a much-needed bath and dinner, we retired to bed exhausted.

There was time to sleep late on Thursday morning and then shave before breakfast. The hostel was a large building located in a grove of trees across the river from the city. It was delightfully cool and pleasant. The innkeepers provided a captured Japanese horse for use of the guests. It was the first horse I'd seen since coming to China. We had hoped to catch a plane at the airdrome but learned [that] Japanese forces had dropped over a hundred bombs only two days prior. It would be a week before it could be made operational again. We decided to go on to Kweilin (Gueylin), where an airplane would meet us. The trip was to be made by train that night. I visited the local station master's headquarters and got our tickets straightened out after some difficulty. The train was packed to overcapacity. It was necessary to put some passengers off to accommodate us.

After loafing around and resting for the balance of the day, we departed for the railroad station after an early supper. It was one of the biggest Chinese cities we had seen, and the shops held all manner of interesting merchandise. Hang Yang is particularly noted for the excellence of the embroidery produced in its vicinity, and we spent some time in a shop which contained some beautiful examples of this art. We all purchased some of the articles and only wished that we had more money and available space to purchase more. I bought two scrolls. Each had an embroidered picture on it with stitches so fine that they appeared to be paintings except under close examination. The Chinese love of symbolism was shown to good advantage in one of these. The picture was of some lovely little birds perched on bamboo, and the inscription read: "The hollow of the bamboo is my teacher." This is taken to mean "My heart is empty when you are away."

Several other shops were visited. In one of these, Mr. Yang (our guide) bought us all sword canes. Then we drove to the station and said goodbye to Mr. Yang and Beep-Beep II. An American-style steam locomotive was tightly coupled to European-inspired compartment cars—a rather strange mix. On boarding the train, I found that our tickets were still mixed up, but with the aid of the conductor I was able to negotiate two first-class compartments for my sickest patients. Dr. Chen, Robert Clever, and I went to the second-class coach, where there were four passengers of mixed company to a compartment.

Everybody got settled and the train started. The smoothness of the train motion was a surprise. Starting and stopping were nearly imperceptible—none of the jerks and jolts we are accustomed to here in America. The toilet facilities of the second-class coaches were crude. Simply an open window. Clever and I were nearly eaten alive by fleas that night but still managed to get some sleep.

The trip was uneventful, and we arrived at Kweilin about 08:00 hours the next morning and were met by a station wagon and an ambulance. After one look at the springs on the latter, Lawson decided to ride with us, and the luggage rode in the ambulance. We drove about 5 kilometers out into the country to the local AVG (Flying Tigers) hostel, a group of nondescript wooden buildings pleasantly located in a grove of trees. They were the largest trees I'd seen in China.

Kweilin was a major American airbase and where our mode of transportation was to shift from surface to air. The airfield was about 5 kilometers away, and we were informed a plane would come for us the next day. We wished to be picked up immediately but accepted the promise instead. It was hot and muggy, but we were comfortable when a breeze was present.

The scenery around Kweilin is very beautiful, and the mountains are characteristic. The vertical or somewhat overhanging mountains of Chinese paintings have their reality here. They go straight up rather like the buttes of our own Southwest. This is largely a limestone country, and the hills conceal many large caves. A cave behind the hostel served as an air-raid shelter. It was stout. Blast walls were constructed at the entrance, and there was nearly 500 feet of solid rock overhead. It was pleasantly cool inside, so we often spent the hottest part of the day relaxing within.

Stationed at the airfield, an AVG radioman with panache first appeared at noon meal that day. His surname was Sasser. (No rank or given name was documented.) He confirmed that there would be no plane that day, but we might get one the next day. Sasser brought with him an attractive Anglo-Burmese girl out of Burma. I treated her for a case of influenza, and so I was endeared to the pair. He told us some hair-raising yarns about his experiences in Burma and China. Ted Lawson also wrote about Sasser—who is not to be confused with Howard Sessler, the navigator with us aboard "TNT."

If a "loose cannon" is a soldier acting autonomously and gone rogue, then Sasser[9] certainly fits that definition:

In their bewildering casual way, the Chinese have an amazing system of air-raid alarms. We were having breakfast when the first warning was sounded. It was a strange sort of "siren"; the noise was made by a Chinese hitting an old automobile brake drum with a spike. As soon as we found out what it meant we started to get up from the table.

"Keep your seats," [Sasser] said, continuing his breakfast. "The planes have just taken off."

We asked him how he knew.

"I can tell by the way the fellow's beating the brake drum," he said, pretty bored about the whole thing. "You'll know when the airplanes get closer. He'll start beating faster and faster," and then he went back to his food while we picked at ours and listened to the brake drum.

He was a nonchalant fellow, that AVG man. He had come up to Kweilin just before the Nipponese had broken through General Stilwell's line and overrun the country. He had gotten out with an American jeep, a tommy gun, a 1-ton truck filled with gas, ammunition, and food. He had a boy drive this for him while he drove the jeep[10]—[with the slender Anglo-Burmese wait at his side.]

Breakfast ended when the diners scurried into a nearby cave. The Nipponese planes arrived promptly and bombed both the airfield and adjacent city.

Sasser was a street-smart hustler who found opportunity by stealing the two vehicles and bringing them from Burma. Rangoon was abandoned on March 7, 1942, ahead of the rapidly advancing Japanese army. He admitted it was common during the evacuation for a savvy chap to go to a motor pool, pick out a nice big truck, drive it to a gas dump, and load up with all the gasoline it would hold—and then just drive around Rangoon filling the truck with whatever his fancy dictated—whiskey, food, guns, ammunition, jeeps, crated light planes, etc. The next step was to mount a machine gun on the hood and drive up the 717-mile Burma Road[11] to Kunming, where all such "merchandise" could be sold for fabulous prices. Sasser told us he had refused an offer of a thousand dollars (US) for his tommy gun.

Another story Sasser told us was that during the evacuation of Lashio, a DC-3 with one DC-2 wing (some 7 feet shorter than the other) had taken off with <u>seventy-three</u> men, women, and children in it and had arrived safely in Kunming. This last story I have authenticated from other sources.

It cooled off after dusk even as a beautiful full moon rose into the star-filled sky. We were all very tired, and I went to bed early after doing the routine dressings on Ted, Dean, and Mac. Ted was still having a lot of pain in his stump, and it was a battle to keep from giving him morphine. There are times when a doctor must be cruel to be kind. So, I had to let him suffer quite a bit of pain to keep from addicting him.

Saturday, May 30, we were up early, showered, shaved, and after breakfast had an air-raid alert. The dozen Japanese attackers circled around overhead above the overcast but apparently didn't dare let down through it because of the mountains. I borrowed Sasser's tommy gun in case any of the attackers came down low enough. Finally, the planes went away after dropping some bombs by guesswork north of the city. Sasser told us about one AVG ground crewman who had shot down a Zero with his tommy gun. The Nipponese attacker came in and strafed the airfield while most of the resident planes were away on a mission. This chap let him have it from a foxhole, and the attacker suddenly half-rolled and crashed into the ground. When they hauled the pilot out of the wreckage, they couldn't find any bullet wounds at first, but on closer examination they found that he had taken a .45-caliber slug dead center in the posterior.

After the alert, I drove over to the local Chinese army headquarters and, after a good deal of "Wa-wa-ing," raised Chungking on the telephone. I spoke to an American officer whose name I never heard clearly. He promised to speak to General Bissell about getting us a plane as soon as possible. I rode to the headquarters and back to the hostel in an ancient 1935 Ford burning alcohol and smelling like a brewery.

The rumors began after lunch about a plane coming, and, sure enough, about 15:00 hours we saw a big, beautiful Douglas DC-3 come floating into the <u>wrong airport</u>. It was a terrible blow to us, and when I finally raised them on the phone, I was told that it was a CNAC (Chinese National Airline Company) plane, not an Army aircraft. Further, they didn't have room for us. Our spirits hit a new low at that, but there was nothing else to do but sit and wait. We watched the plane fly away with heavy hearts. The weather had cleared after the enemy departed, leaving behind a hot day and evening.

Sasser brought with him from Burma a nice collection of purloined native knives. He was tired of lugging them around, so we all bought some. I got a nice set of three, small, medium, and large, within coin-silver scabbards with beautiful cabochon and filigree work, also a more workaday kris. After that, we'd all grab our knives when an alert sounded—in case an enemy pilot had to bail out. Sasser told us that in Burma, very few enemy pilots managed to reach the ground in one piece when bailing out. The natives would cut them to bits before they could set foot upon terra firma.

Sunday was much the same—shave, shower, breakfast, and alert. Again, the Japanese were foiled by the overcast, which cleared soon after they went home. I shot and cleaned Sasser's tommy gun, and the Chinese asked me to look at one of theirs. It was an old Vickers, and it took me quite a while to figure out the complicated mechanism. The ammunition-feeding mechanism had no relation to the action of the bolt. It was worked by the recoil of the barrel. I was able to successfully adjust it, and they were very pleased to have the gun working again.

I borrowed a tin of butter from Sasser's store because it made our meals much tastier. The radio was on the fritz. Sasser was having trouble with his transmitter, and since the telephone was out again, we were out of touch with Chunking. It rained that afternoon and cooled off somewhat. Some of the boys went into town to see the 1939 classic motion picture *Union Pacific* with Chinese subtitles.

Monday was rather a dull day with no alerts, and no news about our plane. In the afternoon the local Chinese station master showed up with word that we might get a plane the next afternoon. He was a nice-looking young chap, thirty-three years old, and had been in aviation for fifteen years; Jimmy Doolittle had been his instructor. He told us that Linhai, the hospital town in which we had stayed so long, had been captured by the enemy. It was expected, of course, but we were naturally worried about the safety of our many friends[12] there. Sasser got his radio operational again and said that the American Military Mission still had us in mind, as we hoped and expected. We were also informed that Chinese decorations might be awarded in addition to our DFC's (Distinguished Flying Cross).

June 2 was a Tuesday, and it dawned cool and cloudy. I did the usual dressings and such. Charles McClure went over to the field with Sasser and Dean Davenport. Robert Clever, Dr. Chen, and I walked across the valley to inspect a junkyard filled with derelict railroad equipment. It was an amazing collection of museum pieces consisting of locomotives made in the US, England, Germany, and Japan and of all vintages. Apparently, the Nipponese airmen had mistaken this scrap pile for an active railroad-marshaling yard because there were several large bomb craters nearby.

After lunch the sun came out, so Robert Clever and I went for a walk and got some more sunburn. We inspected some very cleverly concealed Chinese pillboxes, which covered the approaches to the airport. Later, Sasser took some of us to town in his jeep. We took the top down to keep cool. The storm cleared and we went back to the hostel for dinner. There was no word from our plane, so we had a big bull session and Charles McClure gave us all a lesson in astronomy.

CHAPTER 13

ESCAPE VIA "GOONEY BIRD"

WEDNESDAY DAWNED RAINY but cleared and got hotter as the day progressed. There were many rumors about our airplane—some good, some bad. I spent the day working on the medical histories of my patients so they would be properly documented whenever I got them to a hospital. Finally, after lunch we got word that a plane was on its way to pick us up. After so many disappointments, this news made our spirits rise as nothing else could. The minutes really dragged by slowly until it landed. The Douglas C-47 was the Army paratrooper-cargo version of the DC-3 airliner and couldn't have looked better to us if it had been plated with gold and lined with silk. The official name was "Skytrain," but many called it a "Gooney Bird." Capt. Carlton was the pilot in command, a swell fellow, and a veteran of flying the "Hump."

Two familiar faces then emerged. Copilot Lt. Edgar McElroy (pilot of number 13) and a spare pilot, Capt. David Jones (pilot of number 5), were both Raiders who had been shanghaied (involuntarily requisitioned) by local Army Air Force officials to alleviate the acute shortage of American pilots. "Davy" Jones had been sent as mission envoy. Believe me, we were elated to see both him and McElroy. It was a joyous and emotional reunion as we chatted, endlessly comparing experiences and close calls. Carlton (the pilot) took a shine to my sword cane, so I gave it to him. We all talked until late, and then I shooed my patients off to bed since we were to leave early the next morning. I don't think any of us slept very well that night. We were all too excited.

Davy Jones hand-carried with him our movement orders and some very flattering letters from Gen. C. L. Bissell and Maj. J. A. Mendelson, the surgeon at Chungking. Maj. Mendelson had also sent along stretchers, mattresses, pillows, and blankets, as well as a goodly supply of much-needed dressings, instruments, and the like from his own slender stores. Ted Lawson and Charles McClure were then made reasonably comfortable during our travels aloft.

We got up at 03:00 hours on Thursday, June 4, had breakfast, and were taken to the airfield. We said goodbye to Sasser and our Chinese friends and took off at first light—04:45 hours. It was wonderful to be flying again. In half an hour we would travel farther than we had in five days by chair! We were still talking Davy's ear off and discovered that it had been York (number 8), not Hallmark, who went to Siberia. Hallmark (number 6, named "the Green Hornet") came down in occupied China and was captured by the Japanese.

From the air the countryside looked different than before. The characteristic Kweilin Mountains were still rising on all sides of us, but the rice paddies made a beautiful patchwork of various shades of green below. The country looked like a huge green park with little hamlets scattered about like hunting lodges or guesthouses, their smell and decrepitude lost in the distance.

At 06:25 hours, Sasser called us on the radio and told us enemy bombers were over the field, blasting it to bits. We had dodged yet another close call by escaping with a margin of a mere ninety minutes. Apparently, the Japanese had also heard the rumors about our airplane, but fortunately they arrived too late to thwart our escape.

There is a standing joke in the Air Corps about the pilot who was following a railroad and got off on the wrong branch when somebody carelessly left a switch open. Well, that's about what happened to us that morning. Carleton took a wrong turn, and we flew up into a box canyon. Alarmingly, the walls were getting steeper and narrower. This situation too frequently ends with aluminum shards intermixed with human remains scattered about a remote mountainside. Carlton correctly recognized the trap and aggressively forced the rugged and reliable C-47 to make the sharp turn without contacting any of the nearby crags. It was yet another brush with death, but we were again spared. Kunming was reached about 09:30 hours without further incident.

At that time, Kunming was the only terminus of the "Hump" route, and the first operational airport we'd seen since leaving Japan. It sure looked good to us to see fighter planes and ack-ack (antiaircraft) guns emplaced here and there. It was a busy place, and there were various and abundant supplies stacked about. The Flying Tigers were still operating at the time. In fact, its headquarters were located there. We met a good many American volunteers. The banter with them was enjoyable.

The Burma Road was an invaluable supply link for Allied forces. The Nipponese created a serious logistical problem by severing this overland route. "Flying the Hump" began in April 1942 and continued for forty-two months.

The airlift of 650,000 tons[1] of war supplies across the route was an achievement that significantly bolstered the war effort; however, it came at a steep price: loss of 600 transport planes and airmen plus passengers aboard numbering at least 1,500.

I gave Dr. Chen the letters I'd written to Gen. Bissell and Maj. Mendelson as we disembarked, and arranged for him to board the next plane headed to Chunking. I was committed to getting my charges admitted into a decent hospital as soon as possible; therefore, I opted to decline a side trip to Chungking to meet our benefactors—both Chinese and American. Despite qualms, I decided to bypass that city and proceed directly to India.

We were taken to the Flying Tigers hostel on the other side of the town and got settled, fed, and bathed. They had a small hospital there, and I had the opportunity of meeting Dr. Gentry and the rest of their medical staff. I did the dressings and we compared experiences. They told me of some of the troubles they had experienced in the jungles of Burma. There is a malignant cerebral form of malaria there that can kill in less than forty-eight hours unless treated heroically with intravenous, and sometimes intraspinal, atabrine or quinine. It was learned [that] Dr. Chen had already departed for Chungking upon our return to the airfield. We regretted not seeing him off but were pleased he was able to obtain passage so quickly. I spent the balance of the day writing letters, completing reports, and getting paid. The latter was accomplished thanks to a brand-new Army Finance Office. The Flying Tigers were preparing to disband, and many of them were absorbed into the US Army Air Forces (14th Air Force,[2] to be specific). Provision had to be made to pay them, and my compensation was accomplished on voucher #1.

Friday morning, June 5, we were up early again, ate breakfast, and then drove to the field and reboarded the Douglas C-47 transport. Takeoff was at 05:15 hours Chungking time. The weather was clear, with scattered clouds, as we began the climb for the "hump." Below were villages on steep slopes, broad valleys, deep gorges, narrow streams, and dark-brown rivers. These sights disappeared into overcast while approaching the rugged hills ahead. Lightly loaded, we were able to climb to 21,000 feet to make the crossing, which yielded a greater margin of safety than the usual 18,000 feet; however, there were still plenty of peaks along the route, which went up to 24,000 feet or even higher! Most of this three-hour leg was on instruments flying through sleet, snow, and rain.

Without supplemental oxygen, we as passengers suffered from altitude sickness (hypoxia). Mercifully, Ted and most of the others injured passed out. We bundled them up in whatever blankets we had, since it was bitterly cold, even though the plane heater was going full blast. Davy and I did our best to make them comfortable, but we had to move slowly ourselves and had to rest frequently because of the altitude.[3] The natural hazards were bad enough, but just to make it more interesting, our route passed directly over three enemy airdromes! There were two tommy guns on the plane which we loaded, but they were a poor defense against a Japanese Zero. Finally, Davy Jones and I stretched out between a couple of mattresses and dropped off to sleep from exhaustion.

The descent through multiple layers of overcast on the other side proved nearly as exciting as the actual crossing. Three times we eased down through one layer of overcast only to find another beneath us. A hole was finally located, and we broke out just 200 feet above the treetops. We flew along over the lush jungle of Assam while Carleton picked up his reference points and landed at Dinjan[4] at 09:30 hours Chungking time (08:00 India time). We thawed out rapidly in the damp heat of the jungle and looked about. The dense tropical vegetation with its beautiful flowers and huge trees was a tremendous change from China.

There were eight Gooney Birds at Dinjan (India), each waiting for the weather to lift before making their own eastbound crossing. We didn't envy any of the men on their coming trip but developed a healthy respect for the American Transport Command aircrews who routinely flew the "hump." We also found two more of our Tokyo gang: Lt. Richard Joyce (pilot number 10) and Lt. Robert Grey (pilot number 3)—who were flying Curtiss P-40 Warhawks. They too had been shanghaied on their way back to the US—although they seemed to enjoy their assignment much more than McElroy did. It was good to see them. Another spontaneous get-together erupted with mutual back pounding and everybody talking at same time while trying to outdo each other's stories.

The airdrome commander, Col. Hayes, insisted that we have a meal, so Lt. Robert Grey drove us to their dining facility, which was about 10 miles from the field, where we had a hearty brunch consisting of genuine GI mess-hall cuisine. It was actually a real treat for a change. Then we went back to the field, reboarded our plane, and said so long to Lt. Richard Joyce and Grey. Grey remained on duty in China and died in combat on October 18, 1942. It was part of the ghastly price paid for the mistakes of World War II. His memory should be revered.

The ceiling had lifted a little, and although there was a reported risk of a typhoon, takeoff for Allahabad (India) was at 10:20 hours. It was quite warm as we flew south and west following the course of the Brahmaputra River. We were startled when a pursuit plane dove down upon us from out of the sun, but it turned out to be just a playful RAF (Royal Air Force) chap who put on a show[5] for us before he peeled off and went about his business.

As we flew along, the lush jungle gave away to dusty desert. There was dust in the air in a solid layer up to 9,000 feet, and the free air temperature at 3,000 feet was 113 degrees F. It was a long, dull trip. We were glad we'd eaten well at Dinjan. Davy Jones, Bob Clever, and I played no-bet poker to help pass the time.

We arrived at Allahabad at 16:30 hours and had to make two passes at the field. Edgar McElroy (pilot number 13) was having trouble adapting to a tail dragger and its slower stalling speed after flying the faster B-25s. The first landing attempt overshot the runway, and it bounced on the second. The atmosphere was very hot and dusty, so we all took Col. Tenney's suggestion and went to the officer's mess for a lime squash (nonalcoholic British beverage). They were out of ice, but it was at least cool and wet, which helped a lot. We dropped the colonel there and took off at 17:00 hours for New Delhi (India), where we arrived at 19:30 after another hot, dull trip. It was certainly a far cry from the days when we had made 120 Li in a day riding in sedan chairs and thought that we were doing well. Here we had flown from China over the Himalayas and most of the way across India in a day. These are the advantages of air travel.

A driver in a beautiful new Buick met us at the airport and drove us into town. The weather was a dry heat, but the lack of humidity made it comfortable. The Hotel Imperial was overbooked, so we went on to the Hotel Marina. Subsequently we learned that every British colony town has a Hotel Imperial and/or Marina. All six of us were finally lodged in a single suite. Fortunately, the rooms were large, and it was wonderful to have modern (if British) plumbing after what we had become accustomed to. Everybody bathed, shaved, and had a nice dinner, after which I did dressings. Everybody went to bed exhausted. Charles McClure's foot was acting up again, so I treated it with sulfanilamide powder and dressed it carefully.

Saturday morning, I was up early. After breakfast it was time for a shopping expedition and a real treat to deal with shopkeepers who spoke English. I quickly became accustomed to calling shoes "boots," garters "supporters," and suspenders "braces." All went well. I bought some fine English shoes (I mean "boots"), some tan shorts, shirts, and some nice English woolen socks. I also purchased a "proper" solar toupee (pith helmet) and felt almost civilized again.

It was at US Army headquarters where I next met Davy Jones (pilot number 5). Together we made the rounds for an agenda update. We picked up our DFC (Distinguished Flying Cross) ribbons and ceremoniously pinned them on each other. Lt. Edgar McElroy (pilot on number 13) had developed a painful skin condition. I was trying to get him out of the assignment so he could join the other homeward-bound Raiders. I visited all the Army headquarters I could find—but without resolution. Everything was in the upheaval of getting unpacked and settled in. As is seldom the case, the boundaries of authority were in flux and not yet fully defined.

I was advised not to put my patients in the local hospital because the nursing facilities were substandard. I was further told that they were setting up a big American hospital at Karachi. It would be better to see about taking them there. Carlton would fly us there as soon as we were ready to travel, and we could then revisit the plan. I knew that at minimum, Ted Lawson and Charles McClure would need competent surgery. I wanted to get them into the best hospital. Even then, my end game was to admit them into Walter Reed (Army) General Hospital in Washington, DC.

After lunch, Dean Davenport and I went shopping again. I bought some beautiful gold brocade and tried to find a sari, the characteristic Hindu woman's garment, for my wife, Edith. The shopkeeper finally suggested that he could have one made for me, so I picked out the material and left the order. Our next stop was the Ivory Palace, a retail shop selling all sorts of ivory carvings, and here Dean bought a very ornate chess set for his father. All the men were carved in the shape of Indian soldiers, the pawns being foot soldiers, the knights, cavalry, the kings, queens, and bishops riding on elephants, and so on. I bought an inlayed [inlaid] jewel box.

Wandering along the street, we found a small jeweler's shop and spent a very interesting hour there going over the wares which the proprietor brought forth for our inspection. It was quite an experience; we sat on cushions sipping tea and being fanned by a large punka (operator of a manual fan) while he showed us some of the most-lovely bits of jewelry I have ever seen. One ruby necklace, bracelet, ring, and clip set was worthy of an empress; it was priced at only $50,000! Another beautiful piece was a star-ruby ring for a mere $1,500. I don't really know what the man's idea of a lieutenant's pay was, but I guessed he went on the assumption that all Americans were automatically millionaires. I finally found a nice amethyst ring that was within my means, and Davenport bought some loose stones. The proprietor treated us as if we had bought out the shop, and we had a thoroughly entertaining time.

We went to the town square (actually a circle) and listened to the music of the native bagpipers. It was a creditable performance though it was interrupted by a Communistic demonstration by a gathering of rather scruffy-looking natives. Numerous lemon squashes and some ice cream revived us. We next hired a car to take us into old Delhi and around the old fort. It was an interesting trip, and we returned to the hotel in time for dinner. That evening I purchased a nice big leather suitcase, into which I packed my increasing stock of belongings, attended to the dressings of the ailing, and finally went to bed.

Sunday morning, June 6, I was up early and retrieved my sari. It had turned out very well, and I was pleased with my purchase. I finished packing and then we all had breakfast, paid our hotel bill, and were driven out to the airfield. There we found a full load of passengers and luggage for Karachi (Pakistan). There was little room left for us to be seated, and none for Ted or Mac to lie down. Since it was our airplane, I had them reshuffle the load [and] put off a few of the less essential passengers and much of the luggage. Everybody else reboarded for departure only when Ted and Mac were comfortable.

CHAPTER 14

HOME VIA STRATOLINER

IT WAS BEASTLY HOT inside the plane at first but cooled somewhat after takeoff, which was at 09:00 hours. The trip itself was very uninteresting until we began to approach Karachi (Pakistan), where we flew over supply dumps and encampments, which seemed to reach in every direction as far as the eye could see. We landed at 13:00 hours and first encountered the Boeing Model 307 Stratoliner (with four motors) sitting on the ramp. Further, it was taking off to the US that night. I went looking for someone in authority and finally reached the officer in charge of loading airliners and persuaded him[1] to bump some passengers from the manifest to fully board our party.

After lunch in the mess at base operations came a drive into town in search of a shirt, only to find that all the stores were closed since it was Sunday. Back at the field, I went looking for the big hospital that was reported to be there. What I found was a group of harried medics who were vainly trying to get their equipment sorted out of the general confusion. It seemed that the hospital supplies had gotten lost under the other equipment for a couple of armored divisions and some miscellaneous airplane parts.

The hospital items were only slowly coming to light. They had just gotten a shipment of several hundred bedpans but so far hadn't received either the beds or the mattresses! It was obviously out of the question to leave Ted or Mac. I was glad to have wrangled seats for them on the Boeing Stratoliner. I was trying all the time to get someone to say that pilot Lt. Edgar McElroy could go home with us but had little or no luck. Colonels Tate and Tammerask, while trying to be helpful, unfortunately lacked the requisite authority.

After doing the dressings and having dinner, we boarded the plane at about 22:30 hours. The Stratoliner[2] was a commandeered TWA asset with part of the cabin taken up with auxiliary gasoline tanks. The rest of the cabin retained the original luxurious seats and furnishings. The seats were converted into eight bunks, and there were extra mattresses so the rest of us could sleep on the floor in considerable comfort. The crew were as nice a bunch as you'd meet anywhere, all seasoned airline chaps: Frank Neiswander, the pilot, Charlie Kratovil, Tex Butler, and two others whose names I have unfortunately forgotten. We found to our joy that Maj. Jack Hilger, Charles Greening[3] (pilot of number 11), and Charles Ozuk were to be on the plane with us. We had another bull session and talked endlessly while awaiting takeoff. We finally took off at about 23:00 hours and immediately climbed to 12,000 feet to get over mountainous terrain. I wasn't very happy at that altitude, but we later descended to a more comfortable altitude. Most of us slept well. The plane was insulated against both noise and cold. It was nicely heated, although the pressurization equipment had been removed to save weight.

At about 05:30 local time the next morning (2.5 hours of time change), we landed at Habbaniya (Iraq).[4] We had a "Limey" (British) breakfast of eggs, kippers, and tea for 75 fils (240 fils to the dollar). We appointed Maj. John Hilger (pilot number 14) as mess officer despite his protests, so he settled the bill and had quite a time keeping the various types of currency we ran into straightened out. Back at the field we inspected some old British "Kites," planes of World War I vintage; their top speed was about 80 mph, but they had the advantage for desert work of extremely low landing and takeoff speeds and relatively large carrying capacity.

We took off again at 07:45, crossed the Euphrates River, and flew over the ancient lands of early history. At 11:00 we passed the Dead Sea and the Holy Land, flying over Jericho. We flew along the Palestine oil pipeline to Suez, crossing the famous canal about noon. We arrived at Cairo (Egypt) about 13:00 and were taken by truck to the Grand Hotel. The "Grand" was found in a modern block of buildings in downtown Cairo. Dean, Clever, and I occupied room number 12. Cairo is a modern, noisy city, with enough oriental atmosphere (smells) to make it interesting. The climate was lovely, even in June.

After a decent lunch at the hotel, Dean Davenport (one of the pilots) and I went on a shopping expedition. The bazaar covered quite an area, so we focused our attention on the area with the shops of interest. Our first stop was the "Ding-Dong," a small shop selling mostly costume jewelry and fabrics in addition to the usual tourist junk of imitation scarabs and the like. The salesgirls seem to have been chosen for their physical charms and persistence. I was practically raped before I bought something in self-defense. Further stops yielded a sword cane, a fez, and some native fabric.

Returning to the hotel, we bathed to wash off the grime of the native quarter as well as the numerous and varied scents we had acquired in a perfume shop. I turned in early, but some of the rest went to see Fatima, the famous "belly dancer" (later shot as a spy). They said later that I hadn't missed much. The Western mind just hasn't been educated to see beauty in the gyrations of the navel.

Tuesday the ninth, I was up early and Clever and I went window shopping. We spent most of the morning at Berkeley's Bank (Barclay to you) trying to get a US government check cashed. Finally, three of us were allowed $80 apiece (US dollars) and the balance in Egyptian money. I went to the post office to get some of the current issues of stamps for my collection and bought a few more at dealers. I was also able to get some much-needed shirts. After lunch, most of the gang went pyramiding, but I had more shopping to do. A gun store yielded me two very nice antique pistols, an old Arabian "rat-tailed" brass-stocked item, and a beautifully inlaid and engraved old French flintlock. A pair of antelope-skin gloves completed my purchases for the day.

I was up early the next morning and bought one of these automatic self-winding watches before leaving for the airport. Both Robert Clever and Charles Ozuk (navigator on number 3) had bad stomach aches, which I thought were suspicious enough not to expose them to high altitudes for fear of appendicitis so had them taken to a British hospital for observation. We hated to take off without them, but they were in good hands and it seemed the safest thing to do.

Takeoff was at 10:55 hours, and I rode in the cockpit. It was a thrilling experience because it was my first time in a four-engine aircraft. We passed over the pyramids and flew up the Nile valley. It was very interesting how the green of vegetation stops at a sharp line where irrigation ceases and the desert suddenly begins.

Lunch consisted of Royal Air Force emergency rations, which didn't make bad picnicking. A couple of the TWA crew members were also having stomach aches too, so I also medicated them. I was much interested in a German paratrooper's machine pistol which "Tex" had purchased from some Aussies on leave from Alamein. It looked like a very practical gun, much lighter and easier to manufacture than our tommy gun, though of course its 9 mm slug lacks the authority of the .45-caliber.

Arrival at Khartoum, in the Anglo-Egyptian Sudan, was at 15:30 (one-hour time change). It was very hot and dry, in marked contrast to the pleasant climate of Cairo. We had a delayed lunch or an early dinner and a cold bottle of beer at the Pan American Airways canteen atop one of the hangars. The FAA station there was jointly used by the Royal Air Force, Army Air Forces, and the commercial airlines.

A bunch of us decided to go into town. One of the Pan American Airways chaps drove us. Khartoum (capital of Sudan) is situated at the juncture of the "White" and "Blue" Niles. Both appeared muddy brown to me. I was very much interested in the methods the natives had of raising water from the rivers for irrigation; they were so different from those in use in China. The traditional methods were a water-lifting wheel and buckets on long counterbalanced poles: the "new" method (i.e., only 2,500 years old) was the Archimedean spiral!

We passed flocks of large storks and veritable clouds of bats and arrived in town hot and dusty only to find that there was no beer to be had! We imbibed numerous lemon and orange squashes and looked the town over. It didn't have much to offer except in the line of ivory and native crafts. We met an itinerate knife dealer who had evidently had some dealings with Americans before. His favorite saying was "Come back Christmas!" I bought a nasty-looking old Abyssinian one with the weirdest-shaped blade I've seen in some time. Jack Hilger finally found a chess set he wanted, and several others made similar purchases. Remembering past experiences with sun-cured leather, I persuaded the others to bypass the leather goods—because they stink to high heaven when wet.

Back at the field, we had a snack and got our hands on a copy of *Life* magazine dated June 1, 1942. It had pictures of Gen. Jimmy Doolittle and several of the other fellows in it. It was good to know that some of them had reached the US safely.

We picked up an ailing Army Air Forces officer. The young captain was a B-24 pilot who was suffering some psychological difficulties along with acute depression. He was getting better by the time we arrived, but Army medical officers wanted him sent back to the United States under a doctor's care, so I was elected. He was quite cooperative and not much trouble. I had him admitted to the local hospital at every place where we stayed for more than a few hours. As he got better, I sometimes had to talk fast to get him into a hospital, since he didn't feel sick!

The trip across Africa took us over some Axis-held territory, so the trip was to be made at night to avoid German Messerschmitts. We took off at 23:00 hours and headed west. I rode in the cockpit again during takeoff, which was thrilling since we had a big fuel load, and the field was rather short and rough. I turned in on the floor and got a good night's sleep despite being rather worried about what would happen to us if we had to make a forced landing in the wilds of Africa if a "Messy" (Messerschmitt) got onto our tail. No longer at the mercy of Japanese forces, we were now menaced by the Nazi presence.

It was a smooth trip. We had to climb high to get over the mountains but came down safely the next morning, Thursday, June 11, in Kano, Nigeria, at 06:00 GST (Greenwich Standard Time). Kano is the oldest walled city in Africa and was the western terminus of the old camel and slave trail across central Africa.

We saw Howard Sessler, Griffith Williams (my navigator and copilot), and Jack Sims (copilot on number 14) at the airport and had another noisy reunion. They were waiting for a plane to take them to catch the Clipper[5] which would fly them to Florida. It was good to see them looking so well.

After breakfast we took off at 07:15 and flew over the jungle to Accra on the Gold Coast, arriving at about 13:00 hours. There was a large American base there with modern quarters and a good mosquito control program. We all drew mosquito boots more for looks than anything else. Lunch was at the officer's mess, followed by a shower and a change of clothes. It would take several days to have the Stratoliner's four motors thoroughly gone over before crossing the Atlantic, so we sent out laundry for the first time since leaving China.

It was warm and humid but not uncomfortable. I got mildly loopy on cold beer at the "TWA Stratoliner Club," the informal name for a TWA crew member's room who was blessed with not only a refrigerator but also a large stock of brew. I turned in early and had a marvelous night's sleep. There's nothing like the letdown after some intensive worrying for soporific effect.

The people at Accra (African capital and largest city of Ghana) were very hospitable and the next day arranged a "brush trip" for us. Some of the others had better luck and were able to salvage their cameras (mine went down with "TNT"). A brief safari into the jungle and maybe a chance encounter with a wild animal was my fantasy. Instead, we simply drove through a series of rather civilized-appearing native villages to a botanical garden, where a sumptuous luncheon was served. Accra is famed for its gold jewelry. On the way back we stopped at a native goldsmith's shop. This proprietor had some lovely pieces, both filigree work and engraving, but all had been made to order, leaving no inventory for walk-in customers.

On the way back we saw an old man with four young girls walking along the road. We stopped because the photographers wanted some pictures of the bare-bosomed females. Our driver asked them to pose for us, which they did without protest. The old man turned out to be their father, and he was bemoaning the fact that he had seven daughters and no sons. Trying to scrape up dowries for the girls kept the family broke. We sympathized with him and gave him a few shillings before parting as the best of friends.

When we got back to Accra, we took a tour through Fredericksburg Castle, the old fort guarding the harbor. It had been captured from the Dutch in the seventeenth century. It was Portuguese owned before that—but was still maintained in good repair. As castles go, it was homey, very welcoming, and comfortable;

however, the slaves' quarters didn't look very hygienic. While out on the battlements, we watched the native fishermen bringing their boats in through the surf with their catch. The waves were running tall, and the fishermen had quite a challenge reaching the beach in safety. Just outside the surf they would take in their sails and masts and break out the paddles, then, watching their time, they would try to catch one of the smaller waves and ride it as far as possible before losing it. Some of the more proficient made it all the way into the shore on one wave, a distance measuring a quarter of a mile (or more). One helmsman was either less skillful or unlucky. Riding one of the bigger waves, he lost control, the boat broached, and he fell overboard. The boat rolled over, strewing native fishermen,[6] gear, fish, and sundry items all over the place. The others thought it was a huge joke and really teased the unlucky mariner.

Being rather dry by that time, we went into town, where I had some poor-quality lemonade and some even worse ginger ale. No beer was available. We were highly amused at a rather tipsy Cockney who sang "Doin' Me Duty, Down Old Dakar-Way" to the tune of "South of the Border." The British are great at composing comical songs. Afterward, some of the boys went to a "Jig-jig show" (a popular black and Cuban stage show). I passed on the opportunity and amused myself going through the native market and speculating as to the etiology of some of the skin lesions I witnessed there. Back at camp I took a much-needed shower, shaved, and changed clothing. The base was blacked out toward the sea each night for fear of submarine shelling. Dinner and an early bedtime followed.

Saturday, June 13, we were up early, packed, [and] fed but then had to wait for some last-minute adjustments to the airplane. We finally got off at 10:35 hours after one false start when Jack Hilger nearly forgot his papers, which had been carefully stored in the hotel safe. We had picked up a major with about 500 pounds of luggage for the trip to Roberts Field. Fortunately, it was a relatively short trip, so not much gasoline had to be carried. A circuitous overwater route was required to get around the Ivory Coast, another French colony now in German hands. It was a nice day and an uneventful trip. We arrived at Roberts Field, city of Monrovia, country of Liberia, at 15:45 hours. That airfield was in the middle of a Firestone rubber plantation, and the locale was a perfect movie set for a *Trader Horn* picture (a series of movies filmed on location in Africa); there was even a sluggish river complete with river steamboat nearby. I could almost hear the assistant director yelling: "Lights, music, action, camera!"

A tour of the plantation explained how rubber was grown, collected from the trees, cured, and prepared for shipment. Back at the airfield, a very nice dinner with fresh pineapple for dessert was served. Takeoff for the long hop across the Atlantic was at 18:30 hours. Bearing a maximum fuel load, we staggered into the air—barely clearing the rubber trees at the end of the runway. There was a bright moon shining as we passed under large formations of clouds. It was very lovely; however, I couldn't appreciate it to the fullest because I was thinking about those 2,000 miles of cold, wet, and salty water beneath us. The air was smooth, and despite my anxiety, I dropped off to sleep and didn't even notice the mythical bump when we crossed the equator. The airline people promise there is always a big bump in the air when you cross the equator, one of the new series of legends which is growing up among the navigators of "the wild blue yonder."

We arrived at Natal, Brazil, at 03:45 GST (Greenwich Standard Time) or 00:45 hours local time, after a very quick crossing, due to a good tailwind. We were thoroughly sprayed and inspected for insect pests before being permitted to disembark from the airplane. We had some cider and cookies at the administration building while waiting for the plane to be serviced and then took off again at 02:30 hours for Belem (large city in northern Brazil). This trip was also smooth and fast. We reached the airdrome at dawn and then had to circle for nearly half an hour while the ground fog dissipated. Touchdown came at 07:50 hours.

We were driven into town to the Grande Hotel and were put up in the Annex. This turned out to be an old movie theater with the seats removed and little roofless rooms constructed on the ground floor and balcony. The stage and projection room were still intact, as were the rococo (ornate theater style) decorations. The beds were comfortably soft, the plumbing worked, and we had hot water to shave and bathe. So, we did not complain even though privacy was nonexistent. I had papaya for breakfast, my favorite fruit next to mangoes, and then set out to explore the town.

It being Sunday, most of the shops were closed and there didn't seem to be much doing. Dean and I walked down to the waterfront and along the quays, looking at the fishing boats drawn up there drying their nets and other gear. On the way back we found an open grocery store. I bought cheese. It resided in a spherical tin can and was perfectly round. When we opened it at home nearly a month later, it was found to be excellent, resembling a good moist Edam. It was quite warm and humid. Tired by our walk, we turned in for a "siesta" and slept till 18:30 hours. A nice dinner was followed by performing the routine dressing of my patients, and then it was back to bed again.

We were up at midnight, had breakfast, and then drove to the airfield. I retrieved the psychologically ailing B-24 captain from the infirmary before we all boarded the airplane. After some delay, takeoff was at 03:00 hours, and most of us then went back to sleep. That morning, sunrise was one of the loveliest I have ever experienced. We were flying through scattered white puffy clouds over a calm sea, and the light had a clear golden quality that was breathtaking. For a while, I had the feeling that I was in a different plane of existence, far from the turmoil and strife of things terrestrial.

Heading northbound, the equator was crossed again before arriving at Trinidad (Trinidad and Tobago are islands located 6.8 miles from Venezuela) at 09:00 hours local time (one-hour time change). At the field, we found a typical US Army Post Exchange (PX) that might have been located anywhere in the United States. It had the same type of temporary buildings, the same ambiance, the same GIs, and, wonder of wonders—the same food! We went to the same PX for breakfast consisting of two hamburgers and three bottles of Coca-Cola! They certainly tasted good.

Trinidad is a beautiful tropical island with a very rugged and interesting coastline. It was warm and humid during our brief visit. We were off again at 10:30 and flew over the blue Caribbean to Borinquen Field, Puerto Rico, arriving at 15:30 AWT (Atlantic War Time). This was a nice new camp with many permanent buildings. Officers' row was just being completed and was very impressive. We were billeted in a not-quite-finished house on army cots complete with mosquito netting. I had trouble convincing the unnamed captain (suffering from depression) that he should go to the hospital, but finally got him admitted.

The PX there was really a treat to behold. It was a huge place complete with soda fountain, and the latest magazines. Jack Hilger wanted us to make a somewhat military appearance when we reached the United States, so we all bought some regulation cotton slacks, shirts, ties, and caps. We were rather sorry to put off the rather picturesque but comfortable "uniform" we had been wearing. Most of us had standardized on British shirts, shorts, woolen socks, sandals, and solar toupee (pith helmet). We lost our rather distinctive appearance but certainly did look more like soldiers after the change.

At the post exchange, I also got a much-needed haircut and a strawberry ice cream soda. Later, I made supper of ice cream and Coca-Cola. We went to bed early since we were to take off well before sunrise.

Tuesday morning, June 16, we were up at 02:30 hours. After blundering around in the blackout, we had a snack and collected ourselves. Takeoff was at 04:35, and we headed for West Palm Beach in the good old USA. Months earlier we trained on the Florida Panhandle. With our return to Florida, we had circumnavigated the globe in four months. This part of the trip was smooth and uneventful. I'm a Californian but was so glad to be home that even Florida looked good to me. We arrived at Morrison Field at 09:17 Eastern Time. According to my instructions, the ailing captain was dropped off at the base hospital, followed by breakfast at the PX. My tray was heaped with orange juice, eggs, and fresh milk—the latter being the one article of diet I'd missed even more than Coca-Cola.

We were all given letters from Jimmy Doolittle and Major Swasey (of the public-relations office), warning us not to talk too much and what remained as prohibited information. We were rather surprised that there was so much secrecy about some aspects of the raid, but happy to abide by the instructions. I sent my wife a telegram that I was back in the USA, safe and sound, and expected to see her soon. At 10:00 hours we took off for Washington, glad to get out of the muggy heat of Florida summer. The trip was uneventful except for circling the house where Ted's and Jack's wives were supposed to be staying. We arrived at Bolling Field (Washington, DC) at 15:17 hours, unloaded, and bid goodbye to the TWA aircrew who had carried us halfway round the world so comfortably and safely. They were a swell bunch.

We took our luggage to the BOQ (bachelor officer quarters) and were just finishing a cola when Jimmy Doolittle arrived with Maj. Allyn, who was handling our public relations. Jimmy was resplendent in his new star, and we all kidded him about it. Being a general officer hadn't changed him a bit. He was still the same swell chap we had followed over Japan.

As flight surgeon and prior to our landing, I requested pilot Neiswander to radio ahead for an ambulance to meet us on the tarmac. Ted Lawson and Charles McClure went to Walter Reed immediately upon arrival. I soon received a call from somebody in the admitting office, wanting to know what I meant by sending patients there with no more formality than the written histories that accompanied them. "After all," the chap said, "this is Walter Reed Hospital, you know!" Jimmy then got on the radio and soon straightened things out. It's wonderful what respect you get when you can say, "This is General Doolittle speaking . . ."

Doolittle drove me next to the hospital to see Lawson, McClure, and "Doc" Watson. [As pilot on plane number 9, Lt. Harold Watson broke his arm during bailout.] These wounded warriors were being well cared for. After small talk, we went back to Jimmy's office in the War Department building, where matters relating to the decorations were reviewed. Everybody was to receive the Distinguished Flying Cross (DFC), and Doolittle wanted some to get an additional award. Before realizing it, I found myself chosen to write the citations, a pleasant if arduous task.

On my first free time with a telephone handy, I called my family at home in Redlands, and Edith was soon on the line. It was wonderful to hear her voice again. There had been several times in the preceding three months when I hadn't expected a reunification with family. I next talked with the children, but they were too bashful and excited to answer, though I heard their voices in the distance while Edith was talking. The kids came down with both chickenpox and tonsillitis while I was gone—but were now fully recovered. I also talked to my mother, father, and both sisters.

The next few days were busy ones. We were interviewed by all manner of military debriefers, from the military intelligence office to cartographers (mapmakers); from discussions of the medical situation in China to proposed changes in the B-25s. Col. Grant, the air surgeon, called me into his office, and we had a very pleasant chat. He seemed genuinely interested in my experiences.

One morning I took Gen. Doolittle's car, complete with its big white star, and drove out to the airport to meet Ellen Lawson's plane. I drove her out to Walter Reed and briefly outlined what Ted had been through on the way. She took it all with marvelous spirit and pluck, and the sight of the two of them together again was ample payment for my small part in bringing it about.

Ted Lawson endured a couple of secondary operations on his stump but made a marvelous recovery. He became so skillful in the use of his prosthesis that he could fly a plane and remained on active duty with the Air Corps until the fall of 1944, when he retired for medical reasons at his own request after serving his country long and well. It was a great coincidence, but he was in my hospital, and on my ward, while appearing before the Retirement Board. We had a good time going over old times and catching up on the intervening years.

CHAPTER 15

AWARDS AND DECORATIONS

ON SATURDAY, JUNE 27, 1942, a "March in Review" ceremony was conducted at Bolling Field. The Air Forces band played rousing patriotic tunes interspersed with the command "Call to orders," followed by "Front and center" booming over the public address system. General of the Army Air Forces, Henry "Hap" Arnold, and Jimmy Doolittle came down the line and pinned our Flying Crosses on our palpitating bosoms. Gen. Arnold had a kind word for each of us—which was very gratifying. After the review, we all stood around admiring each other's medals and feeling very self-conscious. Pictures were taken, and several of us spoke over nationwide radio.

Several of us were talking together when we were approached by a jovial chap named Oscar Karnes, who told us he represented the CBS radio network program *We, the People*, and he wanted some of us on the next broadcast. He said that naturally they couldn't pay us anything since we were service personnel, but that it would be all expenses paid. Further, they would provide airline tickets to our homes, where we were to spend our leaves. I was then nearly broke, having just finished buying a new wardrobe to replace the clothing I'd lost. It sounded like a good deal to me. In the tradition of "sticking my neck out," I volunteered while some of the others hesitated. That broke the ice, and most of the others agreed—so now Oscar had his choice. He chose pilots Dean Davenport, Griffith Williams, and me. We were then bundled off to the railroad station and aboard the next New York–bound train.

On the train, Mr. Karnes bought us the best meal from the dining-car menu. Then we retired to the chair car, where we collectively went to work on the script. We pulled into New York about midnight and were put into a luxury suite at the Hotel Pennsylvania.

We freshened up a bit, and then Oscar took us to the Stork Club in a taxi. The dimmed-out streets of the city seemed very strange to us. At the Club we were presented to the manager, Mr. Billingsley. He got us a ringside table and plied us with champagne. Both Mr. Karnes and Mr. Billingsley then brought us a variety of celebrities to meet us. Photographers shot us, and all in all we had an exciting time. At about 04:30 hours Sunday morning, we decided it was bedtime. We had misplaced Oscar in the crush and so taxied back to the hotel alone. The big, soft beds certainly felt good after the cots, mats, and plain dirt floors we had been sleeping on.

We slept late and then had "brunch" in our suite and then went in search of Mr. Karnes and the *We, the People* national radio program. We didn't find Oscar but finally located the program rehearsing at CBS Theater 2. Oscar finally showed up with our scripts, which he had cleared through the War Department, and we ran through it three or four times and then once through the whole program, which included a Russian sailor and a chap from Florida who had salvaged some umpteen tons of rubber. We returned to the hotel for dinner and then went back to the theater for the show. It was great fun. We were so excited that we forgot to be "microphone shy," ran through our scripted lines quickly, and finished three minutes early—so the announcer had to keep the audience clapping to fill up the time!

Dean Davenport's plane left that night, but "Grif" and I waited another day for ours. We left the theater by the back way to dodge the autograph collectors and went back to the hotel and to bed early. On Monday, we slept late again, packed, and then drove to La Guardia Airport. The trip across the country was uneventful, though the plane was late due to bad weather.

Edith and her parents met me at Burbank. Edith looked wonderful. It was grand to see them again. We had lunch at "Melody Lane" in Hollywood. I don't remember what I ate, but we had a good visit. Edith and I then drove to Redlands, jabbered, and held hands the whole way. The first stop was my parental home, where I saw them and my sisters. We then went to our house to get reacquainted with our children. It was wonderful to be with family again.

Raiders were on call for appearances at bond drives and the like—but were able to spend most of our time with family. On the fourth of July there was a review at March Field, and General Barney Giles pinned the Silver Star on my shirtfront.

On July 19, 1942, I flew to MacDill Field, Tampa, Florida, where I was assigned to a new bomber group, the 320th. I trained with the group there and on August 28 left for the port of embarkation with the ground echelon. We spent a few hectic days at Fort Dix, New Jersey, boarded the *Queen Mary* on September 5, 1942, and promptly departed for England. The balance of my military experience was consistent with tens of thousands of others and not particularly interesting.

We were stationed at Hethel, in England, for a while and then went into Oran, Algeria, during the first few weeks of the invasion of North Africa. I spent the first three months of 1943 in the hospital with pneumonia and was then assigned to the 31st Fighter Group, an outfit already famous for its part in the Dieppe show and the initial landings in Sicily and at Salerno. In November 1943 I was assigned to the 34th Air Depot Group in Palermo, Sicily, and spent the next half year trying to think up things to do to keep occupied. I was returned to the United States in June 1944, where I have served ever since.

CHAPTER 16

EPILOGUE

DESPITE OCCASIONAL INTERSERVICE rivalry between Army and Navy, the Doolittle Raid was the epitome of collaboration. Promotions, medals, and other recognitions for Army participants were many; however, the superb performance of the fleet, with its thousands of sailors, was less well celebrated. When President Roosevelt was asked the origin of the attack, a whimsical reference was made to a mythical Asian place called Shangri La. Soon enough, the Navy ultimately seized upon a modicum of glory by christening CV-38 as USS *Shangri La* on September 15, 1944.

The Doolittle Raid against Japan was brilliantly conceived and daringly carried out, but it yielded a tragic consequence. Military leadership in Tokyo fumed about the raid and then sought retribution for any Chinese who might have abetted the Raiders. The brutality was unpublicized during the war and remained hidden for decades thereafter. An early account appeared in Malcolm Rosholt's 1984 book *Flight in the China Air Space, 1910–1950.*[1] The Reverend Charles L. Meeus was a Catholic priest with a mission station in Kiangsi. He was absent at the time of the massacre but returned shortly after to bury some of his parishioners. Invading Japanese troops routinely terrorized local populations. An estimated 250,000 Chinese perished by the most cruel and brutal means, including germ warfare.

American intelligence gathering was improving. Code crackers working in Hawaiian basements contributed to the victory at Midway Island in 1942. Intercepted radio messages also triggered the demise of Admiral Yamamoto (architect of the Pearl Harbor attack). His military transport plane was intercepted and then destroyed in flight by Lockheed P-38 fighters near Bougainville Island on April 18, 1943.

Consistent with the laws of armed conflict, the attack on Pearl Harbor was limited to military assets; however, the conflict with Japan rapidly descended into the most brutal "total" war ever waged. Nippon never signed the 1929 Geneva POW agreement. The Japanese battlefield practices were inconsistent with Western values. The Luftwaffe treated downed Allied aviators with professional respect. Rather than surrender, the Nipponese preferred death for their own men, women, and children. False surrenders, kamikaze attacks, and suicidal banzai charges soon exhausted any goodwill remaining within the Allied side. Some military planners assumed the war with Japan would continue until 1947. Instead, the Japanese capitulated shortly after two atomic bombs were separately dropped on Hiroshima and Nagasaki during August 1945.

Given the horrific fire bombings of Tokyo by B-29s, two atomic bombs, and by silent consensus, any debt owed by the Japan to the Allied nations no retribution for wartime malfeasance at Pearl Harbor (and elsewhere) appeared to be settled. With Gen. Douglas MacArthur's firm hand in control of Tokyo (and everything else Japanese), the rapid rise of the Cold War, and the growing Soviet menace, Americans were ready to bury the hatchet with Japan and then partner on a sustained quest for economic greatness.

With the retention of their own language, religion, and culture, the Japanese people remained cohesive and cooperative after surrender. The Nationalists under Chiang Kai-shek and the Communists under Chairman Mao battled for Chinese mainland supremacy after the Japanese presence was eliminated. The Communists prevailed as the Nationalists under Chiang Kai-shek retreated to Taiwan in 1949.

Executions

It was evident that Dr. White was haunted by the executions of Farrow, Hallmark, and Spatz because of his multiple references to that event. Details of the atrocity emerged only after the war. No civilized nation executes POWs; however, in their ire over the Doolittle Raid, Japanese authorities retroactively imposed a freshly rewritten law titled "Military Law Concerning Punishment of Enemy Airmen." The trial of the eight Americans was a propaganda device intended to dissuade future attackers. All eight Raiders were convicted and sentenced to die. Three were executed, while the five others subsequently received reprieves.

The concocted charges included strafing and killing schoolchildren. It was assumed this landed Spatz, a gunner, the top spot on the list. Farrow, as aircraft commander, was responsible for the actions of his crew. Why Hallmark made the short list remains a mystery. Unlikely to divulge any further useful intelligence, the trio were executed in Shanghai on October 15, 1942.

The 1942 execution of the three Raiders was probed at a war crimes trial held in Shanghai in December 1945. The Judge Advocate's department of the 14th Air Force brought charges against eight Japanese junior officers, enlisted men, and civilians. The American prosecutor was John Hendron, who later lived in Jefferson City, Missouri. The senior Japanese officers deemed most culpable were never found and were presumed to have died previously in actions elsewhere. The defendants were on trial for their subordinate role in an unlawful execution. Relevant events were captured in court records.

The day in question was likely pleasant, with temperatures on that date normally between 57 and 72 degrees:

We arrived at the cemetery in automobiles and dismounted. Captain Tatsuta asked the prisoners if they wanted to have a last word. They did not. After that, the three prisoners were each brought to the respective crosses. They were tied to the crosses with a brand-new white cloth and likewise, a new white cloth was draped over their head. The firing squad lined up a certain distance away from them. By then, we had retreated to the background of the scene. Then the firing squad fired. After the shots were fired[,] an Army medical officer went and examined the bodies to ascertain they were dead. After he was satisfied[,] the bodies were released from the crosses and placed in three separate coffins. The three coffins were arranged side by side. And at that time all those who were present at the execution participated in a short ceremony or service.[2]

Under cross-examination, it was revealed that the cloth around the head of each man had a mark directly between the eyes and over the nose. This was the aim point for the riflemen. A primary shooter and alternate were designated. The crosses were short, and the airmen had to kneel with outstretched arms while their wrists were bound to the cross arms. A Japanese officer explained to Hendron that the commander of the firing squad assumed the Americans were Christians and wished to die in the manner of Christ.

The coffins were taken to a Shanghai crematorium. The ashes were put in boxes. The boxes were put on a shrine, where incense was burned in an unused waiting room at Kiangwan Military Prison. The ashes and other personal effects were returned to the families at the end of the war. The defendants were found guilty of "aiding" in the unlawful murders of the three Raiders. Sentences were rendered: prison confinement at hard labor, with no term exceeding nine years.

Postwar Dr. White

The war-swollen ranks of the US military thinned quickly after V-J Day. Despite rapid promotion from lieutenant to major, Dr. Thomas Robert White departed uniformed military service to resume a full-time, rewarding, and adventuresome civilian life. Dr. White practiced general medicine and surgery in Redlands, California, and Kailua, Hawaii. The postwar era yielded White a third child, plus the six grandchildren who arrived later. Both Mr. and Mrs. White raced automobiles on an abandoned airstrip in Hawaii. A trophy won during the Hawaii "Speed Week" event remains with the family. They recall a person with a great sense of humor who could repair most anything. Most of the family automobiles bore names. One station wagon was called "Babe, the Big Blue Ox." Reading science magazines, farming experimental lab rats, and dispensing vaccinations to family members were all parts of his repertoire.

A Ford laundry truck was handcrafted into a utilitarian homemade RV with four bunks. A seven-week trip ranged from Baja California to the hinterland of British Columbia, where primitive roadways remained common and demanded the fording of small steams. For a time, White lived aboard a 70-foot ketch-rigged schooner that he could sail single-handedly. One memorable trip was from Catalina Island to the mainland through the fog by dead reckoning.

Remarriage followed a divorce. The new family then lived during the summer on their 40-acre apple orchard called "Cold Creek Ranch." Dr. White was a passionate deer hunter and an excellent shot who sought a clean kill with his .30-30 rifle. Family members were treated to an up-close and personal anatomy lesson when the game was carefully dissected with techniques learned in medical school. The wisp of steam rising into the cool mountain air was evidence the peritoneum was breached. A surgeon preparing meat for human consumption takes some people aback. The interior warmth and pungent scent of a large mammal were evident as every internal organ was carefully identified, probed skillfully, and explained (less savvy rifle-toting outdoorsmen describe the process as "gutting" the deer).

Fate of the Fleet Participants

The Doolittle Raid of April 1942 was soon followed by the decisive Battle of Midway in June. Both *Enterprise* and *Hornet* participated in the pivotal encounter, after which the US Navy again dominated in the Pacific Ocean; however, more battles followed. USS *Hornet* (CV-8) was later damaged beyond repair at the Battle of the Santa Cruz Islands by enemy torpedoes and dive-bombers. *Hornet* was abandoned and then sent to a watery grave by Japanese destroyers exactly one year and six days after joining the fleet.

The wreckage of USS *Hornet* was found near the Solomon Islands in 2019 during an expedition sponsored by Paul Allen (Microsoft cofounder). She is lying upright on the bottom at a depth of 17,500 feet (over 3 miles) beneath the waves. USS *Vincennes* (CA-44) was named after a city in Indiana. It was also short lived and was sunk by the Japanese navy at the Battle of Savo Island on August 7, 1942. Built in 1935, the light cruiser USS *Nashville* (CL-43) fared better. It found a new home in the country of Chile and was active until 1985.

The World War II history of USS *Enterprise* (CV-6) is legendary. It survived heroic battles and multiple close calls and ended the war by ferrying ground troops home from Europe. Calls for its preservation fell on deaf ears, and the hulk was scrapped in New York City. A full-sized nuclear-powered aircraft carrier was the eighth US Navy ship to bear the name. USS *Enterprise* (CVN-65) entered service in 1958.

Doolittle Raid: Japanese Documentation

The bibliography references a small paperback book dated 2016 and printed only in Japanese. Scholars Shibata and Hara did their best to research and discretely document the damage inflicted by each of the Raiders on April 18, 1942. Recounting the findings has been avoided in respect for their original research, qualms regarding translation, accuracy of the data after the passage of time, and massive loss of official Japanese records to incendiary-induced fires in the Tokyo region.

Consistent with other battle damage assessments (BDAs), the findings of Shibata and Hara fell into three categories:

First: Military targets that were damaged as intended. Examples: A light aircraft carrier was struck, and construction was delayed by four months. An oil storage facility was also hit, and it delayed the opening by two months. Five women perished and seven were wounded when a small clothing factory was bombed. In any case, the explosive payload, as delivered (size and number of bombs), was inadequate to disrupt heavy industry.

Second: Wasted ordnance. Some bombs exploded but missed their targets. Other munitions were duds that failed to explode (the proper term is unexploded ordnance, which is abbreviated UXO). Some ordnance harmlessly tumbled into the water.

Third: Collateral damage. Urban Japan is tightly packed. Unintended damage included hits at a school, a hospital, and numerous residences. Some buildings were multiunit apartments, while others were single-family homes. Structural damage was broken down between "destroyed" and "damaged." Injury to people was categorized as killed instantly, killed, severe injury, or mild injury. Some air-to-ground strafing (from the nose gun) was noted.

The Japanese researchers relied heavily upon US records. An attempt was made to account for each bomb. Furthermore, discrete routes were mapped over every target. In the end, a list of alleged actions remained but were unattributed to any Raider. These included strafing of three separate fishing boats and a Japanese navy destroyer.

APPENDIXES

APPENDIX A: RAIDER REUNIONS

JIMMY DOOLITTLE[1] HAD PROMISED a memorable party when the crews assembled in Chungking, China, for a postattack gathering, but fate intervened. Doolittle rushed back to Washington, DC. With York and crew impounded in Russia, other survivors exited China helter-skelter. For most of the Raiders, the war continued nonstop with new assignments. Robert Clever, Robert Gray, Paul Leonard, and other Raid survivors perished elsewhere. Sixty-one of the original eighty Raiders were alive on V-J Day. It was not until 1946 when they first gathered in celebration at Miami Beach. An agreement was struck for an annual reunion to be held starting in 1947.

Thereafter, a reunion was organized almost every year (there were a few exceptions). As defined by the Raiders themselves, the purpose of these reunions would be threefold: "to renew old friendships, to honor those who have passed on, and to participate in some activity which is of benefit to the nation, the Air Force, [and] to the community in which they meet."

The gatherings were held in April, on or around the eighteenth—the date of the Tokyo Raid. Presiding over periodic reunions of the Raiders was an apex event of Doolittle's later years. Reunions generally included lectures and talks about the raid, chances for the public to meet and get autographs, book signings, luncheons, and fellowship, with a gala dinner/dance to top off the weekend. The events were held in various cities throughout the US.

One of the most important parts of a reunion was the Goblet Ceremony, which honors those who passed on. Sponsored by the City of Tucson, Arizona, in 1956, a set of eighty silver goblets were crafted. The name of each Raider was inscribed twice on each; however, a few of the names bore minor misspellings.

One moniker was right side up and the other was inscribed upside down. The passing of each Raider would be recognized at a subsequent reunion, when that goblet was turned over. This was a solemn ritual. The goblets were originally housed at the Air Force Academy in Colorado, but more-recent reunions were hosted at the National Museum of the Air Force at Dayton, Ohio. In 2005, it was decided that the goblets would henceforth remain at Dayton.

The lanky young copilot who sat adjacent to Jimmy for thirteen hours on that fateful day was also destined to survive the longest. The reunions ceased after Richard "Dick" Cole[2] passed away in 2019 at the age of 103. The goblet inscribed "Richard Cole" was turned over on April 18, 2022. It was also Cole who fabricated the wooden case in which the goblets were transported. Even at an advanced age, his energy level was remarkable. Reunion participants recall him in the hotel lobby—crisply attired in a sport coat, white shirt, and necktie—eager to socialize late into the evening and then returning fully refreshed, nattily attired, and ready to resume the dialogue early the next morning. His loving daughter was a gracious and constant companion who always advocated on his behalf.

The last Raider Reunion was held at Dayton in 2016 and was hosted by the National Museum of the Air Force. The number of B-25s preserved worldwide is estimated to be about a hundred. Somewhere between twenty-five and thirty-three Mitchells are believed to be airworthy or nearly airworthy. An appeal went out. About twenty of the B-25 operators agreed to make the nostalgic trek. A taxiway adjacent to the museum was cleared and the aircraft were parked in a herringbone arrangement. A huge noise was created when the twenty parked aircraft all started and then revved their Wright R-2600 radial engines. Then a flyover was conducted. The formation was structured with three groups of three aircraft in a triangle grouping led by the balance of the participants in a line abreast formation. It was exciting and memorable for both airborne participants and those on the ground. About seven hundred people were in attendance.

Dick Cole was the only other survivor when former SSgt. David Thatcher[3] died in June 2016 at age ninety-four from complications of a stroke. Dick Hite, the third remaining Raider, had passed away only a month earlier. Thatcher was one of ten children born into a Montana frontier family then living in a sod hut carved into the side of a hill. For Thatcher and others, their wartime service continued beyond the Doolittle Raid. David Thatcher served in England and Africa and flew aboard twenty-six combat missions in a Martin B-26 Marauder. Missions included the first Allied forces bombing raid of Rome. Even as a decorated hero, Thatcher lived an unassuming postwar life in a modest but stately Craftsman home in the western Montana enclave of Missoula, where he earned a living as a post office letter carrier. A son, Gary Thatcher, perished aboard a US Army medevac helicopter that crashed during the Vietnam War in 1970.

The Air Force seldom provides flyovers for deceased veterans—but the passing of one of only two remaining Tokyo Raiders merited special recognition. At noon on Monday, June 27, 2016, an unforgettable dual flyover[4] was held above the burial service at the Sunset Memorial Garden Cemetery. One participant was older and smaller. The other was big and modern. The entire city of Missoula reverberated to the thunder. The big fellow was the Air Force's noisiest bomber flying a simulated attack profile from Rapid City, South Dakota. The supersonic Rockwell B-1 Lancer weighs 477,000 pounds when fully loaded—or roughly the combined equivalent weight of fifteen B-25Bs at takeoff from USS *Hornet*. Each Lancer has four jet engines. In full afterburner, they deliver a combined 120,000 pounds of thrust.

The smaller participant was "Grumpy," a flying artifact in the collection of the Historic Flight Foundation (HFF) that was then kept in a hangar near Seattle. The two planes each took off for rendezvous near the Missoula cemetery. The crews never saw each other because the two bombers were so well camouflaged. The aerial dance was coordinated by radio.

The B-1 appeared first, flying from northwest to southeast. It approached low and slow with wings extended, and then, when overhead, each of the four engines went into full afterburner. The visible flame was accompanied by a window-rattling roar as a steep and sustained climb into the heavens commenced. Only after it disappeared into the ether miles above did the rumble of the afterburners fade. Then, like a delicate autumn leaf caught in an updraft, "a B-25 rumbled in from the northeast. It flew over twice, then circled the cemetery and city of Missoula in ever-higher spirals into the deep blue summer sky."[5] There was not a dry eye amid the gathered mourners—which included Dick Cole wearing his signature white shirt, tie, and blazer.

The Doolittle Raid remains a celebrated event in Air Force lore. All the Raiders have now passed away; however, the legacy of their heroic mission continues. The newest Air Force bomber, the Northrop B-21, was named "Raider" as an ongoing tribute to Doolittle's audacious team and their surprise attack upon Tokyo of April 18, 1942.[6]

Appendix B: Sunshine Assembly Line

North American Aviation, Inc. (abbreviated NAA), built over forty thousand military aircraft during World War II—which is more than any other American company. The airplanes were of three primary types: The AT-6 Texan was a trainer airplane widely used by the US Army, Navy (as the SNJ), and many allied nations. The versatile B-25 Mitchell was designed as a fast-attack medium bomber and first achieved fame with the Doolittle Raid. Finally, many experts consider the P-51 Mustang to be the finest escort fighter of World War II.

"Working on the sunshine assembly line" was an idiom with dual meanings. Many wartime workers moved from frigid northern locations to Los Angeles and found the balmy Mediterranean climate very pleasant during the wintertime. Also, the surge of wartime orders forced additional factory manufacturing tasks to be performed outdoors. Camouflage netting was installed on poles over the tarmac to provide shaded workspace.

The driving force behind NAA was James Howard "Dutch" Kindelberger[1] (1895–1962), who joined a struggling subsidiary of General Motors Corporation (GMC) at Dundalk, Maryland, in mid-1934. Despite the Great Depression, GMC under the leadership of Alfred P. Sloan and Charles Kettering was an economic dynamo and expanded beyond buses and trucks. Kindelberger used his formidable powers of persuasion to convince the owners to move the entire operation to sunny Southern California. Disciplined business practices and a robust balance sheet allowed GMC to invest $697,000 in a freshly constructed sprawling aircraft factory at present-day Los Angeles International Airport (or LAX). As NAA's headquarters and main plant, it was expanded thirty-three times during World War II. (*Note*: GMC ownership of NAA ended in 1948, when GMC quietly sold their final remaining shares of NAA common stock.)

Kindelberger's closest confidant was John Leland "Lee" Atwood (1904–99), his second in command. The son of a preacher, the brilliant but reserved engineer was Kindelberger's lifelong deputy, friend, and key aircraft designer. Work started on a medium bomber called the NA-21 (or XB-21 by the Air Corps). It was eliminated during a flyoff against the Douglas B-18 Bolo. The NAA offering was a better warplane but twice as expensive.

Another attempt at a medium bomber quickly followed with NA-40. This time, rather than a tail dragger, the sole prototype had a tricycle landing gear (the pivoting wheel was shifted from the tail to the nose). An accident occurred near the end of flight testing. After excellent in-flight performance, an Air Corps test pilot deviated from procedure. The airplane stalled, crashed, and burned at Wright Field (Dayton, Ohio). Gen. Hap Arnold dashed off a letter to Kindelberger even before the ashes had cooled:

April 12, 1939: I certainly regret very much what happened to the Attack Bomber. I haven't had all the details yet . . . but was darned glad no one was fatally injured. . . . I just want you to know that it was a great blow to us as to you to have it crack up. . . . Practically all of the tests were completed.

With war clouds looming, the Army Air Corps made a massive announcement of aircraft procurement decisions in August 1939. Those getting the nod included heavy bombers Boeing B-17 Flying Fortress and Consolidated B-24 Liberator. Two medium bombers—the North American B-25 and a similarly sized airplane, the Martin B-26 Marauder—both were awarded production contracts. Other winners included trainers and pursuit planes.

Lee Atwood named the B-25 for Gen. William "Billy" Mitchell (1879–1936). Mitchell was an Air Corps leader and outspoken advocate of airpower. A fast-attack bomber that not only bore his name but also executed his vision would have made Billy Mitchell beam with pride. Relatively small and simple even by the standards of 1940, the B-25 was also intended as an export airplane. Wartime contracts with NAA were managed by Army Air Forces (after Army Air Corps was renamed in 1942). General of Army Air Forces Henry "Hap" Arnold wrote in late 1941:

> One of the latest additions to our air forces, the husky 12-ton baby we know as the North American B-25C. This hard-hitting member of our striking power is one of the speediest bombers in the world, with speed approaching that of the standard fighter-planes in use abroad. It carries a very healthy load of bombs and operates at high altitudes. The tricycle landing gear makes for excellent takeoff and landing qualities, and for a large ship, it handles beautifully in the air.[2]

Designing the Mitchell demanded over 200,000 hours and 8,500 drawings. What B-25 advanced features brought NAA the most pride? That list included tricycle landing gear, low-drag engine nacelles, a top speed (as designed) of 328 mph, and hydraulic flaps, landing gear, cowl flaps, brakes, and bomb bay doors. Redundancy was built into vital functions because warplanes must endure battle damage and keep going.

The Mitchell was a spartan machine. Every part must have military utility. Each Wright radial engine had fourteen cylinders that displaced a combined 2,603 inches—hence the designation: R-2600. The engines burned 100-octane grade 130 fuel and produced almost 1 horsepower per pound of weight. A single collector ring surrounded the engine. It gathered the exhaust from each cylinder and dumped it rearward.

Crew members too frequently suffered hearing loss, because the Mitchell was notoriously noisy. Why? The engines were positioned near the fuselage, the exhaust collector ring was engineered to favor light weight over sound deadening, and there were no blankets. Blankets are the insulation pads found in the walls of modern jet airliners. They insulate the occupants from the cold while also dampening noise. The humble B-25 merited neither the added weight nor expense.

B-25 deliveries were gaining momentum even as the surprise attack at Pearl Harbor struck like a lightning bolt. One B-25 test flight returned to the factory dragging barbed wire snagged in the bomb bay doors, attached to a chunk of well-weathered but broken fence post. It was evident that B-25s were being flown at the extremely low altitudes demanded by the Doolittle attack scenarios.

The Dallas factory assembled trainers, P-51 Mustangs, and eight hundred Consolidated B-24 Liberators on license. Increasing the pace of production to meet wartime demand was the challenge faced by every airplane factory. The Kansas City plant was located on 75 acres in the Fairfax industrial district. B-25s were the sole product. Industrial engineers on loan from the Chevrolet Division established an automobile-style assembly line that ultimately delivered ten aircraft per day, seven days per week. The proprietary "component breakdown method of assembly" providing efficient and low-cost manufacturing yielded (circa 1943, according to the Museum of the Air Force website) a unit price tag of $109,000.

Engineering enhancements for the B-25 were ongoing. Steel plate measuring ⅜" thick protected systems and crew. Self-sealing fuel tanks were added. Anti-icing and cabin-heating systems were refined. More and bigger guns arrived; however, the basic R-2600 engines remained constant. Therefore, top speed retrenched from 328 mph at the start of the war to 272 mph when production ended in 1945.

The B-25 excelled in many roles. Limited to about seven passengers, it was a nimble executive transport when assigned to Hap Arnold, Dutch Kindelberger, or even Dwight Eisenhower during and after the Normandy invasion. As compared to a Douglas C-47, it was faster while burning less fuel. It was also a trainer aircraft for aircrews destined for heavy bombers. The Navy and Marine Corps designator for a B-25 Mitchell was PBJ. A primary mission for the PBJ was maritime surveillance.

Doolittle's armada was equipped with a single .30-caliber gun in the nose and twin .50-calibers in the top turret. Consistent with other early-war aircraft, the traditional .30-caliber machine guns of World War I were standard equipment on the early B-25s (B-25B) but were upgraded later with additional and more lethal .50-caliber armament.[3]

The rock-solid reliability and performance of the B-25B was demonstrated during the Doolittle Raid. Yes, a B-25 can fly on a single engine; however, there was no need on April 18, 1942. All thirty-two engines performed flawlessly. The endurance of sixteen aircraft on a mission of thirteen hours in duration is a testament to the NAA designers, the builders of the reliable Wright R-2600 radial engines, aircraft mechanics, and the capable aircrews.

B-25 Preservation

B-25 production was abruptly halted in mid-August 1945 at just under ten thousand units. Brand-new parts still in the production pipeline became scrap aluminum. Desert airfields were awash with thousands of surplus warplanes, including hundreds of freshly built Mitchells. B-25s were common at many USAF bases until about 1958, when they were displaced by brand-new utility jets, including the North American T-39. For many years, civilian Mitchells also remained plentiful and popular with postwar airplane traders, where they found homes as trainers, utility transport planes, and forest firefighters.

Even after converting production to jet fighters during the 1950s, NAA took great pride in their wartime B-25. In 1958, NAA reworked and retrofitted a newer B-25J into the appearance of a Doolittle-era B-25B. Other than Doolittle reunions, the last big roundup for the B-25 came in 1969. A squadron of them was assembled for Joseph Heller's satirical antiwar motion picture, *Catch-22*.[4] The script consigned one airplane to a flaming crash during the filming on location in Mexico. The other Mitchells received a reprieve and opportunity for preservation by enthusiasts or museums. The few surviving warbirds are celebrated on the annual summertime air show circuit.

Appendix C: The Royce Special Mission

The most-popular World War II stories revolve around a short list of pivotal events that are told, retold, and then told again. They include Pearl Harbor, the Doolittle Raid, Battle of Midway, D-Day at Normandy, Battle of the Bulge, and a short list of others. But some of the most interesting skirmishes took place hidden away in the backwaters. Many historians agree that the China-Burma-India (CBI) is among the least researched (and most forgotten) theaters of World War II. The Southwest Pacific is not far behind. Lacking both embedded reporters and communication links, northern Australia and New Guinea were remote and hostile locations where daily combat missions were undertaken at great risk to first erode and then systematically reverse the persistent Japanese onslaught.

As an outstanding factory mechanic with Air Corps experience, John "Jack" Fox (1910–70) advanced to become a NAA field service representative. "Before departing for my new assignment, I would require some briefing, so I spent a little time with the field services manager, Frank Lyons, in his office. I received my instructions, and we worked out some of the details of each assignment." Field service representatives were the eyes and ears of the manufacturer, and North American Aviation (NAA) employed some of the best:

I arrived at Felts Field in Spokane in the spring of 1941 and reported to the 17th Bomb Group. I became mighty fond of the B-25 airplane. It appeared engineers considered maintenance and repair in the crafting of this jewel. When it became necessary to do maintenance or repair on the B-25, the mechanics didn't have to start off by cussing the knothead and shortsighted engineers for making everything inaccessible. This airplane was relatively easy to work on. It also proved to be one of the most versatile and adaptable of various changes, especially during its combat life in World War II.

The US military was blessed with young men who were overwhelmingly literate. Required was compliance with flight and maintenance manuals (known as "Technical Orders" to Air Force people). Furthermore, many of the American boys had whetted their mechanical aptitude by either tinkering with the machinery on the family farm or a personal jalopy parked in the driveway at home. The experience primed them for mechanized warfare, whereby rigging control cables, trimming engines, and countless mechanical adjustments all became part of the daily routine. The same daily care demanded on the farm was now being showered upon ships, airplanes, and army tanks. Like well-placed reminders from their mothers, the B-25 interior and exterior were rife with stencils, decals, warnings, and embossed messages.

Fox was recalled to Southern California to join a team at the Consolidated Aircraft plant in San Diego and fly aboard the first formation of four B-25C airplanes on their first transpacific flight. Fox was to fix the aircraft, communicate with the factory, and provide customer training:

February 28, 1942: Soon after we made our landing on Hamilton Air Base, the four airplanes scheduled for the Pacific flight were rolled over to the base paint shop where the Dutch markings were painted out and the US Air Corps markings painted on. I made no inquiry nor questions regarding this move as I felt those concerned knew what they were doing—besides, it was no concern of mine.

The destination was Brisbane, Australia, 7,000 miles away. The customer was Netherlands East Indies (NEI) air force. The ferry mission was operated by civilian contractors. Each carried a gunner, and (unlike the B-17s at Oahu, in December) these guns were loaded. A 600-gallon auxiliary bomb bay fuel tank delivered the range needed to fly the critical 2,400-mile leg between San Francisco and Honolulu. This task was separate from (but concurrent with) the project to prepare Doolittle's B-25s for their own extended overwater mission.

Location: 3rd Attack Group, Charters Towers Air Base, Queensland, northern Australia, early April 1942

Lacking supplies while responsible for a starving army in the Philippines, Lt. Gen. Jonathan "Skinny" Wainwright requested in late March 1942 that bombing raids be conducted to lift the Japanese blockade. Brig. Gen. Ralph Royce, a senior staff officer at 5th Air Force, with headquarters in Brisbane, was designated as the leader. Reared on the icy shores of Lake Superior at Marquette, Michigan, Royce graduated from West Point in 1914 and earned pilot's wings in 1915.

	Doolittle Raid	**Royce Raid**
Dates	April 18, 1942	April 11–14, 1942
Leader	Lt. Col. Jimmy Doolittle (1896–1993)	Brig. Gen. Ralph Royce (1890–1965)
Destination	Tokyo, Osaka, Kobe, Japan	Manila, Cebu, Davao, Philippines
Aircraft	16 each, B-25B	11 each, B-25C, 4 each, B-17E
Strategy	aircraft carrier launch (*Hornet*)	remote air base (Del Monte Field)
Result	all targets hit, fires, and other damage	successful missions against Japanese sites
Losses	16 each, B-25B, some crew members	one B-17E destroyed, all crew okay

However, on April 9, 1942, American and Filipino troops on the Bataan Peninsula surrendered. With mission planning well underway, Gen. Douglas MacArthur ordered the risky operation to continue. Given the great military secrecy imposed after the Pearl Harbor attack, it is unlikely that either Royce or Doolittle special missions had the slightest inkling of the other. The Royce mission commenced on April 11, 1942.

After the loss of the homeland (Holland) to the Germans and the colonies to Japan, the NEI air force was decapitated and rudderless. A trickle of American troops and equipment began arriving in Australia. A human tornado named Lt. Col. Jim Davies commandeered Fox and some of the NEI airplanes. Fox was ordered aboard, and a formation of a dozen B-25s headed north to a frontier gold-mining town called Charters Towers. Now embedded with the 3rd Attack Group, Fox settled into his pup tent but soon noted a change to the normal operating tempo:

I was called in with a group of men where I was asked many questions about the B-25[,] especially regarding the fuel system of the airplane, the quantity of fuel that could be carried and how to arrange for it, also cruising power settings and so forth. Much activity was taking place around several selected aircraft[,] and due to my nosy nature, I was fit to be tied in trying to find out what was cooking to cause all this fuss and activity. I was bursting at the seams and kept prying for an answer[,] but those in the know had their lips sealed securely. Finally, my curiosity was satisfied after I learned that a raiding party to the Philippine Islands was being planned and of course Capt. Paul I. Gunn[1] was in the middle of it. In fact, I believe he was the focal point.

We worked feverishly for days in preparing the aircraft to make the forthcoming mission. All was in readiness for the departure as soon as the selected crews were in place. The takeoff would be at night[,] and those of us remaining behind gathered out on the edge of the runway to witness it. All the aircraft were safely airborne. The flight grouped together and disappeared into the darkness. We all returned to our respective areas, hopeful that the flight would be successful and return safely. Capt. Gunn was at the controls of one of those B-25s cutting their pathway through the darkness and onto their rendezvous in the Philippine Islands.

Gunn was the main cog on the mission because [as an experienced Philippines Airline pilot, I later learned] he knew the Islands like the back of his hand. I never saw him use a map or chart. It was uncanny how this man could find his way around in the air. He always managed to find his destination.

Several days passed and still all was quiet[,] then one day a flight of B-25s were seen circling the base. The Philippine flight had returned but there was an empty space in the formation. One airplane was missing. Capt. Gunn's airplane returned with fuel dripping out of the bomb bay fuel tank and the bomb bay doors ajar. The crew emerged all laughing like hell. One would imagine it was all a big joke, but that dripping fuel was not funny. It was a mighty serious situation which could result in fire, but these guys laughed. "Well," Capt. Gunn was heard to say, "we made it despite the obstacles and odds."

[Del Monte Field, their forward operating base,] was found by Jap fighters. Soon after the B-25s landed there, they removed the bomb bay fuel tanks to make room for bombs. It was from this secret base they operated to make their surprise attacks on Japanese forces. On one of these missions, we learned that Lt. T. Gerrity sent a Japanese transport to the bottom.

When the bomb bay fuel tanks were put away under cover[,] it happened that one remained exposed. One of the Japanese pilots got lucky and spotted a shiny surface when scouting for the source of the B-25 attackers. He went around to make a firing pass at the target, putting several slugs through the tank. The fuel tank was from Capt. Gunn's airplane, and he almost blew a fuse—but the damage was done. Of course, the tank leaked but Gunn managed to make some temporary repairs using whatever materials were at hand. Capt. Gunn, being a resourceful man, was not going to let this minor item stop him and flew his airplane back to Australia. This man never did receive the full credit rightfully due him.

The same 600-gallon bomb bay fuel tanks used by the B-25s to island-hop the Pacific were used to ferry them between Australia and Mindanao Island. The Royce Raid consisted of three B-17E aircraft augmented by a larger number of B-25s. The exact number varies by account; however, eleven is likely the correct number. Jack Fox[2] noted the missing airplane and jumped to the incorrect conclusion of a combat loss. One airplane (a twelfth B-25) was left behind at Darwin with a defective tire on the main landing gear.

Capt. Frank P. Bostrom was the officer in charge of the B-17s, which handled missions of longer range. This was the same B-17 pilot who picked up a B-17 at the factory and later ferried it to Hawaii, arriving in the middle of the attack on Pearl Harbor of December 7. He then evacuated Gen. MacArthur from Del Monte Airfield to Darwin, Australia. Bostrom retired as an Air Force colonel after serving as a B-52 pilot in the 1950s.

Del Monte Field was an American forward operating base freshly established in 1941 to augment the main base at Clark Field. Del Monte had fuel, munitions, fighter planes, and uniformed personnel. The name derived from its location adjacent to the Del Monte pineapple plantation and cannery on the island of Mindanao. Lt. John P. Burns, one of the pilots stationed at Del Monte, noted in his diary that everyone there was "startled" at their sight because nobody had previously seen a B-25. After-action reports indicate damage to Japanese-held airfields and hangars, plus enemy ships sunk and aircraft destroyed. One B-17E named "San Antonio Rose II"[3] (serial number 41-2447) was damaged beyond repair by strafing. No aircrew members were lost during the Royce Raid.

The Royce Special Mission concluded on April 14, 1942. MacArthur's Brisbane headquarters downplayed the event. Official wartime records concealed the participation of Paul Gunn. The Royce Raid was heralded in a front-page account that appeared in the *New York Times* during April 1942. Lawson also mentioned it in *Thirty Seconds over Tokyo*, but the story was overwhelmed four days later by news of Doolittle's accomplishment.

As measured by audacity, bravery, and technical accomplishment, the Royce Raid remains significant. As measured by lost aircrew members and destroyed airframes, it can be argued the Royce Raid was more successful than the Doolittle mission. In hindsight, the Doolittle Raid remains legendary while the similar Royce mission faded into obscurity.

Maps

These maps are intended to help the reader follow the unique journey taken by Dr. White and his small cadre of (mostly) patients as they circumnavigate the globe. Each surviving Raider made their way either individually or in small groups. Some Raiders were retained in China to perform military service. The maps are based upon Dr. White's memoir and other sources.

UNITED STATES MAP

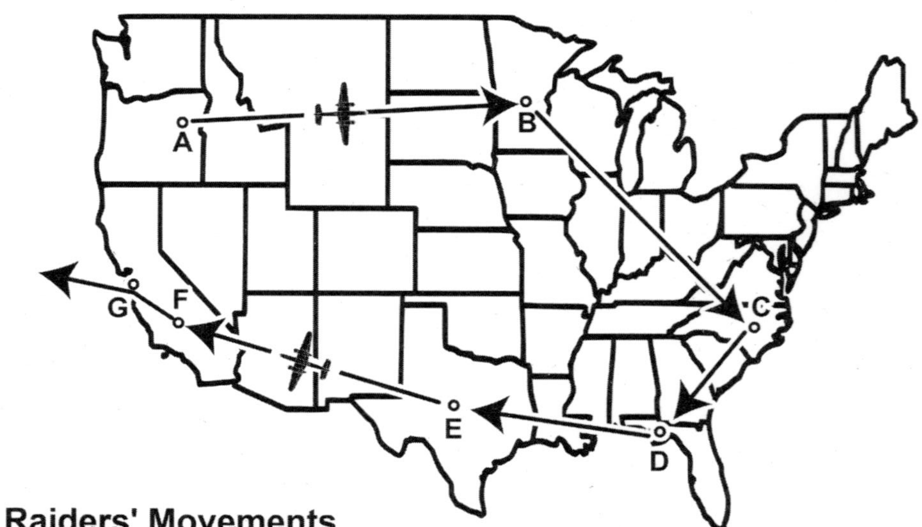

Raiders' Movements

A. Depart: Pendleton - Feb 1942
B. Minneapolis - Feb 1942
C. Columbia, SC - 2/27 to 3/3, 1942
D. Eglin Field, FL - 3/9 to 3/25/42
E. San Antonio (refueling)
F. March AFB, CA
G. Depart: SFO Bay Area, 4/1/42

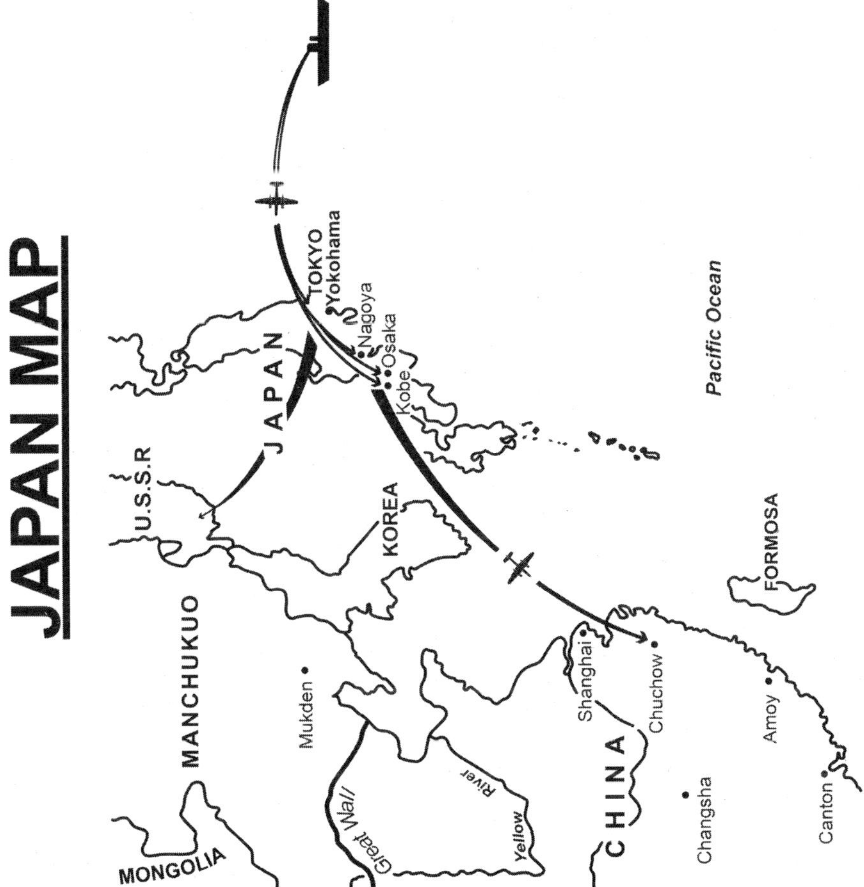
JAPAN MAP
U.S.S.R
MANCHUKUO
MONGOLIA
JAPAN
KOREA
Mukden
Great Wall
Yellow River
CHINA
Shanghai
Chuchow
Changsha
Amoy
Canton
FORMOSA
Pacific Ocean
TOKYO
Yokohama
Nagoya
Osaka
Kobe

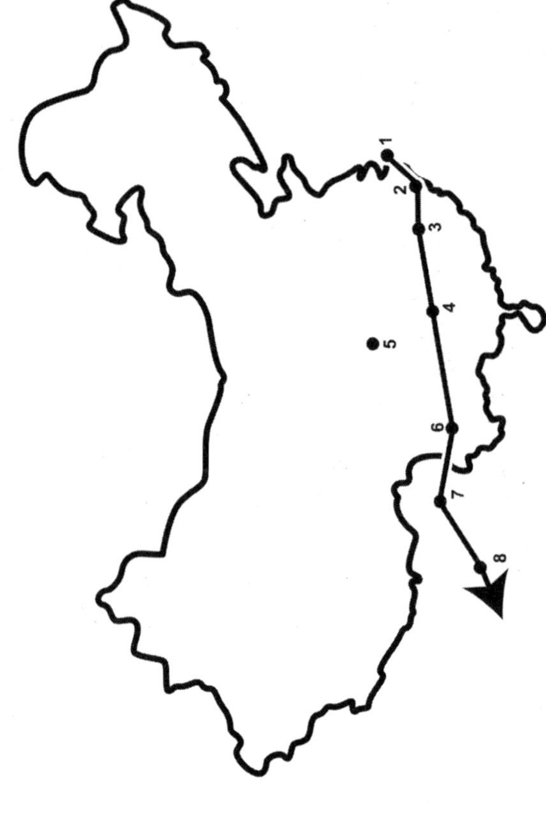
CHINA MAP
CHINA MAP (major cities only)
1. Island of Tan to San (crash site)
2. Linhai (hospital)
3. Chuchhow (now: Quzhou)
4. Kweilin Airbase (now: Guilin)
5. Chungking (now: Chongqing)
6. Kunming (China Hump base)
7. Dinjan (Assam, India Hump base)
8. Allahabad, India

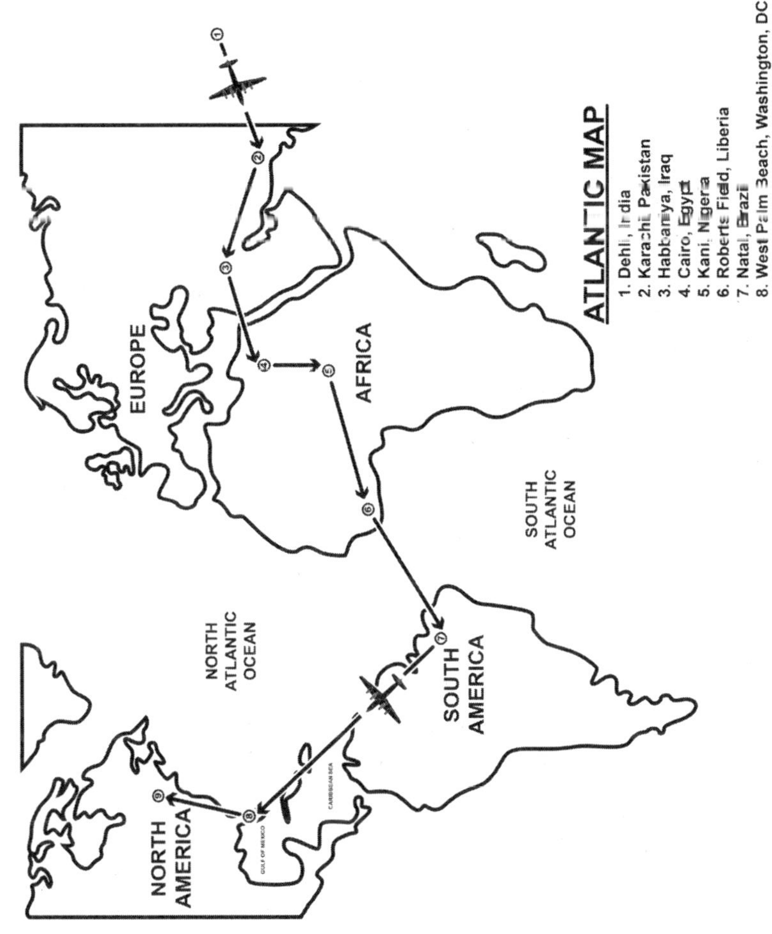

ATLANTIC MAP
EUROPE
AFRICA
NORTH ATLANTIC OCEAN
SOUTH ATLANTIC OCEAN
NORTH AMERICA
SOUTH AMERICA
GULF OF MEXICO
CARIBBEAN SEA
ATLANTIC MAP
1. Dehli, India
2. Karachi, Pakistan
3. Habbaniya, Iraq
4. Cairo, Egypt
5. Kani, Nigeria
6. Roberts Field, Liberia
7. Natal, Brazil
8. West Palm Beach, Washington, DC

ROYCE SPECIAL MISSION MAP

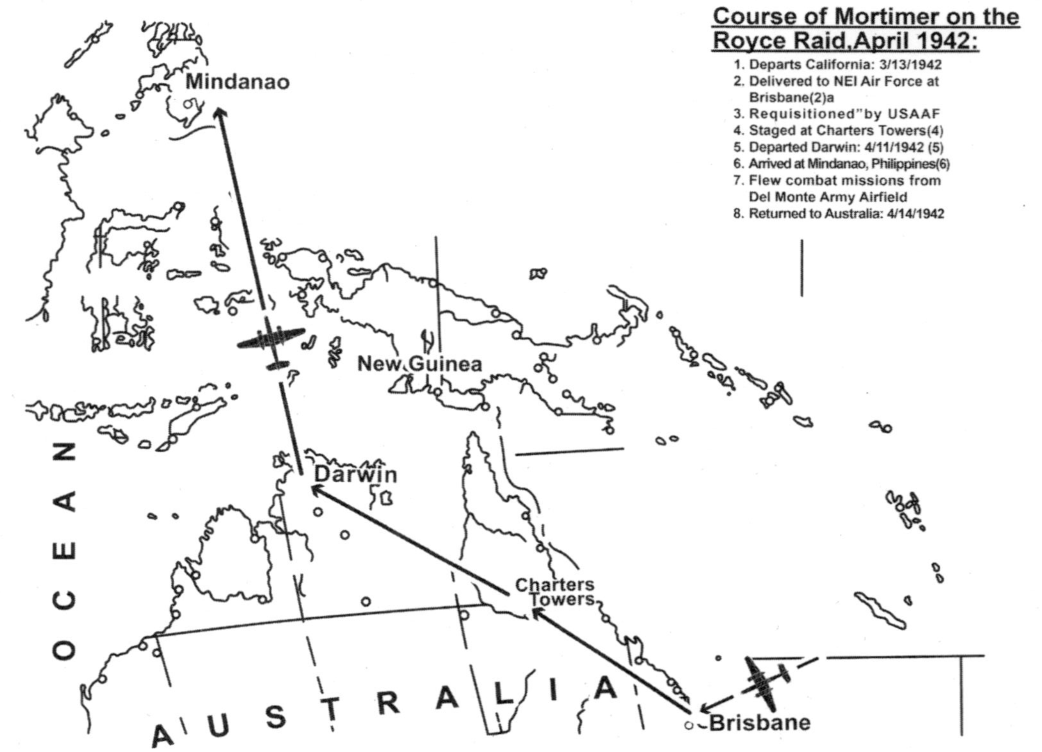

ENDNOTES

Acknowledgments

1. Over two hundred Boeing B-52 heavy bombers participated in the operation also known as the "Eleven Day War" or "Linebacker II." It was the most intensive aerial bombardment in the history of warfare.

2. NARA is an acronym for National Archives & Record Administration, a federal agency.

Introduction

1. The 17th Bombardment Group was the first to receive B-25 Mitchell bombers starting in February 1941. Aircrews were trained at Pendleton, Oregon, but flew coastal maritime surveillance missions from McChord Field at Tacoma, Washington.

2. TNT is short for trinitrotoluene, an explosive substance commonly used for both military and civilian purposes.

3. A lifetime serial number was assigned by Army Air Forces to each acquired aircraft. The leading digit(s) is the year funded. Normally painted on the vertical stabilizer, the tail number is sometimes shortened by left truncation.

4. A daylight departure was dictated by the large number of freshly recruited sailors who were unqualified for night operations.

5. The acronyms FUBAR and SNAFU survived in the American lexicon long after the war ended. The polite versions were "Fouled up beyond all recognition" and "Situation normal—all fouled up."

6. Each aircraft was assigned five crew members, for a total of eighty. They are identified by the rank held at the time of the raid and are accounted for by crew assignment and aircraft number. *Example*: Lt. Thomas R. White (flight surgeon, airplane number 15).

7. Mitsuo Fuchida and Masatake Okumiya, *Midway: The Battle That Doomed Japan; The Japanese Navy's History* (Annapolis, MD: US Naval Institute Press, 1955), 97–99.

Chapter 2: Jimmy Doolittle

1. Kay Summersby, *Eisenhower Was My Boss* (New York: Prentice-Hall, 1948), 187.

2. Modern physiological dogma assumes the human body can briefly endure 9 g, provided that a reclining ejection seat, an "anti-G" suit to squeeze blood out of the legs and lower body, and voluntary muscle contractions (variously called grunting or the Hook maneuver) are all utilized.

3. Like their father, both of Doolittle's sons became Air Force pilots during and after World War II.

4. The military pecking order tends to favor academy graduates (first), regular officers (second), and reserve officers (third). As a "reserve" officer, Doolittle achieved an unprecedented three stars (lieutenant general) by the end of the war. An honorary fourth star came in 1985 at the behest of Senator Barry Goldwater (R-AZ).

5. Some historians attribute the problem with the Martin B-26 Marauder to excessive wing loading. The postwar Douglas A-26 Invader was rechristened B-26 when the USAF was created in 1947. Redesignation caused additional confusion when discussing the B-26 pedigree.

6. Lend-Lease was a term coined by President Franklin Roosevelt to describe providing Allied nations with items needed to fight World War II. Virtually none of it was ever returned or paid for.

7. Generalissimo means supreme commander of all military forces—air, army, and naval.

8. Madame Chiang Kai-shek was nicknamed "Dragon Lady" because of her political clout. She lived to the remarkable age of 105 and died as a US resident in New York.

9. These metrics are from Statistica. Chinese wartime population figures are estimates and vary by source.

10. This is double the per capita US Civil War (1861–65) death rate. An estimate of total losses for both sides during the US Civil War is 620,000, when the combined US population was about thirty-five million people.

11. The often-repeated assertion by Ted Lawson, Dr. White, and various online sources that Japanese submarines were sunk off the Pacific Northwest coast persists to this day but remains unconfirmed by either US or Japanese wartime records. Nor has any wreckage ever been located off the Columbia

River near Astoria, Oregon, despite multiple underwater searches; however, seasonally migrating gray whales may have contributed to this persistent urban legend.

12. William Wolf, *North American B-25 Mitchell—the Ultimate Look: From Drawing Board to Flying Arsenal* (Atglen, PA: Schiffer, 2008), 339.

13. William Halsey was called "Bill" until the name was garbled in a press report to become "Bull." The new version stuck.

Chapter 3: White Joins the Raiders

1. Dr. White's first-person account continues without quotation marks.

2. It appears that both York and White were late additions to Doolittle's project and bypassed the stops at Minneapolis and South Carolina. York was a West Point graduate and (curiously) the pilot of the only plane that ended up in Russia.

3. Lieutenants normally address more-senior officers as "Sir" or "Ma'am." Since the bomber or transport aircrews were bound by mutual interdependence, the military nonfraternization policies between officers and enlisted members were often less formal for aircrews. The flight line is a "no salute" zone. Working efficiently takes priority over courtesy when performing under the constraints of time, battle, or in-flight emergency.

Chapter 4: Life at Sea

1. Eighty of this group (including Doolittle) flew away on April 18. The balance returned to Pearl Harbor aboard USS *Hornet*. Sixty-one of the eighty survived the war. The surviving participants were heartily celebrated in the following decades.

2. The editor can find nothing to corroborate the following assertion: "Scuttlebutt had it that *Cimarron*'s skipper, Commander Ihrig, had an eye for subs and had bagged three so far!" Russell M. Ihrig (1895–1986) was a graduate of Annapolis and retired as a rear admiral. War records attribute sinking of submarines to neither USS *Cimarron* nor Ihrig.

3. Amatol is a class of explosives that includes ammonium nitrate mixed with TNT.

4. The Americans performed European bombing missions during daylight. If the bombardier could see the aim point in the Norden bombsight, it was declared "precision bombing." However, given "circular error of probability" (or CEP), the term "precision" was an oxymoron. Only recently have new technologies (including GPS or laser guidance) yielded the accuracy that was always desired.

5. Adapted from James H. Doolittle with Carroll V. Glines, *I Could Never Be So Lucky Again* (New York: Bantam, 1991), 246–47.

6. Downed Allied fliers handed over to the Luftwaffe were extended professional courtesy and treated with a modicum of decency. Captured Allied aviators (US, British, or Canadian) were sent to one of six special camps called Stalag Lufts and were likely to survive.

Chapter 5: Rage Unleashed

1. Lt. Col. Brian Fredrickson (Ret.) contributed to this chapter. Brian is a student of Japanese language, culture, and history who served with both USAF and Space Force. Three separate assignments of multiyear duration were accomplished in Japan between 2007 and 2024. Each posting was within a different Japanese governmental office.

2. The sinking of USS *Maine* may have been caused by spontaneous combustion in a coal bin. The brief Spanish-American war erupted in April and ended within the single calendar year of 1898.

3. Ultimately, the Japanese government apologized and paid $2 million in restitution for the sinking of USS *Panay* (PR-5); however, that event remained a sore point with the Americans. *The Sand Pebbles* (motion picture, 1966, 20th Century Fox) was a drama depicting a Yangtze River patrol boat circa 1920s.

4. Philippine forces under Gen. Douglas MacArthur were equally unprepared; however, he retained command from Australia after he and his entourage were evacuated from harm's way.

5. Interview with Mr. Abraham M. S. Goo was at his Seattle-area home on December 17, 2021. Three decades after Pearl Harbor, Mr. Goo was a mastermind of Pentagon weapon systems, including Minuteman, SRAM, and defensive and offensive avionics on both the Rockwell B-1 Lancer and Northrop B-2 Spirit. Mr. Abe Goo served as president of the Boeing Military Airplane Company at Wichita, Kansas, and retired in 1990.

6. Quoted text is from the National Park Service website, captured on October 4, 2022.

7. Robert F. Dorr, *7th Bombardment Group/Wing* (Nashville: Turner, 1997), 48.

8. Previous battle cries included "Remember the Alamo" during the Texas war and "Remember the Maine" during the Spanish-American War of 1898.

Chapter 6: Bombers Away!

1. James M. Scott, *Target Tokyo: Jimmy Doolittle and the Raid That Avenged Pearl Harbor* (New York and London: W. W. Norton, 2015), 165.

2. Historians Fuchida and Okumiya in their 1955 book, *Midway*, state that the terse radio message from the fishing boat was flawed. It incorrectly reported three aircraft carriers and made no mention of any oversized aircraft. The Tokyo defenders presumed another day at sea was needed—and therefore prepared their defensive forces for an attack by a larger number of smaller planes on Sunday morning, April 19, 1942.

3. In the era prior to the global positioning system (GPS), the magnetic compass was an invaluable navigational instrument. It was feared that the B-25s may have lost compass fidelity because of weeks aboard an aircraft carrier primarily fabricated of ferrous metals (iron and steel).

4. As configured for the Doolittle Raid, each B-25B carried a crew of five. The navigator and bombardier were normally separate individuals. The bombardier sits in the Plexiglas bubble at the nose and operates the nose gun.

5. Copilot Griffith Williams was a lieutenant, not a sergeant as Ted Lawson said in his book.

6. Seaman First Class Robert Wall was the deckhand who lost his left arm to the B-25 propeller.

7. Only after the war did all the facts emerge. Eight Raiders were captured by the Japanese. Three (Hallmark, Farrow, and Spatz) were executed by firing squad. Meder died of ill treatment (malnourishment) during captivity. Four survived as prisoners of war (Nielsen, Hite, Barr, and DeShazer).

Chapter 7: Flying the Friendly Skies

1. The Mitsubishi G3M was a twin-engine, twin-tail bomber and transport that first flew in 1935. About a thousand were built.

2. Why did the planes climb to drop their bombs? Because the immediate bomb blast at low altitude would pepper the airframe with shrapnel holes. For incendiaries, it gave them time to ignite. The altitude allowed the bomber distance to escape the worst of the blast. Technical solutions including retarder fins and better fusing options came later.

3. The warm tropical ocean current that runs along the heavily populated east coast is known to the Japanese as "Kuroshio" (or "Black" current). Americans call it the "Japan Current" because it brushes against Alaska before turning southward along the West Coast of North America.

Chapter 8: What Happened to the Others?

1. Colt .45-caliber handgun, Model 1911, descended from the dual requirements for a repeating handgun with abundant stopping power at short

range and a mechanism loose enough to reliably operate under the adverse conditions of dirty, wet, or muddy.

2. Bailout was not a panacea. The three enlisted Raiders who perished during their attempt were Faktor, Dieter, and Fitzmaurice.

3. Ted W. Lawson, *Thirty Seconds over Tokyo* (New York: Pocket Star, 2002), 90–91. Both Ted Lawson and Dr. White stated a fondness for their respective planes. Airplanes are warm and comforting. Jumping out into the unknown is frightening. Bailout or ditch? The decision resides solely with the pilot in the left seat and is typically made under duress, with no time for either analysis or consultation.

Was landing and takeoff using the beach viable? Beach sand will support horses and RV-sized vehicles. Aerospace engineers who were contacted on the hypothetical matter descended into babble regarding fractured sand versus polished sand and declared beach sand to have "strange properties." The hypothetical question yielded a hypothetical answer: a firm "maybe."

Next, B-25 owner and pilot John Sessions was confronted with the same question. Sessions owns a B-25D named "Grumpy" and leads the Historic Flight Foundation, located near Spokane, Washington. Sessions wrote, "It is quite easy to pop up the nose wheel early in a takeoff run. Until you achieve rudder authority, your steering is limited to differential power and brakes. I prefer differential power as braking works against the primary goals—to leave the ground at about 90 mph and quickly get to single-engine safe speed of 145 mph. Assuming the Japanese were not shooting at me, I would look for driftwood or anything else on the beach (or nearby) to spread the weight under the nose wheel. In my vivid imagination, I see a small pattern of driftwood sunk into the sand in the shape of a small stage. A crisscross pattern would maximize support. Achieving a relatively flat surface with the sand would require resourcefulness and labor. It would be tough after the day they had been through.

"Tides are the other enemy. An empty Mitchell bomber weighs about 20,000 pounds. Had Lawson arrived in time to see the beach, it would have been a worthy landing option instead of crashing into the sea." Email from Sessions to Fredrickson dated February 26, 2023.

4. Lawson, *Thirty Seconds over Tokyo*, 98–99.

5. After-Action Report of Merian C. Cooper, as reported by Kim Briggeman, *Military Times*, June 28, 2016.

6. Ibid.

Chapter 9: Ditching and Chinese Assistance

1. The names of Chinese location are vexing because of varied spellings and other changes. Dr. White's first reported landfall was Tan Do San Island. Modern sources identify it as sparsely populated Tantou Island. Endowed with a popular sandy beach, it is one of many coastal islands south of Shanghai.

2. Interview with John Sessions, October 8, 2022. Saylor admitted to others late in life that he could not swim and regretted that water survival was omitted from the Raiders' training curricula.

3. Names of the farm couple were found on the Children of the Doolittle's Raiders website, accessed January 4, 2024. The couple saw flashlights and fled because flashlights were associated with either enemy soldiers or pirates. The husband then determined the visitors to be "foreigners, soaking wet, and clad in leather." Then, they were invited in. The "raincoats fabricated of bark" were intended to make crew 15 look like Chinese fisherman.

4. United States military dogma is very specific regarding the person in command. Aboard an airplane, it is always the pilot in command. In this case, it was wise for the "TNT" pilot (Donald G. Smith) to yield leadership in deference to White's greater age and superior education, and because it better fit Chinese cultural expectations.

5. "Shank's mare" is an archaic term that means walking on your own legs.

6. "Jumping sticks" remains undefined, and it is assumed they were an indigenous device for entertainment.

Chapter 10: Hiding in Plain Sight

1. Dr. White's epiphany to persevere was his only (but very brief) expression of self-reflection. The will to survive exceeded the discomforts of sore feet, biting bugs, and the persistent Japanese threats of bombing, strafing, or capture.

2. The term "coolies" was replaced with "porters."

3. The distance of a "Li" has varied over the decades. It is now defined as 500 meters, or 1,640 feet, or about a third of a statute mile.

4. "Farmhands" was substituted for "coolies."

5. The first Chinese woman to visit the United States was Afong Moy, who arrived in October 1834 as a marketing ploy by retailers selling Chinese women's fashion attire. Afong Moy had 4-inch "little feet," which were the result of a cruel Chinese practice called "foot binding."

Chapter 11: Amputation

1. An "airplane splint" holds the arm out and the shoulder rigid. A "cock-up" splint holds the wrist rigid.

2. The Roger Anderson splint was patented in the 1930s and is used to immobilize the leg.

3. In China, the juren (or jurenjang) was a civil service status awarded on the basis of test results.

4. High fever is a symptom of malaria, and it is assumed that the term "bells" refers to ringing in the ears.

5. The Sikorsky helicopter first flew in 1939. Model YR-4B did not arrive in Burma until 1944. Steve Wartenberg, "Send the Eggbeater to Taro," *Aviation History*, Spring 2023, 61–65.

6. Dr. White's attempt to arrange a medevac flight was noble. The inability to move the injured forward by air is probably the biggest missed opportunity of this survival odyssey.

7. Descriptions of medical care are as documented by Dr. Thomas R. White. It is presumed that the medications, surgery, and other treatments were standard and appropriate for the era, location, and extenuating wartime circumstances. Despite multiple serious traumas, Ted Lawson (1917–92) survived the ordeal, wrote a book, remained married, and lived a normal lifespan.

8. Scott, *Target Tokyo*, 331–32.

9. Interview with John Sessions, October 7, 2022. Ed Saylor's hobby was creating stained-glass artwork.

Chapter 12: Dodging a Persistent Enemy

1. China Inland Mission (CIM) became Overseas Missionary Fellowship (OMF) in 1964, and then OMF International in 1994.

2. Robert Clever survived the China trek only to be killed aboard a Martin B-26 Marauder that crashed in Ohio on November 30, 1942. He is buried near Portland, Oregon.

3. As previously noted, silk was superseded by ripstop nylon for fabrication of parachute canopies during World War II.

4. Distances are variously recorded by Dr. White in statute miles, kilometers, or Li. Separately, the abbreviation CBI stood for the China, Burma, and India theater.

5. Here, Dr. White performs as a gunsmith and declares it to be "fun." His grandfather founded the White Sewing Machine Company of Cleveland. Evidently, mechanical aptitude was a family trait.

6. A "pillbox" is a low-roofed emplacement for a machine gun or cannon, often fabricated from reinforced concrete.

7. Colonel Blimp is a British newspaper cartoon character by David Low, first drawn in 1934. Blimp is pompous, irascible, and stereotypically British.

8. "Anvil Chorus" is the rousing Verdi tune from *The Royal Opera*.

9. AVG (Flying Tigers) members were honorably mass-converted into US Army Air Forces on July 7, 1942. One of them was Ralph W. Sasser, and he was enumerated as "communications." *Source*: AVG website.

10. Lawson, *Thirty Seconds over Tokyo*, 190–91.

11. The Burma Road was a primary supply route for US and British assistance to Nationalist China. Its loss in March 1942 dictated establishment of the "Hump," a challenging air route over the eastern Himalayan Mountains between the railhead at Assam, India, and Kunming, China. Fuel intended for Doolittle's planes was one of the first consignments.

Chapter 13: Escape via "Gooney Bird"

1. Soutick Biswas, "World War Two: When 600 Planes Crashed in the Himalayas," online article, British Broadcasting Corporation (BBC), dated December 9, 2023. Challenges included high-altitude operation of unpressurized aircraft, primitive onboard navigation without benefit of ground stations, overloading, and unpredictably fierce weather. Eighty years later, artifacts continue to be retrieved from lofty but isolated crash sites. The artifacts include airplane parts, shoes, wristwatches, and freeze-dried human bones. "Flying the Hump" set precedent for the Berlin Airlift, which ran for almost a year starting in mid-1948.

2. Fourteenth Air Force was established on March 5, 1943, at Kunming, China, and as successor to the American Volunteer Group's (AVG) Flying Tigers.

3. Unpressurized flying is now regulated. Air Force Manual 11-202, dated January 10, 2022, page 37, limits operations at 24,000–24,999 feet to forty-five minutes for prevention of decompression sickness (dissolved gasses emerging as bubbles in body tissue). Obviously, aircrew members must be breathing supplemental oxygen at these altitudes.

4. Dinjan was within the tea-growing India district of Assam and was an important airfield when flying the "Hump" during World War II. The reverse route was a standard air corridor via Africa, Brazil, and the Caribbean. Loads handled on the return journey are called either "backhaul" or "retrograde" cargo.

5. Like a shadow boxer jabbing at nothing, fighter pilots of that era sometimes honed their dogfighting skills by pouncing upon friendly planes in feint aerial attacks.

Chapter 14: Home via Stratoliner

1. Other sources state that Boeing Model 307 Stratoliner service normally ended at Cairo, Egypt. The luxury airliner (now wearing camouflage paint) was dispatched to Pakistan on a special mission to retrieve Dr. White and his entourage; therefore, there was no need to "bump" other passengers. This same airframe delivered "space required" personnel all the way to Washington, DC. Other passengers would have held the lower priority of "space available" and been subject to bumping. The aerial port officer on duty may have had his own "bedside manner" and happily appeased the harried flight surgeon who was traveling with patients.

2. Built between 1937 and 1940, the Stratoliner was one of the biggest and most modern airliners available in 1942. A streamlined passenger fuselage was mated to the wings and engines of a Boeing B-17. Production was halted at only ten units in favor of bomber production. All five owned by TWA were commandeered for military duty, assigned tail numbers, and designated C-75. TWA employees continued to operate and maintain them. Model 307s safely made over three thousand wartime Atlantic crossings.

3. Charles Greening (1914–57) was a gifted artist, pilot of number 11, and inventor of the simple bombsight used by the Raiders, and later earned fame as a German POW. His promising military career ended at age forty-three when he died of an infection.

4. Also spelled Habbaniyah. The airfield is located 55 miles west of Baghdad. Established by the British in 1936, the airfield was abandoned in 1959.

5. Model 314 was a luxury flying boat. A mere dozen had been built for the Pan American Airways (PAA) Clipper fleet before production ceased in favor of Boeing B-17 bombers. The Model 314 Clipper was the airplane of choice when important people such as Winston Churchill or Franklin D. Roosevelt needed a lift over the Atlantic. None were preserved. Decades later, Pan Am directed that some of its features (spiral staircase and multiple decks) be incorporated into the Boeing Model 747.

6. The original term for the native fishermen was wogs. This British term for dark-skinned people is slang and now considered derogatory.

Chapter 16: Epilogue

1. Malcolm Rosholt, *Flight in the China Air Space, 1910–1950* (Amherst, WI: Palmer, 1984), 137.

2. Ibid., 136.

Appendix A: Raider Reunions

1. A still-mysterious but tragic event took place in 1958, when James Doolittle Jr., at age thirty-eight, took his own life by suicide. He was at the time a major and commander of a squadron of McDonnell F-101 Voodoo interceptor jets. John Doolittle retired as a colonel, and his son (Jimmy's grandson) was, for a time, commander of an Edwards AFB test pilot squadron.

2. Mr. John Sessions, proprietor of the Historic Flight Foundation, befriended the final surviving Raiders and speaks fondly of them.

3. Thatcher's obituary is from the *Missoulian* newspaper website, updated August 2, 2016.

4. Interview with John Sessions, October 8, 2022.

5. Kim Briggeman, *Military Times*, June 28, 2016.

6. John Tirpak, "B-21 Shape of the Future," *Air & Space Forces Magazine*, January/February 2023, 36.

Appendix B: Sunshine Assembly Line

1. The story of Anthony Fokker's Atlantic Aircraft (predecessor to NAA) is found in John Fredrickson, *Warbird Factory* (Minneapolis: Quartos, 2015), 21–38.

2. NAA employee quarterly magazine, *Skyline*, January 1942.

3. Undated working papers of NAA field service representative John "Jack" Fox.

4. Stream the first part of *Catch-22* (Paramount Pictures Corporation, 1970) to witness the most-dramatic B-25 action scenes ever captured on motion picture film.

Appendix C: The Royce Special Mission

1. The story of "Pappy" Gunn has been told in multiple books. As a retired Navy enlisted pilot, he was living in Manila with his family when the Japanese invaded. Gunn was commissioned as a captain with Army Air Forces and fought with valor in the Southwest Pacific; however, his actions were concealed to protect his family from harm because they were Japanese captives.

2. John "Jack" Fox was a wartime celebrity who twice appeared on national radio broadcasts; however, riddled with PTSD, his life went into a tailspin. His marriage crumbled, and his status at NAA suffered when he squabbled with others. Fox's wartime account was left unfinished with him waving a gun and chasing phantom Japanese soldiers in total darkness on an island in the

South Pacific. Civilian contractors did not qualify for Veterans Administration healthcare. Fox died at age sixty in 1970.

3. It was the second B-17E named "San Antonio Rose."

BIBLIOGRAPHY

Axelrod, Alan. *Profiles in Leadership*. New York: Prentice Hall, 2003.

Boeing Historical Archives. *Boeing 307 Stratoliner: The World's First High-Altitude Airliner*, 20-page brochure. Seattle, WA: Boeing, 1989.

Boyne, Walter. *Beyond the Wild Blue: A History of the United States Air Force*. New York: St. Martin's Griffin, 1998.

Bruning, John R. *Indestructible: One Man's Rescue Mission That Changed the Course of World War II*. New York and Boston: Hachette, 2016.

Doolittle, James H., with Carroll V. Glines. *I Could Never Be So Lucky Again*. New York: Bantam, 1991.

Dorr, Robert F. *7th Bombardment Group/Wing*. Nashville: Turner, 1997.

Duffy, James P. *War at the End of the World*. New York: New American Library–Random House, 2016.

Fredrickson, John. *Kansas City B-25 Factory*. Mt. Pleasant, SC: Arcadia, 2014.

Fredrickson, John. *Warbird Factory*. Minneapolis: Quartos, 2015.

Fuchida, Mitsuo, and Masatake Okumiya. *Midway: The Battle That Doomed Japan; The Japanese Navy's History*. Annapolis, MD: US Naval Institute Press, 1955.

Gladwell, Malcolm. *The Bomber Mafia*. New York: Back Bay Books, Little, Brown, 2021.

Griffin, Thomas E., Jr. *MacArthur's Airman: General George C. Kenney*. Lawrence: University Press of Kansas, 1989.

Groom, Winston. *The Aviators: Rickenbacker, Doolittle, Lindbergh, and the Epic Age of Flight*. Washington, DC: National Geographic Society, 2013.

Lawson, Ted W. *Thirty Seconds over Tokyo*. New York: Pocket Star, 2002.

Rosholt, Malcolm. *Flight in the China Air Space, 1910–1950.* Amherst, WI: Palmer, 1984.

Scott, James M. *Target Tokyo: Jimmy Doolittle and the Raid That Avenged Pearl Harbor.* New York and London: W. W. Norton, 2015.

Shibata, Takehiko, and Katsuhiro Hara. *Doolittle's Tokyo Raid: April 18, 1942.* Tokyo: Next, 2016.

Summersby, Kay. *Eisenhower Was My Boss.* New York: Prentice-Hall, 1948.

White, Thomas Robert. "The Hornet Stings Japan." *Atlantic Monthly* 171, no. 6 (June 1943).

Wings of a Warrior: The Jimmy Doolittle Story (DVD). New York: Shelter Island, 2013.

Wolf, William. *North American B-25 Mitchell—the Ultimate Look: From Drawing Board to Flying Arsenal.* Atglen, PA: Schiffer, 2008.

Zaunders, Bo. *Feathers, Flaps, & Flops: Fabulous Early Flyers.* New York: Penguin Putnam, 2001.

Unpublished references:

Adelman, Gabrielle; natural granddaughter of Dr. Thomas Robert White, MD. Numerous emails and telephone conversations, 2022–24, regarding White family history.

Carter, Evert D. "Sarge"; first sergeant (grade E-8, retired), United States Army. Unpublished memoir, and numerous interviews circa 2015.

Fox, John "Jack" (1910–70); field service representative, North American Aviation, Inc. Unpublished field notes—North American Collection—Boeing Historical Archives.

Fredrickson, Brian; lieutenant colonel, USAF (b. 1981). A student of cultural and political history of Japan.

Goo, Abraham, M. S. (b. 1925). Interview by John Fredrickson at his Seattle-area residence, December 17, 2021.

Sessions, John S. Interview by John Fredrickson at Historic Flight Foundation, Felts Field, Spokane Valley, WA, October 6, 2022.

INDEX

Note: Dr. White was educated in medicine, but not linguistics. His handwritten notes rely upon phonetic interpretations. Therefore, names of many Chinese people and places are unreliable and are therefore omitted. Furthermore, accepted naming conventions remain in flux; *Example*: Peking is now Beijing, Mao Tse-tung is now Mao Ze-dung.